Alcohol, Binge Sobriety and Exemplary Abstinence

Also Available from Bloomsbury

Alcohol in the Age of Industry, Empire, and War, edited by Deborah Toner
Alcohol in the Early Modern World, Edited by B. Ann Tlusty
The Globalization of Wine, Edited by David Inglis and Anna-Mari Almila
Proteins, Pathologies and Politics, Edited by David Gentilcore
and Matthew Smith

Alcohol, Binge Sobriety and Exemplary Abstinence

Julie Robert

BLOOMSBURY ACADEMIC
LONDON • NEW YORK • OXFORD • NEW DELHI • SYDNEY

BLOOMSBURY ACADEMIC
Bloomsbury Publishing Plc
50 Bedford Square, London, WC1B 3DP, UK
1385 Broadway, New York, NY 10018, USA
29 Earlsfort Terrace, Dublin 2, Ireland

BLOOMSBURY, BLOOMSBURY ACADEMIC and the Diana logo are trademarks
of Bloomsbury Publishing Plc

First published in Great Britain 2022
Paperback edition first published 2023

Copyright © Julie Robert, 2022

Julie Robert has asserted her right under the Copyright, Designs and Patents Act, 1988,
to be identified as Author of this work.

For legal purposes the Acknowledgements on p. viii constitute an extension
of this copyright page.

Cover design: Terry Woodley
Cover image: imageBROKER / Alamy Stock Photo

All rights reserved. No part of this publication may be reproduced or transmitted in
any form or by any means, electronic or mechanical, including photocopying, recording,
or any information storage or retrieval system, without prior permission in writing from
the publishers.

Bloomsbury Publishing Plc does not have any control over, or responsibility for, any
third-party websites referred to or in this book. All internet addresses given in this
book were correct at the time of going to press. The author and publisher regret any
inconvenience caused if addresses have changed or sites have ceased to exist, but
can accept no responsibility for any such changes.

A catalogue record for this book is available from the British Library.

Library of Congress Control Number: 2022932159

ISBN: HB: 978-1-3501-6797-1
PB: 978-1-3503-0129-0
ePDF: 978-1-3501-6798-8
eBook: 978-1-3501-6799-5

Typeset by Deanta Global Publishing Services, Chennai, India

To find out more about our authors and books visit www.bloomsbury.com and
sign up for our newsletters.

To those who learn by doing.

Contents

Acknowledgements		viii
1	Introduction	1
2	Public pedagogy through exemplification	19
3	TSIs as phenomenon	37
4	Reimagining temperance cultures	61
5	Embodiment and affect: TSIs as pedagogues	77
6	Lifestyle heroism: Soberheroes and Dryathletes	103
7	Selfish philanthropists, selfish abstainers	129
8	Unruly examples	153
Conclusion		173
Appendices		181
Notes		195
References		201
Index		226

Acknowledgements

In my 'Introduction to Graduate Studies' seminar at the University of Michigan, our class was introduced to the profession of academe with an invitation, one that still has me question whether it was motivated by humour, prescience or a bit of both. We were asked to introduce ourselves as either amateurs or dilettantes. I professed myself a dilettante, quite unsure of the implications of my self-accusation. While undoubtedly a tongue-in-cheek initiation into the necessary quality of intellectual humility, the exercise has been an enduring one – one that I have revisited on numerous occasions while penning this volume. As someone trained in Francophone literary studies, undertaking a cultural studies project centred largely on Anglo-Australian drinking cultures left me feeling like an amateur. My eclectic (pardon the euphemism) use of theories, scholarship and methods from disciplines not my own leaves me open to accusations of dilettantism. That you are now reading this volume is testament to the guidance and support I have received from many professionals and experts over the life of this project.

I thank my colleagues at the University of Technology Sydney for their inspiration, insights and suggestions as the ideas for this endeavour took shape. The Transforming Cultures Research Centre was the crucible for the project; Meredith Jones and Catherine Robinson in particular were responsible for pushing me to keep pursuing my curiosity into the odd phenomenon I encountered upon landing in Australia. Rick Flowers and Elaine Swan's Public Pedagogies working group introduced me to a number of exceptionally helpful ideas and provided a chance to think about learning through experience while engaged in experiential learning of my own. Alan McKee helped me shape the project into one with genuine relevance while still indulging the quirkiness of the topic. The team in the Research Office in Arts & Social Sciences at UTS were generous in their support for the project in terms of funding and that most precious of commodities: time.

Alexis Bergantz, Nick Manganas and Alice Loda, thank you for your always considered suggestions on the proposal, the chapters as they took shape and for being exceptional friends as well as colleagues. Jarrod Hayes, your friendship and mentorship continue to inspire and be cause to raise a glass. For my many colleagues, academic and professional, in Teaching & Learning at UTS during the crazy pandemic years of 2020 and 2021, you have my gratitude for according me the break to focus on this other side of my intellectual and professional life.

I owe a debt to the team at Bloomsbury, most notably Lucy Carroll and Lily McMahon, who guided me through the publication process with wisdom, understanding and great patience. Given that this book draws on research previously published over nearly six years, I must also acknowledge the careful reading and suggestions from many anonymous colleagues. The insights and incisive suggestions of editors and readers along the way, not limited to David Moore, Henry Yeomans and Waltraud Ernst, are greatly appreciated. I am equally appreciative of the permissions that have allowed me to draw on elements of the research that have appeared elsewhere. In particular, sections of Chapter 4 were previously published in *Alcohol Flows Across Cultures: Drinking Cultures in Transnational and Comparative Perspective* and insights, examples and observations have previously appeared in *Contemporary Drug Problems* and *Health: An Interdisciplinary Journal for the Study of Health, Illness and Medicine*.

I reserve my final thanks for Andrew who has been my sounding-board on this project from its very inception. At every turn, he delicately walked the line between encouragement and constructive criticism. His mastery of the Manhattan has also been a welcome contribution, especially as Covid-19 kept us both at home, working and writing together.

1

Introduction

Sitting in a pub, enjoying a drink with a friend on a wintry Sydney evening in late June 2010, my friend told me that he would be refraining from drinking alcohol for the next month. As a very recent migrant to Australia, I was unaware of any reason for a thirty-one-day abstention in July, and my curiosity was piqued. My unreflexive and potentially impertinent questions of 'What?' and 'Why?' elicited an answer, 'Dry July', pronounced in a self-assured tone that suggested that I was ignorant of a cultural commonplace as elemental to Australian society as the Boxing Day Test (an annual cricket event, as this Canadian later discovered). The look of puzzlement that must have crossed my face prompted a further explanation: 'It's when you give up drinking for a month and raise money for cancer.'

My companion's nonchalant response led me to believe that this must be something that Australians simply 'do', even if none of my newcomer's guidebooks had mentioned the phenomenon. If anything, they and my pre-move online news consumption had warned me of the opposite: this was a society more prone to the excesses of binge drinking than the abstemiousness of binge sobriety. The cultural observer in me (to say nothing of the wine lover) became oddly fascinated by both the individual participant's motivations and the larger cultural relevance of this phenomenon.

From this initial sample of one, I surmised that there were elements of group cohesion, philanthropy, health and financial motivators at play. Dry July, in this case, was adopted as part of an office challenge where individuals signed up to see who could raise the most money by forgoing their usual tipple. The decision to enlist for this particular challenge, when the workplace routinely offered any number of philanthropic schemes with which to get involved, was linked to the enticing prospect of being able to drop a couple of kilos and save a few dollars by not drinking for a month. This mishmash of motivations, and the seemingly arbitrary flip from one day enjoying (more than) a few drinks to forgoing the experience entirely the next, signalled that the undertaking had little to do with the kind of moralistic attitudes towards alcohol I associated with the temperance movement, especially as reflected in Hollywood portrayals of battles between prohibition officers and rum-runners and speakeasy patrons. Instead, it reflected a much more pragmatic and complicated relationship between the temporary teetotaller and alcohol, their health, bank balance, relationship with fellow participant–colleagues, the socially cohesive role of alcohol in Australian society and the charity being supported.

Dry July is now only one of roughly two dozen events of its kind worldwide. The events, most of which were launched after my initial exposure to the idea in mid-2010, differ in terms of timing, causes supported and focus. They nonetheless share important characteristics of being time-delimited, formally backed and often (but not exclusively) philanthropic campaigns that call on participants to totally abstain from alcohol. Most span only a single calendar month or a similarly short timeframe, such as the forty days of Lent in the Christian calendar. Unlike New Year's resolutions, which are often qualitatively vague (to eat healthier, exercise more, drink less) and open-ended, they pitch complete abstinence as the goal, even if many make formal allowances (with financial penalty) for a lapse in willpower or a special occasion that warrants a toast. They are most prominent and popular in contexts with a self-acknowledged reputation for slightly indulgent attitudes towards alcohol. Yet, they are also different from 'sober-curious' communities and groups even though participants, especially since these month-long campaigns have become more commonplace, may have much in common in terms of motivation.

These short-term initiatives are typically backed by an organization that uses the period as a formalized part of awareness-raising, behaviour change and/ or fundraising activities. Like the various 'thons' (swim-a-thons, read-a-thons, etc.) or embodied philanthropy challenges ranging from the heroic (climbing a mountain) to the pride-compromising (shaving one's head or dousing oneself with a bucket of icy water), they are subtly varied but fundamentally related projects that use analogous participatory methods to achieve comparable goals. Campaigns like Dry July might more productively, therefore, be considered iterations of a popular and growing international phenomenon. They have elsewhere been designated 'dry months', 'sober months' or 'voluntary/temporary abstinence campaigns', appellations that speak to underlying assumptions about the rationale for and the nature of the break from alcohol. For my part, I call them Temporary Sobriety Initiatives (or TSIs) in recognition of the overall sobering or tempering effect this period of abstinence is meant to have on both an individual's and society's overall relationship with alcohol.

In more than a decade since the first TSIs launched, they have become something of a mainstream practice, especially in Australia and Britain, but increasingly in Canada and Scandinavian countries. Surveys suggest that as many as one in six residents of the UK intended to abstain from alcohol during January 2017 (YouGov 2017). In Australia, thousands of participants have raised millions of dollars for the causes supported by the three campaigns that entreat drinkers to go dry during February (FebFast), July (Dry July) or October (Ocsober). In other locations – Canada, Ireland, Finland, the United States, even France, Hungary, Slovenia, Belgium and the Netherlands (for a full list, see Appendix A) – the timing and popularity vary, but local adaptations are proliferating and becoming more popular every year.

As TSIs gained in local importance, they transitioned from feel-good public interest stories for local media and fodder for cynical commentators to genuine subjects of scholarly inquiry. Clinical researchers curious about the effects of the trend investigated the purported health benefits of abstaining from alcohol for thirty-day intervals (Mehta et al. 2015; Munsterman et al. 2018). In so doing, they lent some credence to the concept of a month-long break from alcohol having an appreciable medical benefit. Researchers who conducted large-scale studies with participants queried whether particular campaigns, such as the UK's Dry January and Australia's FebFast, have been effective in actually changing drinking habits in the longer term (de Visser et al. 2016; de Visser et al. 2017; Hillgrove and Thomson 2012). Much to the surprise of sceptics, their findings confirm a genuine effect. Larger independent analyses comparing participants to non-participants have nonetheless begun to cast doubt on these claims (Case et al. 2021). Regardless of the findings, such investigations principally serve an evaluative function to determine if TSIs 'work', albeit within relatively narrow parameters of success, defined either by the organizations themselves or by public health bodies. The early results of these investigations have nevertheless buoyed TSI organizers who have been able to draw upon the findings to advertise the reported benefits – better sleep, weight loss, improved productivity and energy, better social relationships, clearer complexions, stronger vital statistics – of the short break from alcohol.

If, however, one considers TSIs not just as sabbaticals from alcohol but as a collection of subtly varied, local expressions of an international trend towards purposive binge sobriety, different questions become relevant. Marketing, communications, legal and public health scholars, as well as professional operators in the third sector, are increasingly looking to dry-month success stories, success defined in a variety of ways, to better understand *how* temporarily giving up alcohol for charity became a new fundraising scheme at the same time as it became an anti-consumption and healthy living movement with even loftier aspirations to change society's relationship with alcohol. Here, comparative analysis of the underlying objectives, campaign structures, timing, messaging and public response – all to be considered within the relevant local circumstances – can provide important insight into the TSI logic and the public resonance of campaigns.[1] Like any coordinated initiative, the choices campaign organizers make provide TSIs with a particular inflection and allow researchers to understand the individual campaigns, and via their similarities in the grouping of like initiatives, as social and cultural actors in their own right.

For cultural observers, the questions are related but slightly different. Where did TSIs come from? Why and how did they spread? What overarching cultural premises and/or local circumstances did TSI tap into or capitalize upon? What is their appeal, especially given that they tend to be most successful in contexts that embrace alcohol as a socially cohesive factor? How do they actually work for the organizations that run them and for the individuals who take part?

This book, the extension of my initial curiosity about Dry July, sets out to answer these questions through a multidisciplinary and cross-cultural analysis of TSIs as complex nodes of philanthropic, health, educational, cultural, consumer and civic activity. Taken as a whole, the enquiry seeks to understand why TSIs have emerged as a preferred means for participants and organizers to effect both personal objectives and advance social goals centring on health, philanthropy, cultural change or some combination thereof. It is not intended to be yet another critique of neo-liberalism or a contemporary history of modern abstinence movements, although TSIs cannot be understood without reference to these phenomena, for it is my contention that TSIs function as networked, neo-liberal temperance campaigns. Where TSIs offer something different – especially when thinking beyond the questions of alcohol, drinking or even philanthropy – is in *how* as a form of social movement predicated on personal choices, they craftily leverage the pedagogical power of individual, embodied examples. In this, TSIs function as a form of alcohol and drinking education, taken in the broad sense Dwight Heath attributes to it, where people engage in a 'more convincing and more lasting process' that addresses alcohol's physiological, emotional and social effects, as well as its role in shaping behaviours when consumed or refused (Heath 2012: 103). By virtue of the extent of participation, these examples both illustrate and enact changes to individual and collective drinking behaviours and the role attributed to alcohol.

Twenty-first-century temperance

Although deliberate periods of abstinence have been practised for centuries and have often been linked to religious customs, the advent of TSIs speaks to logics other than the imitation of a divine example of sacrifice and self-restraint. They similarly differentiate themselves from what linger as the mythologized images of the temperance movement in the American, Northern European and Australasian contexts – staid campaigners railing about the moral perils of alcohol or prohibition officers pouring liquor down the drain – thanks to more permissive views on alcohol consumption from campaign organizers and among the population at large.[2] It is, after all, no accident that TSIs are virtually unheard of in contexts where rates of alcohol consumption are low and/or rates of personal abstinence are higher thanks to either cultural or regulatory factors. Even in their most stridently reforming versions that emphasize individual action as a means to effect moderation and a significant reduction in alcohol consumption on a societal level, TSIs are more neo-liberal than preachy. They envisage and promote demonstrably moderate and considered approaches to drinking, the epitome of 'responsible' drinking, rather than personal teetotalism or legislated prohibition. This approach likely owes to persistent public suspicion of what is perceived as moralism (Berridge 2005) or accusations of regulatory overreach (Valverde 1998), both of which run counter to predominant doctrines of individual responsibility. TSIs nonetheless have a great deal in common with prior temperance logics, if not their outward manifestations.

Like the temperance movement's call to limit alcohol consumption via personal pledges and regulatory interventions, TSIs came about in a general context (with specific local inflections) of heightened anxiety about alcohol (AIHW 2014) that was out of step with the realities of consumption. As Levine (1993) noted of American temperance, the movement arose even though estimated per capita alcohol consumption had been declining for decades. Similarly, Australia in 2008, when all three national TSIs formed, had experienced falling rates of per capita consumption for years (ABS 2015) but was newly awash in media coverage of binge drinking, especially among young people, girls and those more likely to engage in violent behaviour while under the influence (Robert 2016b). This occasioned high levels of public concern for the social problems deemed to arise from the vague notion of 'irresponsible drinking' and the nation's problematic 'drinking culture', a term increasingly unmoored from its anthropological roots (Douglas 1987; Wilson 2005) to instead be used as a euphemism for the most sensational elements and negative behaviours associated with alcohol consumption (Savic et al. 2016). News editors and politicians opportunistically seized upon dramatic scenes of drunken brawls and young women semi-conscious in gutters in their clubbing attire to highlight a handful of severe or tragic cases in their calls to public action. The continual focus on the 'drinking culture' provoked increasing levels of self-scrutiny, but not so much among those who were captured in the B-roll for the evening news. Instead, the messages found purchase among those who already self-identified as 'responsible drinkers' but who recognized the limits or failings of their personal responsibility.

Those decrying the culture of irresponsible drinking stopped well short of anti-alcohol sentiment, especially for the much-touted and epidemiologically over-represented 'responsible majority' of moderate drinkers that Robin Room (2010) argues has become the cultural ideal of self-control in post-temperance, neo-liberal societies. The championing of moderation and responsibility remained unabashed, even though definitions of moderation and responsible drinking have been and remain contested (Yeomans 2013), not least because they are seen as out of keeping with how people interpret them and experience them through daily life (Lindsay 2010). The perceived (and readily perceptible) rather than objective state of alcoholic irresponsibility, not alcohol itself, was therefore cast as the problem to be solved. It was thus the drunken brawler or the staggering clubber rather than those whose overindulgence occurred in the privacy of their lounge rooms or blended into the regular weekly routines of the neighbourhood pub that focused public attention. Demonstrations of responsibility with regard to alcohol, the more overt, the better, thus became central to new temperance thinking and campaigns. As Dorothy Noyes (2016) argues of socially transformative moments, these social circumstances called for gestures, grand or small, that could crystalize responsible conduct, vis-à-vis alcohol, into examples to be followed.

Controlling one's behaviour to achieve socially valued outcomes has long been at the core of temperance thinking. Joseph Gusfield (1986) maintains that nineteenth- and twentieth-century American temperance, which was strongest among the nascent middle class, had always been a primarily symbolic rather than pragmatic campaign: status and recognition for one's way of life – not alcohol control – were the chief objectives of the movement. 'The argument is less over the effect of the proposed measures on concrete actions than it is over the question of whose culture is to be granted legitimacy' (Gusfield 1986: 148). David Wagner (1997) similarly argues that the broader American turn towards 'new temperance', the embrace of lifestyle choices characterized as healthier or less risky, starting in the 1970s, was a strategy of social demarcation whereby behaviour and not relatively stable identity markers, such as race, enabled the increasingly undermined middle class to shore up its social position. Comparable arguments could be made of any number of Western nations, for temperance mentalities became part of larger 'healthist' projects (such as trends towards exercise, dieting, organic eating and anti-tobacco) that were characteristic of the new civic morality – that one shall be self-sufficient in all regards and not become a burden on the state – of the neo-liberal age (Crawford 1980, 2006). Temperance reinvented was therefore most likely to be a lifestyle project related to demonstrations of responsibility for the maintenance and development of one's human capital rather than an overt concern for virtue or respectability, and even less a campaign demonizing alcohol. It is also worth noting that many abstainers (for instance, those who abstain or consume very sparingly owing to factors such as religion or taste) could be accused of missing the point. They perform the right action but for the wrong reason and thus act but do not gesture towards the larger project.

If TSIs are to be considered neo-temperance movements, they must also be seen as paradigmatic neo-liberal projects, but not just for their 'healthy living' orientation. As my friend's example first suggested to me, TSI participants are spurred to abstain (in the short term) to increase their various forms of social capital (Bourdieu 1977), not just to improve their health. They seek to attract the plaudits that come from being part of a socially legitimized initiative, both in terms of society at large and in their own networks. Where societies still regard alcohol as that which facilitates bonding and raises one above the suspicion of either being an outsider (religious minority, suffering from an illness, recovering alcoholic) or judgemental of others who do not belong as a result of their drinking, TSIs purport to champion the ideal of moderation – including the moderation of moderation.

There is an equal, and a more often acknowledged, desire to achieve appreciable and personally advantageous goals related to this capital: to have more energy, avoid hangovers, be fitter, be more productive, save money and improve overall health. Like any accumulation of capital in a late capitalist society, the demonstrability of this capital via achievement is paramount. Such achievement-oriented rationales underpin the Quantified Self movement (the accumulation and analysis of personal data on a range of factors such as sleep, nutrition and activity) and the range of 'tracking' technologies it employs (Lupton 2016; Swan 2013). TSIs leverage the power of such drives by providing (prospective) participants with discursive and calculative tools to quantify the financial and caloric savings of a commitment to temporary abstinence. Participants and organizers alike also conceive of episodic sobriety as a way to direct social and human capital to other socially valued projects. The time saved by not frequenting the pub or nursing a hangover can be directed towards fitness or professional goals, while financial savings can be directed to other purchases or to a charitable cause. These normally hidden opportunity costs of drinking are made visible and, when highlighted through actions such as joining a gym or taking a holiday, become part of the incentivizing discourse.

Scholars of neo-liberalism's influence on healthcare and public health have made compelling arguments regarding the circumstances by which a solicitous concern for one's health and individual productivity came about at the same time – and arguably in response to – the erosion of financial support for erstwhile public services (Brown and Baker 2012; Petersen and Lupton 1996). For decades state funding for medical research, patient support, health promotion and harm reduction for the philanthropically unpopular causes of drug and alcohol dependency support have declined in relative if not absolute terms in many national contexts. Inspired by adages (and evidence) that prevention is more economical (and effective) than cure, governments across Western nations have used disciplining institutions and initiatives such as schools and health education programmes to impose upon individuals a civic responsibility to maintain their health in such a manner that they reduce their chances of having to rely upon services that remain publicly funded.

Philanthropy to support defunded and now (semi-)privatized services in turn became an expectation of responsible citizenship (King 2006), not so much in a nationalistic sense, but rather in regard to an increasingly globalized middle class. Although the secular morality of healthism had replaced the religious morality of earlier years, the services associated with temperance causes still relied on donations for their practical needs, for the work of bringing others into the fold required more than just social capital. Philanthropy was therefore cast as yet another way to allow self-differentiation via one's conduct, for according to pervasive but simplistic logics, being charitable to others elevated the donor relative to those who benefitted from their charity: 'there is a general view that people should look after themselves and not rely on charities, perhaps indicating that charity is viewed as something that exists for the benefit of "other people"

Introduction   9

rather than the reality that most of us are both donors and recipients' (Mohan and Breeze 2016: 14). TSI participants accordingly become not just donors via their own contributions but also fundraisers or philanthropic entrepreneurs for their chosen cause. In doing so, they position themselves on the socially valued side of the false dichotomy between donor and beneficiary, and in the case of health-related charities, as responsible, contributing citizens rather than needy patients or clients.

More so than the viral philanthropic campaigns (2014's Ice Bucket Challenge, as a prime example) or even many of the one-off and especially small-scale sporting events (charity runs, walks, rides that do not require significant training to take part) that also thrust participants into the role of 'fit' fundraiser, TSIs fused two neo-liberal imperatives: philanthropy and individual responsibility for one's health. In the contexts in which philanthropic TSIs flourished (Australia, the UK and Canada), collective charitable activity became an excuse for a still largely impugned or suspect lifestyle choice – alcoholic abstention – albeit temporarily and in service of the more supported aim of moderation or 'responsible drinking'. Taken as a form of contemporary self-regulation, arguably temperance in the truest sense of the word, TSIs are especially well adapted to the present ethos because they blur the lines between individual and collective action and rehabilitate a refusal to consume that is uncharacteristic of its largely middle-class audience as a revenue-generating act. Neo-liberalism alone, however, does not fully demarcate TSIs as a contemporary form of temperance from its antecedent movements.

TSI organizers, whether oriented towards public health or philanthropic ends, emulated the temperance movement's use of networks to extend and enact their activities. TSIs leveraged the increasingly global networks of third-sector actors, particularly among organizations supporting similar causes, to revive the practice – if not always the cause – of temperance internationalism. The spread, popularity and ultimate success of TSIs as public campaigns has been assisted by online networks, apps and social media, especially where English – as with the temperance movement (Tyrrell 1991) – served as a common language. Taking advantage of the global reach of digital technologies is, however, only one of the ways TSIs proved themselves to be digitally adapted.

Although many TSIs began as grassroots initiatives among groups of friends, their expansion utilized the practices and mentalities engendered by digital networks, platforms and technologies. Building on the success of e- and m-health initiatives (Kazemi et al. 2017), TSIs use emails, apps and text messaging to provide just-in-time communication to reinforce participants' commitment to and investment in the campaign's dual goals of behaviour change and fundraising. This strategy provides recognition for adherence up to that point, a reinforcement of participants' self-efficacy, with the prospective intent of keeping them committed to continued sobriety during the campaign and carrying forward an intent to drink less often and/or as much (Bartram et al. 2018). Where TSIs have a philanthropic orientation, there is generally a further dimension to such communications; they thank participants for their fundraising efforts, encourage them to collect more donations and remind them of the implicit contract – the sacrifice of alcohol in return for pledges – they struck with their sponsors.

More than simply being tools TSIs use to reach their participants and donors, digital technologies and online networks function as intrinsic parts of the campaigns. The cultures of self-display and self-promotion that social media promotes give organizers and participants alike platforms to make the temporary non-consumption of alcohol a demonstrative act, a counterpoint to the prominence of performances and displays of drinking and drunkenness (Goodwin et al. 2016). This lifestyle choice is performed and publicized through its broadcast and therein invites not only commendation (Cherrier et al. 2017) but also emulation and financial recognition in the form of donations, which are increasingly collected online.

The broadcasting of deliberate and arguably counter-to-type abstinence to cultivate more responsible or moderate approaches to alcohol consumption is nonetheless paradoxical. It casts what would have been the long-term desire of public health and temperance campaigners – the mundane and easy choice to not drink (as much) – as a radical decision that deserves to be celebrated and financially compensated as a courageous act of social non-conformity and personal sacrifice. Such a contrast is central to the logic of TSIs and explains how, despite their recent spread, they still have not found much of an audience where overall rates of abstinence are higher and alcohol is not regarded as a force of social cohesion. Yet, as the public health backers of many TSIs state, the contemporary temperance goals of changing the (implicitly problematic) drinking cultures depend on making the choice to not drink or to drink only moderately, valid and unremarkable options via a process of normalization (Cherrier and Gurrieri 2013; Fry 2011; Booker 2019). Far from being incidental then, the attention TSIs draw to the participant's non-drinking body and the non-drinker themself – positioning both as noteworthy examples – is central to the campaign's enactment as fundraiser, awareness generator and instigator of behaviour change.

Exemplary abstinence

TSI organizers and participants have attached much significance to the act of temporarily abstaining from alcohol. Why, however, has such a simple act taken on such importance, especially when one considers the range of objectives for which TSIs cater? Within the context of these campaigns, sobriety is treated less as a lifestyle choice in and of itself (even though some may champion that as an ultimate goal) than as a gesture or a performance with specific objectives in terms of social awareness, behaviours favouring long-term moderation and philanthropic engagement. The non-drinking body is invested with the potential to educate, elicit empathy, generate revenue and instigate change because it is posited to be observably different and imitable while in a deliberately sober state. Despite the differences in local contexts and campaign objectives (which range from the mostly philanthropic to the overtly educational with regard to drink driving and alcohol's health effects), the design and discourse of TSIs are strikingly similar when it comes to their core mechanism. They all position the non-drinking during the campaign to be abstention of an exemplary nature insofar as it is demonstrative, but also – and crucially – didactic.

In common usage, exemplarity implies being praiseworthy or the best of a kind (e.g. an exemplary student). This laudatory usage serves as a shorthand for a long philosophical tradition predicated on inspiring particular ways of thinking or acting, the logic being that a superior example invites imitation. Rhetorically speaking, examples illustrate or ground a point to render it more comprehensible; an analogous situation of a more appreciable or familiar nature is often offered by way of explanation for an abstract proposition (Gelley 1995). Similarly, a quality might be exemplified by a person, an object, a case or an instance that demonstrates that quality in an exaggerated or recognizable way (Elgin 1993). Examples are indexical; they carry with them and signal to a larger context even though they are in and of themselves discrete and readily appreciable (Noyes 2016). These largely rhetorical or abstract understandings of exemplarity are not inherently or conventionally pedagogical, although they have long underpinned pedagogical logics and been incorporated into didactic practices.

Examples are increasingly theorized and mobilized as explicit tools for learning, both within and outside of formal educational settings (Warnick 2008). When evoked in their rhetorical sense, examples facilitate comprehension and therein contribute to learning outcomes. Examples, especially human examples, can also be pedagogical insofar as they inspire or guide thinking and action via imitation. Role models, those charged with providing or being 'good' examples and who are entreated to refrain from becoming 'bad' examples, become embodied lessons. In community settings, an example's potential to inspire or effect change, including via imitation, has occasioned renewed scholarly interest, especially in what might be understood as social movement learning (Krøijer 2015; Haenfler et al. 2012) or public pedagogy: the cultural, social and political spaces, discourses, processes and functions that normalize – although also potentially contest and resist – attitudes and behaviours.[3]

The factors that determine whether an example will ultimately be imitated are complex. Traditional philosophical understandings of the matter emphasized judgement and the imitator's rational agency (Kant 2007; Belarmino 2013). Such views have recently benefitted from scientific insights that point to a greater role for affect or a guiding self-narrative to determine whether an example will inspire imitation (Warnick 2008).[4] In both scenarios, the quality of the example itself, specifically its recognizability as a 'paradigmatic example' (Højer and Bandak 2015: 7) and a social proximity that enables identification (Noyes 2016: 78), is determinative of its pedagogic potential and its ability to inspire mimesis.

Understood in the terms of didacticism and demonstrability, exemplarity is the principle at the heart of TSIs. These campaigns use an achievable period of sobriety as a self-generated, embodied example for enacting a form of temperance that holds deliberate moderation (rather than avowed abstinence) to be the ultimate goal. Whether they prioritize fundraising (Dryathlon, Dry Feb) or behaviour/culture change (Dry January, Alcohol Free for 40), or balance these objectives (FebFast, Défi 28 jours), TSI organizers employ a promotional discourse that frames participation as a socially laudable act and participants are cast as literally embodying qualities, such as generosity, social responsibility and health consciousness, that are esteemed. The combination of time delimitation, embodiment and mass participation has proven crucial to TSIs; indeed, these factors speak to the specific ways in which exemplarity is cultivated through embodied public pedagogies.

The time delimitation of TSIs is a central feature of their exemplifying power, for the period of participation is isolated and differentiated from other abstinent phases (Lent, pregnancy and periods of illness being the most common examples) and as an intentionally sober (in the sense of *dry*) and sobering (taken as *tempering* or *moderating*) period in a participant's larger drinking existence. The TSI-aligned abstinence is by consequence not only praiseworthy, including for altruistic reasons, but is also something that is quarantined in such a way that it becomes readily observable as an exaggerated or deliberate state. This isolation and amplification of temperance behaviours allows the exemplary qualities of the abstainers and the consequences of drinking, non-drinking and moderation alike, to become evident and thus richer in didactic potential. This potentiality reaches outside observers – the participant's friends, family, social media followers and acquaintances – and provides them, if all goes according to organizer expectations, imitable and relatable examples of both self-sacrifice and responsibility in alcohol consumption from within their social circle.

The dry period is also inwardly pedagogical, an exercise in self-discovery or learning about oneself through experimentation, insofar as it acts on self-efficacy (Bandura 2006) and the 'skill' of not drinking (Booker 2019: 60–2). A participant may subsequently refer to their (previously) abstinent TSI-self as an example for their own future conduct, for instance to refuse a drink if one is offered or to plan social activities that are not centred around the consumption of alcohol. Failed or misaligned attempts at temporary sobriety can nonetheless generate countervailing examples and nurture beliefs that the paradigmatic example of moderation (or of short-term abstinence) can never be achieved, although this supposition has been challenged by new empirical evidence (de Visser et al. 2016).

The embodied nature of TSI participation allows participants to have more deliberate or conscious experiences with (or without) alcohol. Whether via its presence or absence from the body or social situations, alcohol is experienced affectively and experientially during or around TSI participation in a way that is generally distinctive or better defined than any less than fully deliberate period of non-drinking or modest consumption. TSIs thus concretize the disputed, abstract and potentially ignored messages that alcohol should be consumed in moderation (Barry and Goodson 2010). Viewed from the perspective of the participants themselves, the embodied example created via participation becomes far more than a simple gesture or index case. The participant's embodied experience allows the example to take on its full explanatory and illustrative function, as outcomes, whether the advertised benefits or the less publicized drawbacks, become concretely and affectively linked to the participant's experience of abstaining. Lived experience becomes an alternative and potentially more powerful basis for knowledge about alcohol, its embodied effects and sociocultural function than general advice or abstract knowledge (Newby-Clark et al. 2002; de Visser and Smith 2007).

As *participatory* public health and philanthropic campaigns, TSIs also rely on the body's rich semiotic potential, its ability to communicate via appearance and demeanour (Shilling 2013; Featherstone 2000; Hargreaves and Vertinsky 2007).

TSI participants become behavioural examples in the immediate and over the course of the campaign and thereby communicate, both verbally and non-verbally, the outcomes of participation to others. The example, by virtue of its embodiment, takes on a testimonial function. What is communicated and to whom is nonetheless context dependent and accounts for TSIs, such as the English and French versions of Dry January, that are identical in rationale, structure and execution being seen as promoting either laudable (English) or suspect (French) behaviour.

Thus far, the exemplarity of TSIs has been outlined in ways contained to the participant and circles small enough to know of their participation. As a collective or social phenomenon involving tens of thousands of participants worldwide though, TSIs further engender and function as a form of mass exemplarity or a movement. In countries such as Australia, the UK and Finland, where concern about patterns and rates of alcohol consumption is high, TSI participants en masse serve as an example of how the larger drinking population might shift towards a more moderate approach to alcohol. Individual exemplarity is accordingly compounded and the collective act of temporarily abstaining becomes, as Stine Krøijer (2015) argues of other forms of social activism, both the goal and the means of a public pedagogy based on the demonstrability and imitability of an embodied example. Simply put, TSI participants enact the change the organizers wish to see in society more broadly. In this TSIs might be classified as what Haenfler et al. (2012) have called a 'lifestyle movement' insofar as they 'consciously and actively promote a lifestyle, or way of life, as their primary means to foster social change' (Haenfler et al. 2012: 2). The putative classification nonetheless requires some caveats. Divergences between organizer intent, including between TSIs with different objectives, and participant motivation complicate the defining notion of lifestyle movements, notably that intentionally individualized yet collective action is used to bring about social change. Moreover, TSIs rely on an exaggerated form of moderate drinking behaviour to bring about sustained change. Unlike temperance, which is a lifestyle movement in the traditional sense, TSIs rely on such an extreme example of moderation that it would lose its pedagogical power as a discrete example were it to become an enduring lifestyle choice.

An ideal scenario of TSI participation, one where participant and organizer motivations fully align notwithstanding, the examples generated through and by TSIs do not always support the imagined pedagogical project. During the campaigns, participants might withdraw or be excluded from their normal social circle, feel out of step with their peers or be accused of implicitly (or explicitly) passing judgement on others who continue to drink as before. They may not experience physical or psychological changes that they value or may not attribute positive experiences to their reduced alcohol consumption. They may also be motivated by their own agendas, such as proving to others that their normal consumption patterns are not problematic, rather than those that correspond with the intent of the campaign and risk undermining its objectives. In such cases, TSIs are likely to engender negative exemplarity and work counter to the imputed pedagogies of responsible drinking.

Understanding TSIs

The present volume is a multidisciplinary analysis of TSIs as an emergent international phenomenon. Working in the wide-ranging tradition of cultural studies, it draws on a diverse range of theories and frameworks from health education, philanthropy studies, educational philosophy, social semiotics of the body, marketing and communications to understand what TSIs are, why they have become a phenomenon and how they function. Research has followed the evolution of individual TSIs and the growth of the phenomenon both within and across geographic borders and cultural contexts. It is my contention that TSIs are networked and neo-liberal campaigns that promote a new form of episodic temperance. They have done so via the exemplarity afforded by embodied participation and have consequently enacted multiple public pedagogies centred on changing so-called problematic drinking cultures or irresponsible drinking. At the larger conceptual level, this volume argues that defined embodied examples are the basis of public pedagogies of health that seek to change both individual and collective behaviours through individual action.

To substantiate this view, this study draws on three principal perspectives: participant experiences, organizer insights and public-facing media. These sources allow for a better understanding of how TSIs function as both planned campaigns to generate deliberately pedagogical examples for self and others and as participatory experiences subject to variation that complicate their ascribed objectives.

Participant narratives provide insight into a range of TSI experiences, from elegiac testimonials used in official marketing to dissenting commentary. Blogs, social media posts and media stories speak to much of the public discourse about the experience of TSI participation and temporary sobriety more generally. These readily available accounts are supplemented with over twenty in-depth interviews with participants in a range of Australian TSIs, including self-directed periods of abstinence that are modelled on TSIs but not linked to fundraising or an official campaign. Further information on these participants and the methodology is provided in Appendix B.

Interviews with TSI organizers provide candid insight into the strategies underpinning particular initiatives. Such perspectives are also gleaned from the semi-public documents, such as annual reports, that are a matter of public record for many charitable organizations, but that are not widely circulated. Organizer interviews with third parties, most often third-sector trade publications or forums, further speak to questions of strategy that may not always be apparent in public-facing materials. The main public presence of TSIs, accessible online via official websites, social media platforms and direct electronic communications (emails, text messages and notifications), captures the dominant image of a TSI for any given yearly iteration. Considering that the face and discourse of TSIs have tended to change from year to year, examining such materials over nearly a decade reveals evolutions in the self-image TSIs present, especially in response to market-driven factors.

The chapters that follow explore how episodic and philanthropically directed sobriety has become the twenty-first-century example of temperance and temperance by example. Chapter 2 establishes the theoretical premise of the study, linking educational philosophy about the constitution and function of examples to the context of informal learning. It argues that perceived crises or moral panics, for instance with regard to socially corrosive 'drinking cultures', generate a concern about and efforts to control the instructive power of examples. The chapter takes a step back from the immediacy of the empirical question to consider examples as philosophical and rhetorical constructs. Understandings of exemplarity, notably those that construe examples as didactic and demonstrative, are brought to bear on notions of public pedagogy, lifestyle movements, social movement learning and cultural change.

The next two chapters form a contemporary cultural history of TSIs that interrogate their emergence and appeal. Chapter 3 canvasses a range of international campaigns to argue that TSIs constitute a distinctive phenomenon defined by common features and are classifiable along a continuum that alternately prioritizes one of two neo-liberal objectives: health and productivity related to biopolitical self-governance or philanthropic engagement. This chapter also chronicles how digital networks and established third-sector communities seized upon the successful examples of TSIs in places like Australia to launch an international movement.

The links between contemporary TSIs and the temperance movements of the nineteenth and twentieth centuries are explored in Chapter 4. While most modern TSIs are at pains to distance themselves from the stereotypical images of prohibitionist temperance that dominate the Anglo-American imagination, the campaigns echo many of the practices and discourses of lesser-known temperance movements and other forms of alcoholic abstinence, not least in the ways in which the opportunity costs of drinking are highlighted and in the time-delimited nature of certain historical antecedents. These parallels and divergences are considered in terms of origins, episodic temperance, appeals to scientific and health-based logics, and the role of both examples and public commitment in achieving temperance aims.

The remaining chapters focus on practices of exemplification in contemporary TSIs and explain the various ways in which embodied examples are at the heart of these campaigns, both in theory and in practice. Chapter 5 focuses on the public health objectives of TSIs and analyses the power of embodied and experiential examples to educate about alcohol. The narratives of TSI founders serve as case studies of imitable outward exemplarity, while the embodied nature of TSI participation is explained as a way to turn oneself into a didactic example that speaks to both rationalist and affect-driven realizations about alcohol, for others as much as for oneself. TSIs' emphasis on demonstrability, notably their tactics of exaggeration, amplification and marketing, are explored in Chapter 6. In post-temperance contexts where drinking has become a banal and arguably invisible lifestyle consideration, TSIs have provided a means to make the choice to curtail or responsibilize one's drinking, both an obvious and praiseworthy gesture.

Chapter 7 investigates the philanthropic aspects of exemplarity at work in many TSIs. Practices of exemplification are considered in dynamic tension between individuals, who enact the examples prescribed by the TSIs, and the campaigns themselves, which have proven responsive to participants' priorities and the successes (and failures) of comparable initiatives. The question of failure is explicitly taken up in Chapter 8, which considers the impact of negative examples, which are generated when TSI participation does not adhere to the organizers' plans. The implications for failed exemplarity accordingly put into relief the risks inherent in the generation of personal examples as a form of purposeful public pedagogy.

In the book's Conclusion, I return to the implicit centrality of embodied or lived examples in the processes of awareness-raising, health promotion and behaviour or social change initiatives that have become common objectives in many contemporary social movements or campaigns. The success of TSIs as a phenomenon has seen them and their model of exaggerated individual action become a ready-made response to new societal crises and concerns.

2

Public pedagogy through exemplification

Public pedagogies, and analogue notions such as cultural (Watkins et al. 2015; Hickey-Moody et al. 2010; Noble 2015) or everyday pedagogies (Luke 1996), are the lessons that are both imparted and received via informal learning.[1] An expansive definition, it encompasses any number of objects, events, media, locations and processes. Public pedagogies are used by actors across the political spectrum in both deliberate and unplanned ways. They are associated with a wide variety of objectives, some of which may even be in direct opposition to one another. These pedagogies can 'teach' everything from neo-liberal ideologies to tips for living an anti-consumerist lifestyle. They may also facilitate learning as a process of discovery or validation (Fors and Pink 2017) rather than as a cognitive exercise of linear knowledge acquisition. If there is a definitional predicate for public pedagogies, though, it is their informal nature, which is to say that they are pedagogies, understood as sources of instruction or guidance, that emerge from contexts other than those of formal education or schooling and, indeed, often issue from popular culture and experience.

As in analyses of any pedagogical process, public pedagogies call for a dual focus; on the one hand, there must be a concern for the way learning occurs, and on the other, attention is due to the way in which lessons are imparted. This has led to a concentration of scholarship that focuses on the various forms that public pedagogy takes and on its lessons. Popular movies and television shows (Giroux and Pollock 2010; Warin 2011), advertisements (Giroux 1993; Robert 2015), consumer goods (Fors and Pink 2017), neighbourhood interactions (Noble 2015) and online communities (Sandlin and Walther 2009) are among the most studied forms of public pedagogy. Cutting across much of the scholarship on public pedagogy, however, is an assumption of pedagogic effect, if not didactic intentionality. This owes to the belief that members of the target audience, and the public more generally, are enculturated to particular attitudes and behaviours via either an imitation or a rejection of an imputed pedagogical model (Noble 2015; Flowers and Swan 2015).

Public pedagogies, especially those with the high profile of mass media, tend to attract both scholarly and popular attention in response to a perceived crisis. In particular, there is concern for the ways in which these pedagogies teach by example. For instance, in the most recent edition of his classic sociological account of moral panics, Stanley Cohen (2002) argues that events such as school shootings and other violent crimes focus attention on the modelled behaviours and influences of violence in movies and video games as people seek explanations for unexpected and tragic events. Underpinning the concern for public pedagogy, therefore, is a deep suspicion of not just *what* they 'teach' but also the way in which they use examples – especially embodied examples or role models – for didactic purposes (Rich 2011; Luke 1996). In the case of school shootings, pundits and scholars have sought answers for why movies and video games have inspired horrific violence in a way that news footage has not; in short, what has made them such powerful examples. As framed by analyses of public pedagogy, examples are illustrative of particular qualities and induce imitation, if not by design, then by effect. I therefore propose that public pedagogies of an embodied nature, that rely on both role models and more participatory or corporeal exemplarity, both teach and facilitate learning through a cultivation (which is to say both a generation and a tailoring) of examples.

At the time TSIs first emerged in Finland and Slovenia (2005) and then more significantly in 2008 in Australia, the campaigns were purported to be a means to raise awareness about drinking (especially binge drinking) and its consequences. In that respect they were conceived as public pedagogies that would counter the more obvious influences, such as the sponsorship of elite sport by alcohol companies (Cody and Jackson 2016) and media portrayals (Cin et al. 2008) that normalized alcohol consumption. In subsequent iterations, however, greater emphasis was placed on the initiatives as a framework to modify habits and engage in healthier living, both during and beyond the month of the campaign. Awareness-raising, which has always been concerned with promoting and disseminating knowledge about issues, often as a precursor to planned behaviour change (Ajzen 1985), was replaced by a framework that allowed people, especially participants, to discover for themselves and via embodied experience, alcohol's various and likely previously unnoticed or ignored impacts and entanglements with numerous facets of participants' lives (Hargreaves 2011). As will be set out in subsequent chapters, this process too is fundamentally concerned with the pedagogy of examples of various sorts.

Public Pedagogy through Exemplification

This chapter, however, momentarily steps back from TSIs as a form of public pedagogy engaged with the role of examples in processes of learning and discovery to consider the role of examples in processes of education, teaching and learning more generally. For those most interested in TSIs as social movements or as an expression of drinking and alcohol cultures, the final section is likely to be of greatest interest and empirical import. For those curious about the mechanism that has allowed TSIs to transition from quirky challenge to object of legitimate enquiry in fields such as public health and marketing, though, a deeper study of examples and exemplarity – going back to Classical philosophy, drawing in continental philosophers of the eighteenth and nineteenth centuries and working most concertedly with contemporary educational philosophers and sociologists – provides a crucial insight into how the learning and the change occurs. The approach is intended to be accessible for the philosophically reticent while still providing a common and necessary understanding of the example and its instructive power.

At heart, this chapter offers an exploration of the power of examples (what they can do) and the conditions necessary for them to come into being. It opens new ways of seeing not only TSIs but also social movements and the changes through learning they aim to foster. It elucidates what makes something exemplary and therefore invests it with pedagogic potential. Extending these established educational theories into the more cultural and sociological domains of public pedagogy, I argue that contexts of social movement learning, including lifestyle movements and participatory campaigns such as TSIs, are at their core based on a cultivation of exemplarity. These movements and campaigns reproduce the conditions necessary for exemplarity to effect pedagogic (if not always imitative) outcomes and do so for individuals and society more broadly.

Understanding examples

Scholars of the Renaissance, the period when the Classics were being rediscovered at the same time that vernacular literatures were developing, have noted that the definition of *example* was, both contemporaneously and in the centuries that followed, the subject of much slippage. This was 'probably due to the transformation of technical language under the pressure of common usage' (Rigolot 1998: 557). The two principal definitions – one referencing a normative standard to be emulated, the other an instance that is an illustrative part of a larger group or proposition – remain intertwined. Moreover, these two definitions recognize that the notion of exemplarity extends beyond the discursive to encompass a much wider range of potential examples, including objects and individuals. If there is a common thread, however, it is that examples are defined foremost by their imputed purpose; they demonstrate, elucidate, explain and concretize. On that basis, examples are demonstrative and, by extension, didactic.[2]

For Plato, as outlined in the *Timeaus* account of the origins of the cosmos (Section 1), the example – the archetype – corresponds to the sense of the *exemplar* in today's usage:

> All that becomes and is created is the work of a cause, and that is fair which the artificer makes after an eternal pattern, but whatever is fashioned after a created pattern is not fair. Is the world created or uncreated? – that is the first question. Created, I reply, being visible and tangible and having a body, and therefore sensible; and if sensible, then created; and if created, made by a cause, and the cause is the ineffable father of all things, who had before him an eternal archetype.

Explained by Donna Altimari Adler (2019: 16), 'Timaeus maintained that "the father" (the Craftsman or creator of the universe) must have looked toward an eternal exemplar in the world's fabrication, since it would not otherwise be beautiful.' In this sense, the example is normative (setting the standard) and also superlative: it is the model that epitomizes a concept or a kind and that, by consequence, lends itself to reproduction or emulation. For Noyes (2016: 78), it is this kind of example, the *Vorbild*, that is endowed with the necessary and sufficient gestural qualities for role models, such as Rosa Parks and the student standing against tanks in Tiananmen Square, to emerge from the performance of simple actions. The Platonic example is in this way didactic, for it evidences that which is worthy of emulation and therein facilitates what we commonly refer to as 'learning by example'. Most discussions about the power of role models and the very concept of imitative learning harken to these Platonic understandings.

In Aristotle's *On Rhetoric*, the example is discussed more overtly. It is not to be imitated but is instead an instrument to illustrate and explain for the purpose of persuasion. It uses a familiar or relatable instance to propound the logic of a corresponding but lesser-known situation that must be understood in order to convince. Aristotle rejects the idea of the example as a particular expression of the general or as a subordinate notion – he emphasizes the lateral movement from 'part to part, like to like' and explains, clarifying, 'When two statements are of the same order, but one is more familiar than the other, the former is an "example"' (Aristotle 1991: Part 2, 44). His arguments nonetheless provide the foundation for inductive reasoning's progression from the readily comprehensible instance to the unfamiliar, abstract or general. The Aristotelian example, contends François Rigolot (1998: 557), was accordingly also didactic in intent; it was 'an illustrative anecdote with a moral point' where the quality of the illustration, the art of the rhetoric, determined the example's effectiveness as a form of pedagogy.

These Platonic and Aristotelian concepts of the example – the model and the illustration – are not mutually exclusive in contemporary understandings of examples and exemplarity (Gelley 1995). Instead, they exist in a tension of differentiated emphasis. Plato's accentuation of the nature of the example as self-evidently worthy of emulation leans towards the didactic. Educationalists from Locke to Rousseau, to modern theorists such as Dewey, have accordingly been concerned with the latent potential of examples, especially the moral and rational model of the teacher, and their ability to influence conduct and thinking, in essence, to engender learning (Warnick 2008).

Aristotle, by contrast, argues that for examples to be didactic, in the sense of being persuasive, they must be crafted to be unambiguously illustrative of the proposition being exemplified. What is exemplified, as the general class, is not taken to be self-evident but is instead rendered appreciable via circumstances or skills that can reinforce or undermine. For Aristotle, the art in crafting examples to demonstrate one's point is the measure of the rhetor. Kant's *Critique of Pure Reason* correspondingly deems one's ability to parse the appropriateness of an example for a general principle to be an exercise in judgement and, as Scott Stroud (2011) argues, a form of educative rhetoric: 'Indeed, the grand and only use of examples, is to sharpen the judgement' (Kant 1781: 105). To wit, Bryan Warnick's (2008: 31) comprehensive genealogy of human exemplarity ventures that an alternative definition of education could well be 'the ability to recognize things as examples of something else in increasing levels of complexity'. At both the point of crafting and comprehending examples, though, demonstrability acts as a key determinant of the quality of an example's didactic potential.

Preconditions for learning by example

An example's potential to influence behaviour or understanding, whether through imitation or elucidation, helps to explain the interest in exemplarity among those concerned with education and pedagogical processes more broadly. Philosophers of education, among them Catherine Elgin and Bryan Warnick, contend that the pedagogical or didactic effectiveness of examples is the result of a number of factors that speak to their 'demonstrability'. Educators of various sorts, both formal and informal, have accordingly endeavoured to maximize the instructive utility of examples to enhance their demonstrative and, by extension, didactic potential.

One of the key elements in the demonstrability of examples, in both the Aristotelian rhetorical and Platonic normative senses, is context. A well-chosen example hinges upon a shared, or at least mutually comprehensible, frame of reference. In the case of deliberately articulated examples, the context must be shared between the giver of the example and those interpreting it – for instance, between a teacher and students or author and reader. Where examples are not consciously framed or given but are instead recognized, the example is also context dependent. Building on the work of both Goodman (1976) and Elgin, Warnick argues 'a context of similarity is just as important as difference in directing our attention toward examples. An exemplar has to be recognizably part of a community of things, but also recognizably different from other members of the community' (Warnick 2008: 43). This explains how we can regard a high-achieving student as an exemplary student, as they are part of a class of peers but distinguish themselves from their classmates through their studies and results. Recognizability here underpins context and accordingly emerges as the crux of demonstrability.

Recognizability depends on what first Goodman, but later and more persuasively Elgin, refers to as 'expressive reference' or the example's demonstration of its instantiated epistemic qualities within a context of sameness and difference.

> Exemplification requires instantiation. But instantiation, even obvious instantiation, is not enough; for exemplification is a referential relation. An exemplar refers to certain of its properties; it exhibits them, highlights them, shows them forth, makes them manifest. Exemplification requires both reference to and instantiation of the properties exemplified. Because an exemplar is itself an instance of the property it refers to, it affords epistemic access to that property. (Elgin 1993: 400)

Elgin nuances this proposition by noting a number of caveats, which I will attend to in turn. First, exemplarity may be either unintended or deliberate. Second, exemplarity can be non-verbal, symbolic, even embodied so long as it is recognizable. Third, although exhibition is a necessary precondition of exemplarity, exhibition need not be conspicuous.

First to be considered is the matter of intentionality. While rhetorical examples are most often deliberate, as they are carefully selected to illustrate a proposition, normative examples may be either chosen or accidental. One can hazard upon a rose that exemplifies a particular shade of red or one can seek out a paint swatch exemplifying that same colour. Normative examples may be defined in either form or significance, but not both simultaneously, as the example must reference the singular class of which it is defined as a part. The exemplification of 'red' may take either the form of a flower or coloured ink on paper. If, however, asked what the rose in question exemplifies, one may well answer with reference to its scent, its thorniness, its cost relative to other flowers or even its symbolic meaning of love. Insofar as examples are involved in the construction of meaning, they are subject to the same variables that affect the making of meaning more generally; they can be faithful to an original intent or introduce unanticipated alternatives, including those that depend on context and individual interpretation.

As the case of the rose illustrates, examples can take many forms, including those that are unmediated by words. The rose, owing to a shared cultural system of signs (Barthes 1957), can symbolically exemplify love. Absent an understanding of the symbolic meaning of a red rose, it fails to exemplify in this way. Examples, however, often exist outside of semiosis, especially where they take the form of normative models for imitation (Elgin 1993). The dance instructor who performs a movement expecting his class to repeat it provides an example for the students. Performed outside of the dance studio, this same movement may not be an example but, rather, be a mundane act or even an involuntary twitch. The context of the studio and the instructor's acknowledged role nonetheless allow his movements to be recognized as examples. The students, especially depending on their level of skill and experience, are similarly likely to be attuned not to the most conspicuous elements of their teacher's embodied model but, rather, to the nuances that mark his dancing as an imitable example.

The theorizing of exemplarity in educational circles, as in philosophical ones, more often focuses on the power of examples to sway someone to a predetermined conclusion or to engender imitation. Examples and processes of exemplification can nonetheless be crucial to processes of discovery or of forming new meaning. Thomas Kuhn suggests that examples of as yet undiscovered or unarticulated phenomena – counterinstances – are at the root of discovery. They provide a basis from which to experiment and extend knowledge, including where the examples no longer align with the apparent rule: 'If, therefore, these epistemological counterinstances are to constitute more than a minor irritant, that will be because they help to permit the emergence of a new and different analysis of science within which they are no longer a source of trouble' (Kuhn 1996: 78). While Kuhn is more concerned with the empirical evidence, Donna Haraway argues that even the metaphors used to illustrate and explain scientific concepts can occasion moments of discovery: 'A metaphor is important to the nature of explanation because it leads to the testing of the neutral parts of the analogy. It leads to the searching for the *limits* of the metaphoric system and thus generates the anomalies important to [scientific] paradigm change' (Haraway 1976: 9, original emphasis). Affect theory and the sensorial ways we come to know is the personalized extension of this scientific and linguistic precept. 'The success of the example', argues Brian Massumi, 'hinges on the details. Every little one matters. At each new detail, the example runs the risk of falling apart, of its unity of self-relation becoming a jumble' (Massumi 2002: 18). The imperfection of examples therefore risks undermining any deliberate pedagogy at the same time that it contributes to their function in processes of discovery-based learning. Examples thus have the potential to both concretize and to destabilize knowledge.

Such views are informed by an acknowledged relationship – one inherent in all processes of discovery and learning – between the particular and the whole, the already experienced or known and the potentiality of the future. There is therefore an implicit temporality in examples. Illustrative examples draw upon a familiar past or are invented in a mutually understood present (Lyons 1990: 8). Normative examples, by contrast, are inherently more future-oriented in their temporality. A model from the past or present inspires imitation in and for the future, or in the words of Lars Højer and Andreas Bandak (2015: 10), 'a possible figuration of the future'. Reflecting on an example's possibility to influence who we will become, Irene Harvey (2002: 123) alludes to an embryonic future self when someone takes something or another person as an example to imitate. It is for this reason that educationalists gravitate towards the normative definition of exemplarity and seek to harness the power of examples.

Effectively employing or harnessing examples for didactic purposes depends on two key factors: one, understanding what constitutes exemplarity and two, how examples incite imitation. For centuries, educational theorists and practitioners have contended with such questions, as they have sought to mobilize examples with didactic intent – in essence to teach in the conventional sense of the term. As educational precepts have become embedded in everything from marketing to leadership to public health, however, the questions have become salient for a wider audience. In these broader circles, the emphasis is less on teaching and

Public Pedagogy through Exemplification

27

more a question of how best to influence people towards particular behaviours or beliefs.

The models for influencing behaviour that dominated up to the late twentieth century suppose that people are actors who will imitate behaviours that lead to results they esteem for themselves. The biblical and hagiographic narratives that circulated in the Middle Ages were examples of pietist devotion and moral conduct leading to divine reward; ergo imitative piety and moral conduct were promoted, and in some cases taken up, on the basis that they would lead to similar rewards (Warnick 2008). This kind of consequential thinking, the logic of imitating actions that led to esteemed outcomes in the hope of achieving similar results, endures in the rational choice models of political and economic theory (Fishbein and Ajzen 1975). In these models, which have extended into myriad other domains, people are presumed to make choices that will be in their logical best interest. The limits of rational choice models – social, environmental or psychological factors, habit and emotion, to name but a few – that sway people away from rational actions are frequently prioritized in decision making or prevent any potential planned action from even reaching a stage of cognitive contemplation. As such, these factors have been a vexing problem for, among others, public health professionals who would seek to change behaviour. Where appeals to reason have proved to be ineffective pedagogies, those seeking to influence or shape behaviour have had to develop alternative strategies and pedagogies, such as reframing the choice architecture (removing unhealthy options via legislated prohibitions) or appealing to emotion or affect (Maziak and Ward 2009; Hansen et al. 2010; Lupton 2014).

Both imitation theorists such as Ellwood (1901) and Tarde (1903) and behaviourists like Skinner (2012) have positioned their ideas in contrast to the imputed calculation of rational choice models in imitative learning. Observing the behaviours of crowds, young children and animals, they identified deeply submerged patterns of reward-seeking for the imitative behaviours in and of themselves rather than for the outcomes of these actions. In these frameworks, the rewards for imitation are likely to be more immediate: a sense of belonging or positive emotional reinforcement for the imitative behaviour can serve as a reward before the longer-term consequences of successful imitation, such as professional success, could be expected to bear fruit. More recent psychological theories informed by cognitive science and neuropsychology posit a still more innate tendency towards imitative behaviour (Meltzoff and Prinz 2002). The default position in such frameworks is towards imitation; failure to conform to the example is consequently either problematized as a condition of aberrant or atypical circumstances, or is regarded as a choice. In these framings of imitation, which resemble the pre-cognitive act of mimicry, understandings of what is being exemplified or modelled are not necessary (Warnick 2008).

Between the purely rational and the unthinkingly imitative, Warnick argues that a 'narrative sense of self' or a narrative about who we perceive ourselves to be is a determinant element in human imitation: 'Those perceptions of human action that provoke imitation are those that, all things considered, are classified such that the action is not incompatible with the narrative self and that exist within an enabling context that allows the imitation to take place' (Warnick 2008: 69). Citing experimental psychology, he contends that we will default to imitating examples unless imitation is in some way discordant with our understanding of ourselves or our circumstances. While it is beyond the scope of this project to thoroughly evaluate this contention in both philosophical and empirical terms, the concept of narrative sense of self provides a plausible basis for both a choice not to imitate when we are confronted with an exemplar we reject and the ways, planned and unplanned, in which we find ourselves conforming to an example.

To recap: examples can serve their demonstrative and didactic functions where shared context makes them comprehensible. Examples, whether rhetorical or normative, must both be that which they exemplify and must be recognizable as an instance of that phenomenon or class. These two necessary conditions can either be crafted, where there is pedagogical intent, or can be accidentally instructive, as is the case in processes of discovery. Examples establish a relation between the past/present and the future that is based on the potential for greater understanding or having a model to recreate (or to guide an antithetical refashioning). Whether or not a model will be imitated, especially in the case of human conduct, has been a contested issue, with perspectives from numerous disciplines articulating theories that range from an innate tendency to imitate to a rigorously rationalist approach to behaviour.

Exemplarity in embodied public pedagogy and social movements

The various theories of how and why people imitate examples underpin enquiries into how examples can be constructed and deployed pedagogically or as method. In explicitly didactic scenarios, where both content and form are purposeful, for instance as one might find in schools or instructional settings, examples are prominent elements of the pedagogy, 'the instances serving as a guide and stimulus to practice' (Gelley 1995: 8), and act as vehicles for greater understanding. Exemplarity, however, is just as often subtly pedagogical as it is manifestly so, and elements of both overt and hidden pedagogies may intermingle. This situation more accurately reflects the role of examples in public pedagogies, which are often effected via the anodyne or unobtrusive rather than the obvious, or via a combination of these elements.

Human examples of conduct are seen as an especially potent form of pedagogy and are at the core of much of what is considered public pedagogy. Such examples include both the lofty and likely to be inimitable (Jesus, Mohammed, the Dalai Lama) and the more likely to be imitated (a parent, a coach, a colleague). The process of exemplification may be conscious (a social media influencer) or unbidden (the embarrassed parent of a toddler who repeats an expletive), just as the act of being influenced by examples can be willed (copying the training regimen of a star athlete) or can sneak up on us (realizing that we have become 'just like' our parents). The imputed power of the human example underpins everything from advertising (Leiss 1983) to religion (Mellor and Shilling 2010), from the cultivation of habitus (Bourdieu 1977) to the cautionary tales employed by groups such as Mothers Against Drunk Driving (Reinarman 1988).

Warnick maintains that human exemplarity is bound up with a self-narrative, but it is also tethered to the questions of temporality inherent in any example: 'Human examples function in education as representations of a self that is not yet realized. They act as mirrors that reflect not who we currently are, but who we could one day be. Through examples, we come to see our future selves in those around us' (Warnick 2008: 32). He further nuances this position, noting that human exemplarity can function in both the affirmative and the negative, as well as for collectives, not just individuals. Warnick's formulation of the human example as the unrealized future self (or a present self articulated in relation to a prior self) presupposes the example as a spur to change, whether in the form of learning or of imitation. As encapsulated by Shilling in reference to embodied ways of learning, including by example, 'there emerges distance between the previous and present bodily self, knowledge and capabilities, and new distinctions between those with whom one now shares this skill and thought patterns and those bereft of such abilities' (Shilling 2017: 1217). The human example's potential to inspire or drive change and to generate new solidarities explains why social movements, which often rely on public pedagogy, have concerned themselves with lived exemplarity.

Social movements, which both advocate for change and call on adherents to live the change sought, readily employ human exemplarity as both tactic and strategy of their public pedagogies. This has long been true in new social movements such as feminism, queer politics and environmentalism, where awareness-raising combines with activism of various sorts (Martin 2015; Laraña et al. 1994). It is also increasingly so in lifestyle movements – green living, voluntary simplicity, slow food or purity/virginity movements – that focus on lifestyle, or that which 'connotes individuality, self-expression and stylistic self-consciousness ... [as] indicators of the individuality of the taste and sense of style of the owner/consumer' (Featherstone 2007: 81). Lifestyle movements, however, use 'lifestyle choice as a tactic of social change' and foreground 'personal identity work', which often entails work on the mundane practices of lifestyle without necessarily having the same structures of formal organization of the more established social movements (Haenfler et al. 2012: 2). Lifestyle movements also tend to accord a greater role to embodiment and lived experience than social movements. Shilling (2010) notes that the latter tend to be more tethered to a Foucauldian primacy of discourse than they are to phenomenological ways of apprehending the world. Lifestyle movements nonetheless share with social movements a corrective impetus, as they are often formed in response to the perception of either a crisis that requires intervention or an impending 'tipping point'. Where they differ is in the way that they 'encourage participants to demonstrate their commitment to change, to lead by example' (Haenfler 2019: 432) and in doing so, to engage in public pedagogy.

Dykstra and Law (1994) contend that movements that focus on lifestyle rely on experiential learning as part of their public pedagogy. As analysed by adult learning scholars, participants experience the movement through some form of involvement and gain an appreciation of the need for the movement, about ways to advance its objectives, about how to do so at scale and about how to accommodate that commitment at a personal level (Choudry 2015; Sandlin and Walther 2009). Where these movements 'often involve personal and intimate aspects of human life' and 'extend into arenas of daily life: what we eat, wear, and enjoy' (Laraña et al. 1994: 7), the pedagogy too is not just experiential but frequently embodied and reliant on phenomenological ways of apprehending the world. The examples upon which lifestyle movements rely as part of their public pedagogy therefore become embodied too.

As a case in point, Stine Krøijer's (2015) study of radical left activists in Europe identifies a tradition of producing examples, for instance, of anti-capitalist resistance such as squatting and dumpster diving, as the means to enact a theory of change. 'Living change through exemplification' (Krøijer 2015: 90) becomes the means to set an example for others and indeed for oneself as it galvanizes adherence to the cause and its actions. These movements act as public pedagogies insofar as they produce and use examples to demonstrate that alternatives to the current state of affairs are possible. For instance, sourcing a healthy and nourishing meal from produce discarded by a supermarket becomes an object lesson in a public pedagogy of anti-capitalist lifestyles. The very act of exemplifying in such cases, harkening back to the need for an example to instantiate that which it exemplifies, becomes a counter to arguments about the immutability of the capitalist status quo.

The exemplarity Krøijer identifies in her case study applies to individuals, both the leaders of these movements and the individual participants themselves. The leaders or spokespeople become examples that are publicized; whether entirely localized or global in scale, they function as role models. The rank-and-file participants who enact changes in turn become examples for others, but also for a potential or future self who can refer to their own anterior situation as a counter to a past self that could not, would not or had not performed in the way that created the example. There is accordingly an element of demonstrative exemplarity, but also of self-efficacy (Bandura 2006, 1986) inherent in the pedagogy of embodied examples employed in social and lifestyle movements. In a class of 'versions of the self', the iteration of the self that makes the change both demonstrates and explicitly references a changed self, whatever the tenor of that change might be. Making the change becomes a means to prove to oneself (and others) that living that change is possible. Creating and becoming an example in this way thus reinforces the self-narrative of accomplishment around the quality or behaviour being exemplified, which in turn sets up further imitation. This sense of efficacy may extend to groups of peers, where one person becomes an imitable example for others. These peers may judge, whether consciously or not, that they are similar enough to the exemplary individual (thus forming a class) and that their actions, the example, may be either imitated or rejected.

The self-efficacy inherent in the personal exemplarity of social or lifestyle movements also extends to the collective. While lifestyle movements prioritize individual engagement over the more collective action of social movements, there is in both a 'subjective understanding that others are taking similar action, collectively adding up to social change' (Haenfler et al. 2012: 5). Latent in this argument is the function of the individual's example (or the example of a small group) as a key driver of a kind of mass exemplarity that is generated when a movement grows beyond circles of immediate (arguably personal) influence. The personal example writ-large and reproduced at scale becomes bound up in the generation of collective self-efficacy and, therein, becomes entangled with and generative of an ever-greater potential for social change. As with individuals, but extrapolated to a group, the more people live the change, the more society in itself changes. This in turn reinforces the knowledge that the actions, whatever they are, are effective and thus exemplary as a means to effect social or cultural change.

By seeking social change through the modification of routine practices and consumption, facets of daily life that are deeply connected to people's sense of who they are, lifestyle movements sometimes run the risk of their didacticism being interpreted as judgemental or strident. Thus, the exemplarity in service of a cause cultivated as part of these movements risks becoming a liability or a jarring impediment to their pedagogical objectives. A pedagogy of examples nonetheless allows for didacticism through the subtler means of demonstrability. Shilling's theory of body pedagogics acknowledges this as 'immanent sensory understanding', where individuals are afforded the possibility of learning 'pre-reflectively through their senses and actions' (Shilling 2017: 1213). By exemplifying that an alternative lifestyle or social organization is possible, lived examples provide a new or alternative normative model to be emulated. Change is accordingly led by example rather than by rhetoric, a situation especially useful when lifestyle becomes entwined with questions of ethics and morality.

Alcohol, lifestyle pedagogies and exemplification

The practical implications of a shift towards greater attention to educative examples, including embodied examples, are potentially far-reaching, not only for lifestyle issues related to moral or ethical stances (e.g. purity movements, veganism) but also for other domains – such as health education and philanthropic awareness-raising. The case of TSIs reverses the normal concerns about exemplarity that arise in response to a perceived crisis; rather than seeking to downplay, regulate or censor bad examples, TSIs followed in the model of lifestyle movements and proposed a cultural, embodied solution to create alternative examples as a way to change drinking cultures. While the full discussion of the ways in which TSIs create and use examples will be the focus of the volume as a whole, I propose to here outline the divergent strategies with regard to negative and positive examples that arose at the time that TSIs began operating on a large and replicable scale.

In 2008, Australia initiated a number of measures, including localized restrictions on trading hours for licensed venues, to call out and redress problems with youth intoxication, a rise in consumption among young women and growing attention to 'alcohol-fuelled' violence (AIHW 2008; Department of Health 2014; NHMRC 2009, 2007). The identification of these problems corresponded with a threefold spike in media coverage centring on the adverse effects of a destructive drinking culture and 'binge drinking', especially among young people (ProQuest Australia & New Zealand Newsstand 2014). One part of the ensuing official public health messaging was to focus on the influence of poor role models. In addition to the usual culprits in the media such as advertising and sponsorship of elite sport (Hill and Casswell 2004; Anderson et al. 2009), parents were also identified as a key part of the larger preventative strategy, and a number of government and private/industry initiatives began to draw attention to their role in setting examples for their children.

DrinkWise, the Australian Alcohol Industry's corporate social responsibility arm, launched its 'Kids absorb your drinking campaign' in 2008, with airings of public service announcements in 2009. 'The key to this campaign', explains the organization, 'was "holding up a mirror" to parents' drinking, to increase their awareness of the effects of role modelling and to positively influence their children's future drinking behaviour' (DrinkWise Australia 2009). The underlying strategy of DrinkWise and other initiatives was to change *what* was being exemplified by making parents conscious of their status as norms-givers for alcohol consumption (DrinkWise Australia 2021).[3] The tagline 'DrinkWise in front of your kids' reminded parents of the demonstrability of their normative example.

The call to action was a reduction in the demonstrability of a poor example – not drinking in front of the kids or drinking only so much that it would not be apparent to them. The organization championed their intervention as a success based on this reduction in demonstrability: 'The campaign achieved positive results with almost three in ten parents reporting that they had subsequently reduced the amount of alcohol consumed *in front of their children*' (DrinkWise Australia 2009, emphasis added). A cynical interpretation (perhaps warranted given that the campaign is an act of corporate social responsibility on the part of an industry body) would see the call to action as tokenistic. The campaign's focus on how pedagogies of drinking operate rather than on the content of these pedagogies could nonetheless be anticipated, as alcohol is still widely endorsed in the Australian context as an agent of social cohesion. In line with other campaigns promoting some version of responsible drinking, what constitutes responsibility is ill-defined (Wolburg 2005).

TSIs, which came about at the same time as the strategy to diminish the impact of poor examples, instead created conspicuous counterexamples in line with the strategies of exemplification used in social and lifestyle movements. The result is an approach to alcohol education – in some cases deliberately planned, in others more serendipitous – that fully exploits the power of individual and collective examples, those within oneself and those observable in others. While overt pedagogical rationales feature in some (but not all) early statements from TSIs about their mission or vision, they did seek to disrupt, challenge and provoke reflection on the drinking culture by temporarily prohibiting the consumption of a largely taken-for-granted substance.[4] Shilling argues that such disruptions, 'novelty or problems in the material/social environment' (Shilling 2017: 1209), render it 'impossible to maintain a "business as usual" approach to life' (1210). Adaptation, both corporeal and cognitive, is required. This process is enacted in numerous ways, although many centre on heightening the demonstrability and thus didacticism of counterexamples to the dominant or normative drinking culture.

By their very structure, TSIs make temporary abstinence a demonstrably and deliberately sober (and where fundraising is involved, also self-sacrificing) period in an individual's life. This period both functions *as* an illustrative example and *produces* imitable examples of temperance and moderation. TSIs accordingly draw on the complexity of exemplification, as represented in the educational and anthropological theorizing of examples, and provide rich case studies of multilayered public pedagogies using embodied exemplification. While not initially designed as a large-scale cultural behaviour-change solution, and thus arguably lacking the purposiveness of lifestyle movements, their embodied 'pedagogy of the possible' (Fors and Pink 2017: 6) nonetheless allows for alternative examples, individually and organisationally, that may bring about change that has been sought, often ineffectively, via various other educative and regulatory means (Heath 2012).

Conclusion

Learning, whether seeking to increase knowledge and comprehension or to develop capabilities and dispositions, has long (arguably always) relied on the pedagogic power of examples. As the ways we live our lives, individually and collectively, have become a focus for social, cultural and health education employing both formal and informal pedagogies, lived and embodied examples have come into focus as an area of greater theoretical and practical interest. For lifestyle movements, including temperance and episodic neo-temperance, which operate at the levels of both individual and collective action, embodied examples instantiate and thus demonstrate to didactic effect the public pedagogy of the movement. This volume will continue to explore in greater depth how TSIs have masterfully created embodied examples and leveraged their range of affordances as public pedagogies focused on not only health education but social and cultural values as well.

3

TSIs as phenomenon

The casual, nonchalant way in which I first learnt about a friend's impending July hiatus from alcohol suggested that the practice was an almost idiosyncratic undertaking. It struck me as a whim: an unusual idea concocted as part of a team-building exercise or a social media phenomenon with no substantive backing. The notion of giving up drinking for a month and raising money for charity while doing so hardly seemed like part of an international philanthropic and health promotion movement. To be fair, in June of 2010, Dry July was more of a local initiative, albeit one with a growing national profile in Australia. Now though, such undertakings are recognizable through their analogues in a number of contexts, and their status as legitimate and popular events, predictable occurrences on an annual calendar, is assured. There is a consistency to the TSI experience and structure regardless of where the campaign operates, and this relative homogeneity suggests TSIs warrant consideration, and definition, as a genuine popular phenomenon.

By way of orientation to the phenomenon that TSIs have become, this chapter performs three principal functions. First, it presents a richly descriptive, ethnographic-style account of TSIs. The intent is to chronicle, taking a yearly 'life-cycle' as the unit of observation and analysis, how TSIs operate, engage with participants and publics and how participants, construed as models for a particular campaign, enact their participation. Rather than profiling a single campaign, this analysis draws upon approximately two dozen TSIs operating in different contexts to identify common features and to describe a composite or general TSI. Owing to the location for the primary research with participants, the Australian context is nonetheless the point of departure. While scholars have rightly warned against generalizations given the diversity among TSIs (Bartram et al. 2018), I contend it is the commonalities that allow TSIs to be constituted and analysed as a movement and for the variants of individual campaigns to be more readily considered and interpreted.

Second, the chapter maps and contextualizes the spread of TSIs. Working historically, it traces how a historic Finnish practice (that was re-launched in 2005 as a public health campaign) and a Lenten fast in Slovenia (that was rebadged as a road safety initiative), despite occurring in relative isolation, became widely emulated examples for grassroots and philanthropic undertakings. From there, it documents how TSIs, leveraging familiar self-responsibilization techniques such as New Year's resolutions and cycles of increased and decreased consumption, gained in both popularity and prominence. Of particular importance is online media and established third-sector networks, which inspired imitation and allowed the model to spread from Australia to New Zealand, then to Britain and Ireland, and eventually to Canada, the United States and other parts of Europe.

It is from the survey of the range of TSIs and their evolution that the third objective emerges: proposing a typology of TSIs based on two identified poles or orientations that help to define them and account for the differences that have, in some cases, become wedge issues within the TSI community. On the one hand, TSIs exhibit a social focus that prioritizes health, responsibility and 'changing the drinking culture'. On the other, there is a philanthropic orientation that accentuates fundraising and awareness for a charitable cause (other than changing the drinking habits of society at large). Understanding where on the continuum between social and philanthropic objectives a TSI positions itself allows for a greater appreciation of how TSIs operate, where they came from, how they engage participants and publics and, not least, what impact they have.

TSIs up close: Defining a phenomenon

TSIs, in the simplest of terms, are time-delimited periods of planned abstinence from alcohol. While potentially resembling other periods of abstinence or strict moderation undertaken for medical, religious or purely circumstantial reasons, TSIs invite participation on their own terms, as they are undertaken as part of an organized campaign centred on temporary abstinence as a means to an end. Increasingly, they are highly coordinated initiatives, either as part of a larger organization or as an independent venture, often with staff and/or volunteers to manage fundraising, online platforms and apps, and communications, as well as routine matters such as accounting, governance and human resources. They operate on a yearly cycle of campaign build-up, activity and consolidation. These operations, vital as they are to TSIs, largely remain hidden from the public who experience TSIs as prospective participants, adherents, donors or observers.

From the perspective of a member of the general public, the TSI cycle begins when one is entreated via conventional and/or social media, colleagues, members of a social circle or even a medical practitioner (Pennay et al. 2014) to participate in a TSI, whether formally or informally. Such requests, whether the result of advertising, news stories or personal appeals, typically come in the three to four weeks leading up to the official start date of the campaign, which is generally the first day of the nominated calendar month: January, February, March, April, July, September, October or November, depending on where one is located and which campaign is in question; or on the first day of Lent. Even in the first week in which a TSI commences, latecomers are still encouraged to join.

Not all, however, are likely to be so interpellated, either directly or indirectly, by these incitements. This is because TSIs both target and exclude certain segments of the population. Excluded are the minority in Oceania, Europe and North America who have either never consumed alcohol or the growing proportion of those who have abstained over the previous twelve months (WHO 2018: 44–5). Whether motivated by religious, cultural, medical or any number of personal reasons (ranging from apprehension about family histories of addiction repeating themselves to a simple dislike of the taste of alcohol), this group has little to gain from what TSIs offer and consequently provide little incentive for the initiatives to target them. They require no (further) education about the risks of alcohol and would not be seeking a mechanism to help them moderate their alcohol consumption. There is no challenge for them in the undertaking, and thus they provide little fundraising potential because their abstention is unrelated to the campaign and its logics of sacrifice for a cause. Similarly, there would be no social reward or kudos for a demonstration of responsibility with regard to alcohol; if anything, they could be accused of looking to baselessly attract plaudits to themselves for tokenistic effort.

The second group excluded from the appeals of most TSIs – the in-house fundraising campaign of American mutual-help group Moderation Management aside (Moderation Management 2016b) – are those who suspect they might be alcoholics or otherwise alcohol-dependent. Because TSIs make no claims of competence in the treatment of such conditions, legal disclaimers stating that TSIs are not intended for such persons and referrals to qualified medical professionals and treatment services are the norm. Dry January, for instance, is quite detailed in its advice to daily drinkers, those who score more than twenty points on their Alcohol Use Disorders Identification Test (AUDIT) questionnaire, those who have had alcohol withdrawal seizures in the past or those concerned about the likelihood of physical symptoms upon the cessation of drinking to self-identify as unsuitable or potentially unsuitable candidates (Booker 2019: 47). More common, however, are general disclaimers that advise potential participants who are 'heavy drinkers or people dependent on alcohol to speak with their GP before signing up' (Dry July 2015a). In practice, and largely depending on the thresholds set by local definitions of problematic drinking, some very heavy drinkers may find themselves participating.

The polar ends of the alcohol consumption spectrum are tacitly, if not officially or practically, excluded from participation, and the target audience for TSIs is, by consequence, those who find themselves somewhere in the middle of this continuum. In regions that run TSIs, this equates to the approximately 50 per cent of the population that drinks alcohol, but that is not considered to have an alcohol use disorder, defined as either dependence or harmful use (WHO 2018: 44, 72). Given that potential participants would need to self-identify as alcohol-dependent to see themselves counselled against TSI participation, the group of potential participants effectively includes a broad range of drinkers: social, moderate, occasional, heavy, binge, regular and (ir)responsible drinkers. In short, TSIs effectively target anyone who is not an abstainer and who does not already identify as an alcoholic or dependent drinker.

In practice, TSIs tend to recruit their participants from those who drink somewhat more than is considered safe or low-risk, as defined by the various national health authorities governing the locations in which TSIs operate (de Visser et al. 2016). TSIs may also define a yearly target group whose alcohol consumption either attracts considerable public attention (university students) or that is less obvious (women) (Kékpont: Alkohol Drog Karantén 2020). In terms of dispositions, participants may include the intrinsically motivated as well as those who are recruited into the undertaking at the behest of others. Making some allowances for historical and geographic particularities, TSI participants tend to be members of the middle class, have formal higher education and are employed in professional roles. They are likely to define themselves as part of the ethno-cultural majority and act in ways typical of its norms of behaviour. Reflecting the patterns that alcohol consumption tends to gradually decrease after marriage and the onset of family responsibilities, participants are often between thirty and fifty-five and are in stable relationships. Participants are slightly more likely to be female.

The would-be participant, where formal campaigns are concerned, then signs up via the campaign's website, supplying basic demographic information (name, gender, age, etc.), contact details and opting either in or out of communications from the organizers. In some campaigns, participants will complete their registration by using a bank or credit card to pay a nominal fee – typically equivalent of what one might pay for roughly three to four standard drinks in a bar or pub. In the case of TSIs that double as fundraisers, the fee also acts as one's personal and (in many jurisdictions) tax-deductible donation to the nominated charity, usually one that has organized the TSI as a fundraiser or that has been identified by the organizers as the beneficiary of their efforts. In recent years, some TSIs (such as FebFast) that had been charging for registration have forgone these fees in favour of a suggested donation to one's personal (or team) fundraising tally. Where no registration fees are levied, for instance Dry July (2017b), participants can direct their strictly voluntary contributions (or a portion of them) to a particular charity from a list of sponsored organizations or to the organizing entity itself. Not all TSIs, though, expect either a financial contribution or an official registration.

Once registered, and even before the campaign officially commences, participants in TSIs that involve some element of fundraising are requested to solicit donations from their friends, family and colleagues, a standard strategy in peer-to-peer fundraising (Scaife et al. 2016; Breeze and Scaife 2015). These appeals, following the suggestions of campaign websites, can be outright requests – either in person or using social media – or more elaborate exchanges, for instance of donations in lieu of small gifts or fees for services rendered. Refusing an offer of a drink during a round, for example, can result in a monetary exchange in which the cost of the participant's libation is converted into a cash or electronic contribution to a personal fundraising tally (Go Sober 2019) so long as the participant plays their part in purchasing a round of drinks for the rest of the party. Sobriety can also be the precondition of labour, for instance as a compensated designated driver service in lieu of a taxi or ride-share (Cowra Guardian 2014). These exchanges of funds have increasingly been facilitated by smartphones that allow for the easy electronic transfer and the attribution of these funds to a participant's personal fundraising tally. The fundraising efforts of participants are tracked online, and leader boards for both individuals and teams are used to encourage friendly competition and boost the total of funds raised.

To enhance the monetary yield of this fundraising, abstinence is discursively positioned to take on various positive connotations. For TSIs with a strong philanthropic orientation, images and text reinforce notions of sacrifice, martyrdom and/or heroism. Here, participation is cast as an act requiring considerable effort or suffering, and this in turn is posited as worthy of monetary compensation (Olivola and Shafir 2013). Discourses of heroism additionally confirm for participants the social value of their effort, the impact of their efforts to date and the importance of persevering with both their embodied commitment and their fundraising (Bartram et al. 2018). For unlikely participants, typically those whose consumption patterns suggest that a month without alcohol would be especially challenging, sobriety can even become the object of a wager, where the participant and a potential donor agree to contribute the sum wagered in the event that the participant goes the distance. For TSIs that downplay their fundraising to instead focus on other objectives, abstinence is framed as an intrinsically worthwhile undertaking (Yeomans 2019) with corollary virtues, such as helping out those in need, that extend to others. Where drinking in cultures that have adopted TSIs is largely a socially cohesive practice associated with being part of an initiated community or notions of 'mateship' (a concept that in Australia is linked to military camaraderie) and abstention is regarded as 'a deviant form of behavior' (Heath 2012: 100), these framings ascribe social value to a normally suspect and anti-social practice.

Pre-TSI activities have, over the past decade, increasingly included detailed data collection. Across many TSIs, especially those that position themselves as wellness activities or campaigns that aim to reform the local or national drinking culture, it is increasingly common for participants to be prompted to report their baseline data. Campaign organizers, often working in tandem with researchers, have become progressively more interested in the changes that TSIs occasion for participants' normal drinking habits (volume, frequency, cost) and overall state of well-being (weight, subjective ratings of health, energy, sleep). In order for claims about TSI effectiveness (in a medical or health behaviour sense) to be validated, both pre- and post-campaign information is requested, with the first dataset typically collected just before participants cease drinking (e.g. see de Visser and Piper 2020). Regardless of the formality or methodological rigour of the collection process in terms of programme evaluation or publishable research, the mere fact of asking for this information may prompt participants to reflect on and take note of their drinking habits and overall health, or even modify their behaviour owing to the awareness of external scrutiny (McCambridge and Day 2008).

The campaign underway, TSIs use social media and various forms of electronic direct messaging – emails, text messages, in-app push notifications for smartphones – to keep participants engaged, committed to their pledged action, fundraising and ascribing value to the campaign. The discursive framing of the participant might liken them to a superhero (Go Sober 2016), an endurance athlete (Dryathlon 2016b) or somebody simply looking after themselves (FebFast 2013); each framing pitched to have participants think of themselves in a particular way, whether that be as a particular kind of heroic figure (Bartram et al. 2018) or simply as a new version of themselves (Yeomans 2019). The timing of a given message is often just as important as its content. Participants might receive an encouraging text message timed to coincide with the end of the workday on a Friday afternoon, the just-in-time communication both calling attention to the ritualized social expectation to drink at certain points in a week when the transition between work and leisure is most obvious (Heath 2012) or to mark particular occasions and bolstering willpower (Emanuel 2014). Communications that celebrate milestones in the participant's temporary sobriety (one week, the halfway mark) or that herald the final days of the campaign (see, for instance, Lansdown 2018, for Dryathlon's badges) both champion achievements to the goal-oriented participants and reinforce their commitment.

Although online participant-to-participant interactions did not feature prominently in TSIs in the early years, online communities of participants have become important virtual networks and the way in which many TSIs launch (Pados et al. 2020; Irish Heart Foundation 2017). These forums allow participants to speak to each other and offer support via hosted blogs linked to official websites and social media interactions on a campaign's official page or feed. Participants often report that this dialogue reinforces the feeling of solidarity among the temporary abstainers, especially as they might be feeling left out of offline social activities centred around drinking or alcogenic environments with offline friends, family or colleagues (Cherrier et al. 2017).[1] These official online exchanges, often seeded by TSI staff or volunteers, can spur participants to reflect on and assess the larger cultural relationship with alcohol from a standpoint, one defined if only temporarily by a sober or non-drinking identity, they might not otherwise have consciously adopted.

The social media platforms participants use to engage with each other via official pages and closed groups also provide a means for them to broadcast their involvement to non-participants who are members of their online social networks. These posts enable them to attract kudos, but more importantly to articulate a self-presentation (Yeomans 2019) as goal-oriented, philanthropic, health-conscious individuals. Participants post photographic evidence of their involvement (photos of non-alcoholic beverages such as elaborate mocktails feature prominently) and its effects, which range from early morning fitness activities to selfies showing off trimmer figures and clearer complexions. TSI-produced collateral (i.e. digital badges, images and text that can be copied and shared) for achievements in fundraising and/or sober endurance allow participants to be self-congratulatory by posting these tokens or statements to their own social media profiles.[2]

Despite efforts and stated intentions to keep participants sober throughout the month (or other designated period), most TSIs concede that several weeks of total sobriety may not be feasible for all, especially when alcohol is so often used as a social lubricant or a marker of celebrations (Pettigrew and Pescud 2016; Heath 2012). This recognition underpins the logic of TSI timing, as most initiatives avoid both December, the month associated with Christmas and end-of-year festivities, and the months coinciding with summer holidays (with allowances for one's position in either the northern or the southern hemisphere). To accommodate events with variable timing (such as birthdays and weddings), many campaigns offer participants the chance to buy a short dispensation from their commitment. For a fee roughly commensurate with the registration cost or the cost of three or four standard drinks in a bar or pub, participants (or those who are willing to pay for their drinking company) can purchase a 24- or 48-hour break from the commitment to abstinence. These reprieves are often given a slightly humorous name – Golden Tickets, Time-Out Passes, Leave Passes, Joker, Tipple Tax – as a way to tacitly authorize their modest use without stigmatizing the participant as a failure or a cheat for using one.

At the conclusion of the campaign, TSIs thank participants for their contributions to a cause, update them on the impact of their collective efforts – typically in terms of a total amount of funds raised for TSIs with a philanthropic component – and congratulate them for their commitment and for setting a good example among their social circles. They often entreat the participants to take stock of how they feel and, for those that are more oriented towards health, wellness or overt alcohol-related objectives, suggest that participants carry on their sobriety – or at least a more moderate approach to alcohol – and extend the health, lifestyle and financial benefits into the coming weeks and months.

Participants, for their part, may mark the end of their teetotal month in a variety of ways. Some participants count down to the end of the month as though it were New Year's Eve and time their first sip (of many) to the stroke of midnight. Reports of this type of prompt and/or excessive celebration, despite figuring as the common cautionary tale about TSIs being a form of binge sobriety encouraging an equal and opposite response of binge drinking, are less common (de Visser et al. 2016) than the sceptical and frequently sensationalizing press (Lees 2012; Pryor 2010; Hamilton and Gilmore 2016) portray though. Some participants will go to the other extreme and will extend their sobriety by significant periods of time, going for months without drinking. It is more common, however, that temporary abstainers will resume drinking shortly after the campaign's end, albeit at rates and volumes less than before they gave it up (de Visser and Piper 2020). Curiously, it is what is (erroneously) hypothesized to happen at the end of a campaign that tends to attract the most public scrutiny.

Ever eager to improve upon their reach and impact – number of registered participants, funds raised, social media trending and overall positive media exposure – TSIs seek feedback from participants. This feedback is often used to inform the next year's strategy, as many TSIs operate in contexts where they are not only competing for participants, dollars and attention with different kinds of campaigns and issues but also against other TSIs, some of which – for instance, Dry January and Dryathlon in the UK, or the Défi 28 jours and Dry Feb in Quebec – are even scheduled for the same timeframe.[3] Participant feedback is also used as evidence of efficacy in annual reports, with both quantitative indicators and qualitative feedback in the form of quotes and testimonials featuring prominently. Participant surveys, the prime vector for obtaining this information, have accordingly become the unofficial end to a TSI's annual cycle.

More than just gathering useful feedback and testimonials though, these surveys prompt participants to adopt a reflective and evaluative stance on their period of sobriety. Even if no pre-campaign questions were sent out, post-TSI queries about a range of probable outcomes and effects solicit participants to assess whether benefits assumed to be applicable (improved sleep, weight loss or financial savings) extended to them. Posing such questions can spur retrospective realizations about outcomes for participants and guide them towards interrogating and ascribing value to elements of their experience, including those that had previously gone unnoticed but that retrospectively become 'learnings' and 'realisations' (Robert 2016a). To return to the framing of exemplification, these questions can help participants to determine if they exemplify an anticipated TSI-induced effect.

The traits and activities above occur in the vast majority of the campaigns that can be classified as TSIs. Each nonetheless responds to local conditions to realize their objectives, and this results in distinctive features, such a timing, duration, discursive and visual strategy, technological sophistication and the extent of collaboration with researchers. These differences can be determinants of success or failure, as some TSIs have grown from year to year while others, such as FebFast in New Zealand (NZ Drug Foundation 2015), Australia's Ocsober (Life Education Australia 2019), Ireland's On the Dry (Irish Heart Foundation 2016)

46   *Alcohol, Binge Sobriety and Exemplary Abstinence*

and Big Easy Dryout (Big Easy Dryout 2017), diminished in importance and scale before ceasing official operations.

Explaining the spread of TSIs

TSIs are typically regarded, much like temperance, as an Anglophone phenomenon. The largest and most influential campaigns certainly originated in Australia and Britain. A cataloguing of official TSIs (see Appendix A) nonetheless reveals the TSI model is increasingly returning to its roots and is tentatively finding new audiences throughout Europe and North America. The popularity of the phenomenon has seen both charities and alcohol awareness groups imitate the example of long-running campaigns like Dry July and Dry January to establish their own local initiatives, including in partnership with these well-established Australian and British organizations.

The first modern TSIs, albeit without a philanthropic component, began in Slovenia and Finland. The Slovenian initiative, 40 Brez Alkohola (40 days without alcohol) (2021), began as a campaign of the Public Agency for Traffic Safety and was timed to coincide with Lent. In the context of this staunchly Catholic country, however, Lenten abstention – even when linked to larger social objectives – attracted little outside attention.

By comparison, Finland's Alcohol-Free January, subsequently rebranded in 2005 as Tipaton Tammikuu (Dropless January), was cited in a German Ministry of Health initiative collecting information on novel approaches to combat binge drinking (Varamäki n.d.). The report speculates about origins linked to a political campaign in 1942 and ties to the labour movement, a feature of Finnish temperance in the nineteenth century (Sulkunen 1990). It asserts that the modern iteration launched in earnest on a national scale in 2007 as the initiative of various, unnamed, non-governmental organizations concerned with combatting substance abuse (Varamäki n.d.). Subsequent to the popularization of the Tipaton model beyond their borders, the Finns have reclaimed the concept, citing it as an exemplary practice of self-correction developed by a population aware of its own alcoholic excesses (Cook 2012; Tolvin 2020).

Despite being first, 40 Brez Alkohola and what became Tipaton Tammikuu appear to have grown in relative isolation both from each other and from the larger group of TSIs that emerged in Australia in 2008. One possible explanation for this disconnect is a simple language divide, for neither Slovenian nor Finnish are languages readily understood or often encountered outside of Slovenia or

Finland or their small expatriate circles. The differences between an abstinent Lenten period that took on a public health inflection and a secular dry month also suggest that these two campaigns, despite their obvious roots in public health, had little in common with each other.

In contrast to these initiatives, the next volley of TSIs all claim to have their origins in private actions that snowballed of their own accord into larger movements. The public self-presentations of these campaigns champion a founder's moment of inspiration that was able to be capitalized upon in a socially entrepreneurial way, expanded and turned into a successful philanthropic and public health initiative. Thereafter, these campaigns spread to other contexts, including to some that had already developed their own successful TSIs. The lag between the introduction of TSIs in Australia and the first of the British (2011) and Canadian (2012) TSIs suggests that the claims of innovation on the part of both Dry January and the Défi 28 jours must be weighed against ubiquitous but subtle processes of cultural transfer occasioned through what Manuel Castells refers to as mass self-communication. This process refers to the widespread adoption and use of internet-enabled horizontal communications (those other than traditional, corporate or state media) that are 'self-generated in content, self-directed in emission, and self-selected in reception by many that communicate with many', enabling local phenomena to quickly reach global audiences (Castells 2007: 248) where such communications find pathways and can be understood.

The first of the TSIs to claim spontaneous, grassroots origins is Australia's FebFast, which recounts the story of its founding in banal terms:

> The idea for turning an alcohol free month into a fundraising activity was conceived at a barbeque a few days before Christmas in 2006. A guest at that barbeque, and now FebFast's CEO, was Fiona Healy. She and a friend, Eliza Anderson, then followed through on what they thought was a good idea in February 2007. The pair raised $910, which they donated to YSAS Pty. Ltd. (the Youth Substance Abuse Service) Victoria's largest service provider for young people who have problems with alcohol and substance use. From there Fiona decided to turn the concept into a fully-fledged charitable trust. (FebFast 2009)

FebFast, as the public iteration of the campaign became known, launched in time for February 2008 and ran four more campaigns as an independent organization. It folded as a separate legal and financial entity in October 2011 when it was acquired by YSAS Pty Ltd, the charity it first supported, to be an in-house fundraising campaign (YSAS 2011).

Dry July similarly began as a small-scale philanthropic project among three friends – Brett Macdonald, Phil Grove and Kenny McGilvary – in Sydney in June 2007. A health scare and relative's diagnosis had prompted the trio to raise money to support adults in their community undergoing cancer treatment through a donation to the oncology unit of their local hospital (Dry July 2009). The next year's campaign was intended to be only slightly less modest in scope: a group of ten friends working towards a target of AU$3,000. A presenter on a national radio station based in Sydney nonetheless heard of the initiative and launched the group's challenge to a wider audience, and 1,049 people wound up raising over AU$250,000 (Dry July 2009). That year, Macdonald and Grove created the Dry July Foundation to run the annual event and disburse funds to the beneficiary organizations.

As I have explained elsewhere, a peak in public discourse and concern about binge drinking and alcohol-related violence contributed to launching both FebFast and Dry July as successful public campaigns in Australia in 2008 (Robert 2016b). Discourses of both acute and generalized risk as a result of drinking were at maximum levels, and a largely middle-class constituency of not fully responsible but self-responsibilizing individuals took up the TSI challenge. These cultural circumstances alone, however, do not fully account for their quieter private origins some years earlier. Indeed, the inspiration for the independently conceived ideas to forgo alcohol as a way to raise money for a worthy cause is difficult to trace. Nonetheless, there are common antecedents – the New Year's resolution, the Lenten fast, various detox diets and embodied philanthropy – that primed the public to be receptive to the idea of a temporary break from alcohol, including for altruistic reasons.

The tradition of the New Year's resolution, a vow of self-discipline after the excesses of the festive season (which in Australia and New Zealand extends until the end of January on account of summer holidays), is widespread. Indeed, the notion was at the heart of both the long-standing and recently rebranded Finnish TSIs. In the UK, the alcohol-oriented variant of the phenomenon was even rebranded, thanks to a *Daily Mail* article from 2002, as 'Janopause' (Friedland 2015). The neologism, used to designate a teetotal January in a generic sense rather than as a concerted campaign, received much more publicity after the British Liver Trust criticized the practice as a faddish, hollow gesture (BBC 2012), a position it has since reversed.

Periods of self-sacrifice are also common religious practices, and the Christian tradition of a Lenten fast, which is often enacted through the forgoing of a particular pleasure such as sweets, smoking and alcohol, are part of the cultural vernacular for many people in contexts with a predominantly Christian heritage (even if the practice has been popularly abandoned as societies have secularized). That said, an alcohol-free Lent was recently reinvented as a secular TSI in the New Orleans *Times-Picayune*'s Alcohol Free for 40 campaign, begun in 2016, as a lifestyle and wellness challenge following the customary excesses of Mardi Gras and carnival season (Kimball 2016), and in the Dutch IkPas initiative, which has both a thirty-day version commencing with the new year and a forty-day Lenten variant (IkPas 2019).

The logic of correcting a period of overindulgence (the holiday season, the pre-Lenten carnival tradition) with a corresponding period of relative privation was not just culturally entrenched in many contexts (Heath 2012) but was also gaining in pseudo-scientific importance. The early years of the new millennium saw a proliferation of short-term 'detox diets' and 'cleanses' that, while unequivocally rejected by the mainstream medical community (Dixon 2005), proved immensely popular as a form of self-help via highly restrictive nutrition and lifestyle modification.[4]

These potentially unacknowledged precedents of abstinence, which amount to demonstrations of compensation for previous overindulgence, were likely to have coupled with larger patterns within the philanthropic sphere. Embodied philanthropy – the process of channelling philanthropy through the body's actions, habits and surfaces – had been gaining in popularity, both through durational campaigns centred on a calendar month, such as the international Movember initiative (launched in Australia in 2003) and event-style fundraisers (long-distance walks for breast cancer, charity runs and marathons), which were at peak popularity around the same time as TSIs launched (Jacobson 2010; King 2006). The public in many of the contexts in which TSIs first took root had thus already accepted the premise that charitable activity could come from doing something unconventional and potentially also a little self-serving with one's body insofar as one could use a charity campaign as a way to get fit, lose weight or justify a radical change in appearance.

It was into this larger and shared cultural ethos, with both FebFast and Dry July already in full operation, that British and Canadian TSIs began. Each of these campaigns claimed that they too were the inspired idea of their founders. The UK's Dry January, run by the public health and advocacy group Alcohol Concern, report their origins as the personal health project of Emily Robinson (Dry January 2017). Robinson gave up drinking for the month of January in 2011 to help her train for a long-distance run. Having begun work at Alcohol Concern in the intervening year, Robinson repeated her personal project in

2012 and, inspired by her initiative, her new employer hosted a kick-off event for Dry January in May 2012 in advance of a first public outing in January 2013. This opening campaign attracted 4,350 participants. By 2014, Alcohol Change UK had trademarked the name, which is still widely used in a generic sense rather than in reference to this particular TSI.

In the Canadian province of Quebec, the Défi 28 jours ran for the first time as a major public event in 2014, albeit under the bilingual and oddly translated banner of Soberary – *Les 28 jours les plus longs de ta vie* (Soberary – The longest 28 days of your life). The event is cited as the brainchild of friends Jean-Sébastien Chouinard and Antoine Théorêt-Poupart (Défi 28 jours 2017; Fondation Jean Lapointe 2015). Chouinard notes the genesis of the campaign as a December 2012 idea that took root among a small group of friends who abstained from alcohol in February 2013 and used Facebook to motivate and publicize their project (Chouinard 2014). The founders encouraged participation by hosting an exclusive party, to begin at midnight on 1 March, for those who managed to abstain for the whole month (Chouinard and Théorêt-Poupart 2013). The Jean Lapointe Foundation, a Montreal drug and alcohol charity running both residential treatment and education programmes, subsequently approached them about launching the idea on a larger scale, incorporating it as an in-house fundraiser, much as Youth Support and Advocacy Service (YSAS) had incorporated FebFast into its organization.

Explaining the emergence and spread of TSIs can be summed up in two hypotheses: the first, the notion of multiple discovery, the second that of networks. Theories of multiple discovery, which hold that innovations are often made independently and in many cases simultaneously (Simonton 1979), may explain the claims of independent grassroots action concretizing into highly similar campaigns in different locations, in some cases at a few year's remove from one another. Australia, Britain and Canada share a number of cultural factors that suggest a common cultural ethos. All three have traditions of Lent (now largely secularized) and New Year's resolutions, trendy experiences with embodied philanthropy and larger neo-liberal preoccupations with health and wellness – all of which might have made the TSI premise a logical response to local circumstances.

The emphasis on TSIs being homegrown solutions to local problems enacted by inventive individuals, a discourse reinforced in 'Our Story'–style narratives, is nevertheless a strategic framing of the creation accounts. Every one of these narratives emphasizes the ordinariness of the founders in their local context. The notion that they also drink and enjoy doing so helps to position them as an everyday person, a 'Joe Sixpack', in societies that still presume drinking to be the norm (Bartram et al. 2017). They are (or at least were) neither authorities on the alcohol question nor exemplary individuals, just people who acted on an idea that had no particular moral, public health or scientific inspiration, but that intuitively made sense given both cultural practices and norms, and recent trends.[5]

Discourses of TSIs as solely sui generis programmes or grassroots initiatives nonetheless need to be weighed against the highly visible and mediatized way in which they operate. When considering Australian, British and Canadian claims to founding TSIs as grassroots undertakings, it is important to remember that English functions as a lingua franca and movement (e.g. gap years, working holidays, study abroad) between the countries, especially among younger people at the start of their professional lives, means that many from one country have developed both immediate and more distant ties to people in these other locations. It is therefore likely that individuals in one context would have enduring networks, including in the virtual space, that connect them to these other contexts. The founders of Dry July, for instance, are British expats in Australia, which makes the news of their Dry July initiative quite likely to have travelled back to the UK.

TSIs have, from the outset, encouraged participants to blog, post and fundraise online. They operate as digital entities that have successfully employed the connectivity of the internet, the viral potential of social media and even digital giving platforms and apps to publicize their presence and objectives (Scaife et al. 2016). The practices of mass self-communication have been pivotal in the spread of social movements (Castells 2015, 2007) but have also led to unprecedented levels of information exchange about lifestyle trends and even more banal phenomena (recipes, household 'hacks', etc.). Participants accordingly use social media and other platforms to broadcast their involvement or even their reactions to TSIs. As my own introduction to TSIs proves, non-participants, through their reactions to TSIs, can also disseminate information about local campaigns among their potentially international networks, communicating the core premise (whether they are in favour of it or find it implausible) to potentially vast audiences. Even the reporting on TSIs in conventional media has become integrated into these communications networks through the practices of hyperlinking and sharing. The concept of the TSI had thus been circulating freely for more than a decade, a situation that may contribute to explanations of how TSIs were able to arise 'organically' in a number of locations.

The network hypothesis of TSI proliferation also presents traceable evidence that is less dependent upon vast, potentially global networks of individuals than it is on existing professional or organizational networks within the philanthropic sector. Excavating these networks helps to explain how TSIs moved from Australia to New Zealand, the United Kingdom, Canada, the United States and a number of European countries.

Overwhelmingly, TSIs operate in alliance with (either being an undertaking of and/or supporting) two types of charitable initiatives: drug and alcohol education and treatment services or cancer support and research organizations. Each of these sectors operates as an international network of charities and community service organizations with similar aims. Moreover, the sharing of information and the showcasing of exemplary strategies through publications, conferences and personal connections are common (Breeze and Scaife 2015). These specialized circles operate in addition to the broader philanthropic or third-sector forums, such as the Showcase of Fundraising Innovation and Inspiration or *Third Sector* magazine, that promote novel and successful approaches to shared concerns (see, for instance, Chapman 2015; Emanuel 2014). TSIs, as will be outlined later, have been able to spread internationally thanks to these networks, which are the empirical basis for the majority of 'new' fundraising campaigns and awareness initiatives in the third sector (Bennett and Savani 2011). Local successes were publicized and exported, much like franchises of a highly successful business. Individual participation too came to be linked to joining up to a 'global phenomenon' with hundreds of thousands of participants (Dry January France 2020; Dry January Suisse 2021).

Within the drug and alcohol treatment and education circles, FebFast is the foundational TSI. Having noted the success of both FebFast and Dry July's first public campaigns in 2008, Life Education, an Australian charity promoting healthy living education programmes for children, founded Ocsober in time for October of that same year (Ocsober 2016). FebFast was also the first TSI to generate an international spin-off, FebFast New Zealand, which ran in support of the New Zealand Drug Foundation. It began as a loosely allied campaign of its Australian inspiration in 2011 (NZ Drug Foundation 2015). In that interval, after the expansion to New Zealand, Dry January came into being in the UK and the campaign that would ultimately become the Défi 28 jours allied itself with the Fondation Jean Lapointe. Although all save the New Zealand iteration of FebFast claim origins independent of one another, they share a common model of being in-house fundraisers for alcohol and drug prevention and treatment organizations, a situation that suggests a unity of operational strategy if not of inspiration.

Dry January's focus on changing participants' relationship with alcohol has since become the pre-eminent objective for TSIs in the northern hemisphere and especially in Europe, where the European Union facilitated greater information exchange, especially around public health measures. Imitator campaigns have accordingly sprung up in the Netherlands (IkPas 2019), the Czech Republic (Suchej Únor 2020), Estonia (Septembris Eij Oo 2020), Hungary (Kékpont: Alkohol Drog Karantén 2020), Denmark (Hvid Junuar 2020), France (Dry January France 2020), Belgium (Tournée Minérale 2021) and Switzerland (Dry January Suisse 2021). Some – notably the Dutch, French and Swiss campaigns – are formal partners of Alcohol Change UK while others appear to be more inspired by example (including by the original Finnish TSI), than officially linked.

The spread of TSIs within the international network of cancer charities is more directly traceable to Dry July and its influence. The campaign, which began in Sydney thanks to three British expats, launched publicly in 2008 and expanded to New Zealand in 2012 using the same fundraising model: an independent foundation serving as a clearing house to make grants to other charitable interests supporting projects related to cancer treatment and patient support (Dry July New Zealand 2014). Dry July is also credited as having inspired Cancer Research UK's Dryathlon, which launched in December 2012 in time for a January 2013 event; Macmillan Cancer Support's Go Sober (for October), which is now an official partner of the Australian Dry July initiative (Birkwood 2014); Dry Feb, the Canadian national campaign that launched in 2015 (Dry Feb Canada 2015); and British Columbia's Lose the Booze, which began only in February 2018 (BC Cancer Foundation 2020). Unlike the Australian and New Zealand versions, these adaptations of the campaign were typically incorporated into or partnered with established, national or regional cancer charities as fundraisers. A small amount of local adaptation was also employed in the shift from the southern to the northern hemisphere, as a mid-summer period of sobriety would have met with significant popular resistance, even for the worthiest of causes. The links between these four major national campaigns were further cemented through the use of a common peer-to-peer fundraising platform (Macdonald 2020), a commercial venture spun off from Dry July in 2016 by the Dry July founders as CHIL Fundraising, which has appointed Brett Macdonald, one of the founders of Dry July, as its managing director (2020).

As new TSIs have emerged, they are likely to have been inspired by both the freely circulating ideas for TSI-style experiences and the formal fundraising apparatuses that have developed around such campaigns. American journalist

John Ore (2015) claims to have quietly begun the practice of what he dubbed Drynuary in 2005, although he concedes that interest in it began to accrue mostly once Dry January had launched in the UK. The Drynuary designation remains a generic one, unaffiliated with any particular campaign or cause, although Dryuary (absent the *n*) commenced in 2015 as a fundraiser for alcohol self-help group Moderation Management, whose programme has always included an initial month-long period of abstinence before returning to moderate drinking (Moderation Management 2016a, b). Molly Kimball, founder for Alcohol Free for 40, cites no specific inspiration for her campaign, although as a registered dietician with a newspaper column, she professes that she was always searching for novel ways to promote healthier food and beverage choices.

The TSI model has influenced other health-related charities to emulate the success of cancer and drug and alcohol organizations. The Irish Heart Foundation launched On the Dry for January 2015 as a campaign derivative of earlier examples, even somewhat replicating Dry January's logo – a cup of tea adorned with cocktail garnishes (including the iconic umbrella) – in its visual branding (Irish Heart Foundation 2017).[6] The American Liver Foundation's small-scale Go Dry initiative (American Liver Foundation 2020), which launched in 2019, has also made use of the same secret superhero imagery (inspired by Superman baring his costume under business attire) used in Go Sober's campaigns for a number of years prior to their association with Dry July. In the United States, non-alcoholic beverage producers such as WellBeing Brewing have created Dry January communities that are unaffiliated with formal TSIs but capitalize upon the concept for commercial purposes (WellBeing Brewing Co. 2018).[7]

Divergence: Socially and philanthropically oriented TSIs

TSIs, whether direct offshoots of earlier movements or loosely inspired by the concept of a month away from alcohol, share many commonalities that allow them to be recognized as a phenomenon. As TSIs have proliferated, both within and beyond national borders, the concept has taken on a variety of local variations and nuances, not least as a result of the different objectives that the various initiatives set for themselves.

Perhaps the most notable distinction between TSIs is their framing of alcohol itself. On the one hand, there is a discourse centring on the social, physical and psychological drawbacks of alcohol, a framing more in line with the behaviour-change motives of temperance or health education. On the other, TSIs frame alcohol as a sacrificed pleasure, a strategy that drives fundraising and that wards off potential accusations of moralism. Similar splits – for instance between evangelical, experimental and charitable abstention – have been observed in relation to sugar, a legal but increasingly suspect foodstuff from a health point of view (Throsby 2018).[8] This distinction allows for a differentiation of two main types of TSIs that function as poles at either end of a continuum. On one extreme are the TSIs that prioritize social objectives, and on the other, those that champion philanthropy.

For most TSIs, social and philanthropic objectives exist in productive but occasionally contradictory tension. Over the dozen years that TSIs have been in widescale operation, there has also been a movement away from defined positions at either end of the spectrum, although this centring impetus has not always proceeded in a linear fashion. Likely motivated by desires to secure the largest possible number of eligible participants, whose own reasons for engaging in a TSI are varied, most TSIs now occupy a middle ground where social and philanthropic orientations coexist, often in ways that are outwardly contradictory or even, according to more cynical commentators, hypocritical. Where multiple TSIs emerge in the same national context and vie for limited charity dollars, participants and publicity, tensions between them have also arisen. The major point of contention is the priority accorded social versus philanthropic objectives.

Socially oriented TSIs, such as Tipaton Tammikuu, Dry January (and its affiliates) and Alcohol Free for 40, downplay philanthropic objectives. This is not to say that they do not accord some place to charitable motives, but in contrast to other TSIs, financial contributions or fundraising are not implied requisites to official participation.[9] Tipaton Tammikuu, for instance, remains unaffiliated with any fundraising effort, noting that the charitable angle is a curious Anglophone variation of their tradition (Tolvin 2020). TSIs with a strong social orientation tend not charge a registration fee, do not allow for purchasable reprieves and accentuate their educative and social impact, either by calling on participants to reflect on and evaluate their changed alcohol consumption, drawing attention to the social ubiquity of alcohol and the impacts of associated exclusionary practices, or by engaging in formal evaluations of their impact. Belgium's Tournée Minérale (2021), for instance, explicitly links reflection, and arguably the dry month needed to facilitate this reflection, with better health: *Faire une pause et réfléchir à sa consommation, c'est contribuer à une meilleure santé* (Pausing to reflect on your drinking contributes to better health). Where reflection is a common pedagogical strategy employed in forms of both formal and informal experiential learning (Jordi 2011), these evaluative exercises double as reinforcements of the participant's more individualized learning.

Socially oriented TSIs most strongly align with the neo-liberal discourses of taking responsibility for personal health and well-being as part of an improved societal relationship with alcohol. Ocsober touts the intertwined benefits of participation for self and society: 'you will be seen as actively supporting a positive campaign that aims to reduce the impact of alcohol abuse on everyone in our communities – children and adults alike' (Life Education Australia 2018). Such TSIs position themselves as tools to enable individuals to take control of their drinking and their health and are often run in collaboration with either government or non-governmental public health organizations or healthcare providers. This is especially the case in the more recent Western and Eastern European iterations, which take place in contexts that have more limited historical engagement with temperance movements. This recent spate of socially oriented TSIs also began subsequent to the publication of studies, such as Richard de Visser's work indicating a verifiable effect on medium-term alcohol consumption subsequent to TSI participation, including for previously heavier drinkers.

Alcohol Free for 40 presents a peculiar example of a socially oriented TSI. It engages in no fundraising and charges no registration fee. A sponsorship arrangement with a regional hospital network, founder Molly Kimball's employer at the time, even provided a financial benefit to participants. The Oschner Health System arranged pre- and post-campaign blood tests for hundreds of participants as a means to empirically demonstrate to them the ways in which abstaining from alcohol could have significant and quantifiable effects. In the American healthcare system, such tests could cost thousands of dollars for the under- or uninsured. While participants were encouraged to make a blood donation, a form of medical philanthropy (Meslin et al. 2008), when they came in for testing, the provision of the tests as a means of alcohol education and as an imputed kick start to a changed pattern of consumption was not contingent upon giving blood.

For socially oriented campaigns, personal and embodied action is posited as a means to educate participants – and through them society more broadly – about alcohol's effects on health, wellness, productivity and finances. These TSIs consciously seek to develop a successfully abstaining self as an exemplar for both a future self and others. As framed by these TSIs, there is a high degree of public ignorance or disbelief about alcohol's mundane effects and little consideration about how they compound and contribute to larger social and health problems, such as traffic fatalities, public and domestic violence (40 Brez Alkohola 2021), and chronic illness (Kimball 2017). Alcohol's ubiquity and central role in social interactions are also identified as problems and are, at least temporarily, redressed by creating experiential empathy (Reynolds and Reason 2012) by providing greater support for and recognition of those who choose to drink less or not at all or who, in the case of addiction, struggle to do so.

Philanthropically oriented TSIs, such as Dry July and Dryathlon, by contrast, do not overtly cast themselves as agents for healthier lifestyles or alcohol reform. Participants may draw personal benefits – physical, psychological, emotional, financial – from the experience, but these are not the intentions and annual reports first and foremost tout the revenues raised (see, for instance, Dry July 2016, Dry July New Zealand 2014). These TSIs instead align themselves with the philanthropic objectives to frame abstaining from alcohol as a vehicle for supporting worthy causes that require resources from engaged, civically minded individuals. Dry July's first annual report lists three vision statements:

(1) leadership in the not-for-profit sector supporting cancer and hospitals
(2) leadership in 'web-based community fundraising'
(3) 'to make Dry July the standout campaign of the calendar year where not consuming alcohol for the month of July is considered the "thing to do"' (Dry July, 2009, 3).

Their marketing positions them as clever enablers of good works, including by developing enabling technologies and involving those who do not normally donate to charity or engage in fundraising (Robert 2013).

These more philanthropically oriented TSIs refrain from broadcasting overtly negative judgements about alcohol. Indeed, it is the normalcy and ubiquity of alcohol, and its recognition as a (guilty) pleasure for many, that is so valuable. For participants to give it up and to thus buck social conventions by 'depriving themselves' for a short time (as opposed to renouncing it altogether) is what is worthy of compensation. The more normative and enjoyable alcohol is represented to be, the bigger the sacrifice and thus the fundraising potential (Olivola and Shafir 2013).

In light of this martyrdom effect, philanthropic TSIs emphasize the sacrifice or effort required to abstain (Bartram et al. 2018) and enact strategies to encourage fundraising that paradoxically monetize both drinking and sobriety. Reprieves such as 'Golden Tickets' (Dry July 2017a) and the payment of a 'Tipple Tax' (Cancer Research UK 2020c) acquiesce to the notion that sobriety is hard. Staying sober and forgoing the use of a free pass is a reinforcement of the overall social contract of the TSI between the participant and their sponsors or donors (Cherrier and Gurrieri 2013), yet it is often the case that these same supporters will be the ones to make an extra donation or payment to enable the participant to imbibe for a special occasion. Fundraising strategies encourage participants to make sobriety the object of a wager, the basis for an exchange of or a competition (Cancer Research UK 2020c; Tonkin 2008). Lest the prospect of a month away from drinking be too daunting, shorter or intermittent versions of TSIs have recently been introduced. Dryathlon, for instance, piloted a change to allow a week-long version for a £10 registration fee in lieu of a month-long initiative for £25 (Cancer Research UK 2020b); the decision to extend one's sobriety (within the framework of the TSI) would therefore be costlier by a considerable margin.

Some initiatives, however, have never been defined by one pole or the other on the spectrum. FebFast and the Défi 28 jours, which both operate as in-house fundraisers for drug and alcohol support services, have always purported to speak to both social and philanthropic objectives. When TSIs function as fundraisers for health-related charities, as is the case in Lose the Booze and Go Dry, there also tends to be a dual emphasis on health outcomes and philanthropy (BC Cancer Foundation 2020; American Liver Foundation 2020).

TSIs that used to be more obvious in their orientation, however, have increasingly found themselves balancing their focus. From 2016, Dry January began partnering with other charities in a revenue-sharing arrangement (May 2016). While it still charges no registration fee and sells no reprieves to participants, the concession to fundraising for causes that participants can select themselves is recognition that philanthropic TSIs attract a share of the market for a reason. From the opposite angle, Dry July temporarily made concessions to feature more health and wellness information on their website. In 2014, the site began to resemble those of more socially oriented TSIs, with recipes for healthy non-alcoholic drinks, a wellness blog and even yoga videos featuring prominently (Dry July 2014b) on what its annual report dubbed an embedded 'micro-site' (Dry July 2015b). The shift marked a recognition that participants engaged in TSIs just as much for health reasons as for altruistic ones.

Conclusion

TSIs are now an identifiable and even internationally franchised phenomenon. They are highly successful examples of health behaviour-change campaigns and habit-based embodied philanthropy initiatives that were widely disseminated through personal and professional networks using both mass self-communication and specialist media. Based on their success, they inspired imitation. Exemplarity, whether via grassroots or organizational pathways, allowed TSI organizers to replicate successful models, expand their reach, diversify their operations and internationalize.

At its core, the idea of the TSI was so simple – you quit drinking for a month and, possibly, also raise money for charity – and it is that simplicity that allowed TSIs to flourish in a number of different linguistic and cultural settings. Within these contexts, inflections towards either collective social or individual responsibility, and via either personal lived example or through philanthropy, allowed TSIs to differentiate themselves from one another and, in so doing, to appeal to different kinds of participants. The situations in which TSIs are most established and successful as organizations, however, are those that have had a long history with the impetuses for self and social control that expressed themselves in temperance movements.

4

Reimagining temperance cultures

As outlined in Chapter 3, there is a history of modelling TSIs off each other and following the examples of success (or avoiding examples of failure) in each national or regional reinvention of the concept. For socially oriented TSIs in particular, the examples that inspired imitation go back much further than the early years of the present century. Today's TSIs, as experiential alcohol awareness campaigns, owe much to the temperance movement of the late nineteenth and early twentieth centuries.

Harry Levine (1993) identifies 'temperance cultures' as the English-speaking (Canada, the United States, the United Kingdom, Australia and New Zealand) and Nordic (Finland, Sweden, Norway and Iceland) countries that were among the staunchest supporters of temperance organizations and regulatory campaigns. They were primarily Protestant and enjoyed spirits-based drinking cultures. Not coincidentally, this group includes the societies that have been the earliest and most enthusiastic adopters of TSIs.

Organizers of TSIs have not always been keen to have their initiatives associated with the lingering image of temperance prevalent in most former temperance cultures, though. The reputation of the temperance movement, often erroneously understood as a homogenous entity with uniform objectives, tactics and structures, centres on its most extreme forms, which championed both total personal abstinence and state-imposed prohibition. In reality, temperance organizations advocated for a range of state controls, such as licensing and limits on trading hours, to various forms of moral regulation (Yeomans 2011) centring on promoting overall moderation and/or banning the consumption of certain types of alcohol, namely spirits (Roberts 1982; Sulkunen 1990). Their positioning relative to commercial and consumer interests was also far from uniform, with only the more extreme elements of the movement centred on wanting to eliminate or diminish the sectors of the economy that derived profit from the production and sale of alcohol. Virginia Berridge encapsulates these

62   *Alcohol, Binge Sobriety and Exemplary Abstinence*

beliefs with a disclaimer that prefaces her report on the potential lessons of temperance for twenty-first-century policymakers: 'most people associate it with outdated attitudes, rigid moralism, narrow religion and an uncompromising attitude towards the consumption of drink' (Berridge 2005: 1). Anti-temperance attitudes, epitomized in Australia by the maligned figure of the *wowser* (Room 2010) and the American post-prohibition backlash (Travis 2009: 61), are thus never far from TSIs and are guarded against in the public image these campaigns cultivate.

The apprehension about unflattering associations notwithstanding, TSIs have largely taken these earlier temperance movements as normative examples. They have capitalized on many of their legacies, including their international philanthropic networks, their mustering of both medical and economic arguments, the utility of public commitments and even some of their lesser-known forms of involvement (such as time-delimited initial commitments) to create popular campaigns. The origins, rationales, forms, discourses and even exemplifying practices of temperance have nonetheless been reimagined and made palatable to contemporary audiences in a way that 'temperance' as popularly understood could not be.

Temperate values on display

Temperance, as Gusfield (1986) established, is often framed as a response, admittedly a symbolic one, to a 'moral panic' (Cohen 2002) about alcohol consumption. This is to say that temperance was a reaction to the popular perception that alcohol was a problem that was worsening and that would continue to worsen without intervention. Analyses of both temperance and neo-temperance contexts reveal that in objective terms, alcohol consumption prior to the initiation of renewed calls for regulation and prohibition was in decline (Hunt 1999; Reinarman 1988). Images of alcoholic excess and sensationalist headlines – whether the gin drinking of nineteenth-century working-class England or the binge drinking of young women and 'alcohol-fuelled violence' that began to claim the attention of modern news outlets in Britain in 2004 (Berridge 2013) and Australia in 2008 (Azar et al. 2013) – nonetheless presented alcohol as an emergent threat to social order rather than as practices whose effects were mostly felt by individuals, most often individuals who were virtually unknown to the advocates of temperance. The order in question, albeit in different ways, relied upon self-governance as a means of distinction and differentiation. Temperance activities (both old and new), as Levine (1978) influentially argued, were accordingly predicated on the overt manifestation of restraint and responsibility as the symbolic solution to the perceived problem of rampant alcohol consumption.

Temperance was most often associated with the upwardly mobile middle classes amid urbanization and industrialization. 'In most societies', note Barrows and Room, 'temperance started as the concern of a relatively elite group, sometimes about their own drinking but more often about the drinking of others in less privileged positions' (Barrows and Room 1991: 14). Those of greatest interest were the workers, whose sobriety and productivity were of direct pecuniary interest to industrialists and an emerging managerial class (Douglas and Wildavsky 1983: 59). A 'politics of moral superiority', which justified imposing on others a way of life that temperance supporters felt respectable for themselves' (Sulkunen and Warpenius 2000: 424) accordingly emerged.

Temperance, however, was primarily a middle-class endeavour, at least in the Anglo-American tradition, and as such was not as overtly disciplining as the framing of industrialists seeking to control the productivity of their labour pool implies.[1] Instead, the movement's emphasis on moral superiority allowed it to operate as a lifestyle and arguably a social movement concerned with 'secular self-mastery' (Bernard 1991: 347), a behaviour-based principle of social distinction that at least partially supplanted the era's dominant social stratification based on fixed categories, such as class and religion, and to a lesser extent, race and gender (Wagner 1997). The emergent middle class's aspirations of social differentiation and advancement, more so than those of the working class, could accordingly find a 'productive' outlet in temperance. This is because temperance was an imitable form of conduct that could be modelled, taught and incited, and once enacted, elevate the temperate citizen above his or her intemperate counterpart.

David Wagner contends that 'new temperance' movements emerged in the 1970s and 1980s, at a time when the middle class in the United States and Britain in particular were gripped by significant economic (and ergo class) anxiety. As class security began to give way, these new movements – which encompassed a turn away from alcohol, tobacco and other recreational drugs, with a new focus on diet, exercise and wellness – replicated temperance's earlier behavioural demarcation of society into its respectable elements and an underclass that failed in its social obligation of self-mastery. 'New Temperance is, in many respects, a reassertion of the ideology of middle-class respectability' (Wagner 1997: 103). Alcohol control strategies as part of the neo-temperance movement followed closely in this vein, as they targeted 'the self-regulating capacity of the many rather than . . . the propensity to excess of the few' (Valverde 1998: 13–14). The focus therefore shifted to the responsible enjoyment of alcohol, for instance, via campaigns aimed at preventing impaired driving or moderation for reasons of health.

TSIs are a late manifestation of this larger neo-temperance trend, including its economic underpinnings. The emergence of TSIs in Australia in 2008 coincided with the Global Financial Crisis and the Great Recession, a period in which the middle class came under tremendous pressure subsequent to the collapse of whole sectors of the global economy. Comportment in line with the dictates of respectability for the time – living within one's physical and financial means and thus ensuring one's future security – once again became civic and social imperatives and, in line with lifestyle movements more generally (Haenfler 2019), a means for people to use conduct and consumption to fashion a valued identity for themselves.

Writing in 2005, before the emergence of TSIs in the UK, Virginia Berridge remarked that 'society now has no mass movement focused on individual abstinence as a route to working-class respectability and advancement' (Berridge 2005: 11). Arguably true at that juncture, TSIs have since emerged to prioritize individual control of alcohol consumption as a means of advancement. Granted, their focus is no longer on the sworn commitment to prohibition or total abstinence, outcomes that run counter to the compulsory consumerism of today's culture, but rather on promoting the 'moderate' and 'responsible' use of alcohol to show personal mastery over that which threatens disorder, abnegation of responsibility and loss of productivity (Room 2011). Such consumption poses minimal risk of harm to others – in simple terms, it does not lead to violence or disorder and does not impinge on responsibilities such as driving or care-giving (Berridge 2013: 234; Gusfield 1981) – and the overall risk to individual and population health is kept within acceptable limits. More than just propping up the alcohol and hospitality industries, moderate and responsible alcohol consumption had to become an equally performative means to evince respectability balanced with consumerism.

TSIs are accordingly conceived to elicit the continual demonstration of this respectability – the ability to be moderate and responsible in one's alcohol consumption – as a form of 'visible achievement' (Wagner 1997: 104) of aspirational values. The act of 'drink refusal', whether in the form of an alcohol-free day (or month) or the cessation of consumption after one or two drinks, acts as the epitome of neo-temperance. In this, TSIs are more akin to the form of Finnish temperance from the 1870s and 1880s propounded by A. A. Granfelt, who saw total abstinence as 'a drunkard's resource' (Sulkunen 1990: 64) insofar as it required less fortitude to enact than moderation. Long-term abstinence may be a consequence for some TSI participants, but the lessons to be learnt, and the examples to be repeatedly enacted as proof of this new respectability are those of continual self-restraint and self-responsibility, which function as 'protective behavioural strategies' (Pearson 2013) over a lifetime.

As evidence of this penchant for demonstrative responsibility, TSIs encourage participants to use their break from alcohol to initiate a more judicious use of their personal resources of time, energy and money, for instance, by channelling their efforts towards achieving a fitness goal or by saving up for a major purchase (FebFast 2015). Blogging or posting to social media about one's progress, including using pre-developed content (Cancer Research UK 2020c), is promoted as a routine part of TSI participation, a feature of the experience that drives fundraising, personal commitment and, increasingly, cynicism about grandiose displays of small-scale martyrdom (Frizzell 2014).

One feature of TSIs that underscores the performative nature of this self-restraint is the way in which participants are encouraged to frequent (or are not actively discouraged from frequenting) drinking venues that earlier temperance movements, such as the Anti-Saloon League, would have seen shuttered. Philanthropic TSI participants in particular are entreated to continue to accompany members of their circle to drinking establishments and to put themselves in settings where refusing a drink or being alone in their sobriety is linked to fundraising. A drink that would be bought for them is to be monetized as a small donation (typified by Dryathlon's 'make mine a donation' strategy (Vahdati 2014)), a lift home is to be converted into a donation equivalent to a taxi fare (Go Sober 2019; Cancer Research UK 2020c, also see Chapter 6). In a nod to the paradoxical centrality of alcohol in these neo-temperance cultures, advice to TSI participants accentuates the continuity of behaviour, including in alcogenic environments:

> Just because you're giving up drinking doesn't mean you have to stay home while your social circle is downing shots at a dance club or sampling the vino at a new bistro. In fact, not showing up might just give you a case of FOMO [fear of missing out], which could cause you to lose your resolve later in the month. Instead, do the same things you would usually do with your friends and loved ones, but just do them without drinking. (Gold 2018)

Drinking venues and beverage manufacturers have responded to this need for demonstrative moderation by crafting and selling non-alcoholic drinks –

mocktails and non-alcoholic beers, wines and spirits. Major producers such as Heineken have even acceded to the pressures of the consumer trend (Bird 2019; Hooper 2020).

TSI participants themselves express a variety of views with respect to the practicalities of carrying on as they normally would while simply abstaining from alcohol versus modifying a wider range of habits and behaviours, especially their ways of socializing. Roughly half of participants interviewed for this book concede that they prefer not to put themselves into contexts where they will be tempted to drink or will be the only sober person. Where the Australian context involves considerable drinking outside of the home, this meant the avoidance of licensed venues. They opt out of social events in bars or pubs, make earlier exits than they otherwise might have had they been imbibing, or choose to organize social events in contexts that do not lend themselves to an assumption of drinking. Morning or daytime gatherings, trips to the cinema or family-friendly venues (the zoo) and even a preference for restaurants without a liquor licence were all mentioned as alternatives that could provide sociality without an expectation of drinking.

Louise (n.b. all names have been changed), a habitual FebFast participant, takes the opposite view and is an example of the (neo-)temperate individuals who 'enjoy the ability to righteously resist and refrain' (Wagner 1997: 59). She recounts typical encounters with her friends and neighbours at beachside barbecues:

> Now that I do it every February (that's right, every February) they're: 'Oh, there she is again, she's mad, that woman' . . . and I say 'Oh shut up . . . I don't want to have a drink' . . . I'm fine. I'll drink bloody Diet Pepsi. Or I drink my water like my daughters do. . . . If anything, they don't realise that it actually spurs me on.

She is proudly defiant about being the only non-drinking adult in the alcogenic environment of the beach party. Her satisfaction, arguably her sense of superiority, comes not from being a teetotaller but, rather, from having the fortitude to withstand especially pressured situations where drinking would be the norm.

TSIs as neo-temperance initiatives are fundamentally aligned with the deep-seated ideological and even economic imperatives of older temperance movements; this is true even if their outward objectives, such as constraints on the supply of alcohol and their overall view on alcohol as a suspect or dangerous substance, appear to be at odds. In both TSIs and earlier temperance movements, participants used their adherence, the overtness of their choice about their conduct and their continued focusing of attention on what could be a rather banal choice (what to drink) as a mark of distinction, a signifier of their adherence to the dictates of middle-class respectability of their era.[2] Moreover, in the contemporary context of TSIs, many participants use the structure of the campaign and its fundraising schemes to repeatedly assert their ability to moderate their consumption, to refuse a drink and to redirect their personal resources to socially valued projects, such as fitness, well-being, productivity and consumerism.

Scientific temperance: Appeals to hip pocket, health and harm reduction

The demonstration of respectability is characteristic of temperance movements, both old and new. In the context of neo-temperance, it is fundamentally an expression of internalized neo-liberal logic. The defunding of public services for healthcare, addiction support and the larger social safety net has resulted in preventative measures – responsibility for one's own health, welfare and economic standing – being reframed as the proactive imperatives of new civic life (Foucault 2008; Rose 1999; Brown and Baker 2012). While these logics explain the drive towards neo-temperance, direct health and economic motivations were also important but frequently overshadowed parts of earlier temperance movements.

Temperance mythology in popular culture favours explanations and motivations centred on religiosity and morality, thinking reinforced by images of firebrand revival tents and terms such as 'demon rum'. Fictionalized portrayals of American temperance during the prohibition era such as the HBO series *Boardwalk Empire* (Winter 2010–14) popularized these stereotypes for those unacquainted with temperance as a historical phenomenon. The movement's 'scientific' arm nonetheless sought to understand and educate people about alcohol's social and economic effects through lenses that would now be understood as social scientific (Berridge 2005). At the same time, scientific temperance highlighted alcohol's effects on individual and population health. Education was central to this mission, for although temperance campaigners embraced moral suasion arguments, 'they were confident that, since sin was due to ignorance, knowledge would turn men from vice to virtue' (Krout 1925: 125). Scientific temperance thus positioned itself in alliance with public health, and at a time when science and progress were fuelling economic advancement, temperance 'was pragmatic and appealed to science for legitimacy' (Edman 2015: 37).

Specialized temperance groups, among them the Scientific Temperance Federation and the International Temperance Bureau, were active temperance educators (Woiak 1994; Edman 2015). The tenor of temperance organizations in France, a nation where moral arguments about temperance have held little sway, reflected the views of bourgeois professionals and was strongly medical and scientific in nature, often inflected with the same Lamarckian eugenic thinking on heredity that underpinned much of the country's contemporary public health policy (Prestwich 1980). Groups such as the Woman's Christian Temperance Union (WCTU) also routinely advanced economic and medical arguments for abstinence and prohibition alongside their moral campaigns, and it was this scientific line of reasoning that secured them the greatest inroads into some societies, such as Japan (Tyrrell 1991).

Temperance organizations employed public pedagogy in terms of both moral and scientific objectives. Berridge's (2013: 41) report on the mid-nineteenth century 'Malt Lectures' of Joseph Livesey, the founder of the British temperance movement, stresses these intertwined objectives. The lectures, which were franchised to other temperance speakers to aid in wide dissemination, involved arguments hinging on national virtue, economic rationalism about the costs of intemperance and a pyrotechnic demonstration involving the evaporated alcohol from a quart of ale – a display that countered the popular belief that the alcohol in ale was categorically different from that in spirits. Such performative education reinforced Thomas Laycock's (1857) contention that medical and scientific arguments were more effective than legal means or moral suasion in converting people to the cause of temperance (Woiak 1994).

In contrast to the relative earnestness, and arguably, censoriousness, of scientific temperance, TSIs have often employed a light touch when engaging in temperance education. The websites or smartphone apps for a number of TSIs – among them Dryathlon, the Défi 28 jours and Dry January – feature calculators participants can use to determine both the financial and caloric costs of their usual drinking habits (Fondation Jean Lapointe 2015; Dryathlon 2016a; Zanec Soft Tech Private Limited 2017). Participants enter what they deem to be their average weekly consumption of wine, cocktails, spirits and beer and embedded formulas approximate the costs of their usual drinking. In the case of the Défi 28 jours, the sum of the calculation is expressed in relatable in-kind units: the number of tickets to Montreal Canadiens' hockey games that could be bought and how many servings of the infamous artery-clogging, post-drinking snack of poutine could be consumed for an equivalent amount of alcohol. Without veering into economic or health moralism, these calculators serve an educative purpose and employ rational choice models (sometimes with a bit of affect and humour) to change attitudes and behaviours. It is precisely this kind of scientific reasoning, always expressed in terms of cost to the individual rather than to society at large, that medical temperance campaigners argued, more than a century earlier, would prove decisively influential.

Perhaps because TSI participants tend to be professionals and members of the middle class (Robert 2016b), for whom alcohol consumption is not so subject to the pressures of price elasticity, health has proven to be a greater motivator (and thus focus) for TSI discourse than economics. Dry July reported that their Wellbeing micro-site, which launched in 2014, attracted more web traffic than their main website (Dry July 2015b). The branding strategy of Dryathlon plays up the associations with sport and sporting charity challenges; its website features 'Dryathletes' in athletic gear (Dryathlon 2016a), connoting both the health benefits of exercise and the kudos that tends to accrue to those who undertake sports-based charity fundraisers (Palmer and Dwyer 2019). FebFast, one of the TSIs that most accentuates health outcomes – a logic confirmed by its now equally prominent campaign revolving around sugar abstention – used participant testimonials to suggest that a month off alcohol will improve everything from skin complexion to workplace productivity (FebFast 2013). This information, which has been legitimized via research (Hillgrove and Thomson 2012; Robert 2016a), has now become so common that TSIs worldwide replicate it on their websites to incentivize participation.

If for many temperance organizations health and other scientific arguments were important but subordinate to the persistent and central concerns of morality and social order, TSIs have overwhelmingly elevated health to the pre-eminent position. Alcohol Free for 40's encouragement of – and subsidies for – before and after medical tests consisting of seven separate blood tests to provide an empirical basis for the health benefits of temporary sobriety is the most extreme example of this trend (Kimball 2016). The priority accorded to health reflects its status as what Robert Crawford (2006) identifies as its 'super-value' status in many Western societies.

Following neo-liberal currents of individualized responsibility, however, TSIs often interpret health as physiological – sleep, digestion, weight, hepatic function, energy levels – and less as either psychological or mental health. Where alcohol, in modest amounts, is frequently used to calm nerves, reduce anxiety or stress, and facilitate social interactions, TSIs emphasize finding 'healthier' means to achieve what they concede are important aspects of mental well-being. TSIs also prioritize individual health over population or public health, especially concerning matters such as the aggregated population-level impacts of alcohol consumption. Socially oriented TSIs such as Dry January and Alcohol Change UK are more willing to engage with population-level scientific temperance arguments and to not subsume alcohol education to an overall focus on personal well-being, a trait that Berridge (2005) cites when she links them to temperance organizations insofar as their main aim is to change drinking cultures. Socially oriented TSIs in non-Anglophone European countries have been more overtly aligned with public health objectives and organizations, including government organizations. For instance, the fledgling French iteration of Dry January controversially sought, but was ultimately rebuffed in its efforts, to secure official sanction from the French Ministry of Health's Santé Public France (the country's peak body for public health) owing to the impacts of alcohol on the overall disease burden in France (Santi and Horel 2020).

Even among philanthropic TSIs though, there is evidence of change. TSIs that support cancer charities had until recently been conspicuously silent on the carcinogenic properties of alcohol, yet Dryathlon's homepage now links to a site detailing this connection (Cancer Research UK 2020a). Peak medical bodies and governments have also recently become more proactive in endorsing and promoting well-known TSIs. Most recently, Australian minister of health, Greg Hunt, recommended Dry July participation: 'Dry July raises funds to improve the comfort and wellbeing of Australians diagnosed with cancer. Not only that, it delivers health benefits to every person who takes the pledge and gives up alcohol for the month, or part of it' (Hunt 2020). The final clause in the minister's statement reflects the evidence that successful completion of the TSI is not a precondition for reduction in medium-term drinking.

The care for or treatment of those affected by alcohol dependence, a lesser-recognized part of scientific temperance, has also been taken up by TSIs. While earlier temperance organizations mostly lobbied the governments to assume such functions, TSIs operate in a neo-liberal climate of increasing privatization of social services. They have thus become more directly involved in care for individuals who abuse or are dependent upon alcohol and other drugs. FebFast and the Défi 28 jours serve as in-house fundraisers for drug and alcohol education and treatment services, and many socially oriented TSIs in Northern and Eastern Europe – such as Száraz November and IkPas, to say nothing of Dry January's links to Alcohol Change – are run by drug and alcohol treatment organizations. These TSIs fuse the educational and activist elements of scientific temperance by using embodied forms of philanthropic engagement to raise money to support these endeavours. They also create a context for empathy (Reynolds and Reason 2012) among participants for the clients of these services, a concept to which I will return in the next chapter.

Where temperance aims were from their inception closely allied with public health and the medical professions (physicians, such as Benjamin Rush, often being prominent temperance advocates), TSIs were initially met with limited but arguably disproportionately well-publicized misgivings from within these communities. In 2012, the British Liver Trust dismissed the TSI concept as one that created a false sense of security and, echoing early Finnish temperance promoter A. A. Granfelt's views, noted that TSIs failed to have participants query their overall relationship with alcohol (BBC 2012). British public health researcher Ian Hamilton (2019, 2016; Hamilton and Gilmore 2016) in particular emerged as an unofficial spokesperson from within the health community for the much larger contingent of cynics in the general population. Hamilton's critiques, now reinforced by emerging research (Case et al. 2021), were more scholarly than ideological, as he pointed to potential gaps or limitations in the evaluation research. His methodological critiques and questions about the campaigns were nonetheless amplified by editors, even of reputable academic journals, and transformed into overdetermined headlines that zeroed in on the dangers – potentially even fatal ones – of TSIs (Hamilton and Gilmore 2016; Manning 2019). Some clinicians, among them Mark Wright (University Hospital Southampton 2018), and 'sober-curious' organizations such as Hello Sunday Morning (2019) have identified and publicized the 'dark side' of TSIs.[3] Their criticisms include the way a month of sobriety can mask a genuine dependency and promote a feast-or-famine mentality, including via an implicit moral licensing of abnormally excessive post-campaign binge drinking that is (often erroneously) forecast.

Critiques of TSIs have nonetheless become less vociferous than they were at the midpoint of the 2010s. This shift in discourse is largely attributable to work – most notably by Richard de Visser and his collaborators (de Visser et al. 2017; de Visser and Piper 2020; de Visser and Nicholls 2020; de Visser et al. 2016) – to evaluate the effects of TSI participation on post-campaign alcohol consumption. Having an evidence base provides greater legitimacy for TSIs and has led to a decisive turn towards the concept of a sober month. Former critics have also reversed their earlier positions; in 2018 the British Liver Trust became an official partner of Alcohol Concern for Dry January 2019 (British Liver Trust 2018). Short-term abstinence was granted scientific legitimacy as a neo-temperance concept.

Episodic temperance

The stereotypical (but often mistaken) image of temperance is that members of temperance organizations, motivated by morality, forever forswear alcohol. Their allegedly lifelong commitment is taken to be akin to that of other contemporary groups of abstainers, such as those who eschew alcohol on religious grounds or who adopt a sober lifestyle as part of a programme of addiction recovery. Temperance history nonetheless suggests that permanent abstention from alcohol has not been the universal objective, let alone outcome, of the movement.

The British temperance movement began in the Lancashire city of Preston in 1832 at the urging of Joseph Livesey and got its start not as an enduring pledge but, rather, as a year-long experiment in total abstinence (Berridge 2005). Its novelty was a change from earlier temperance objectives, which had focused only on refraining from drinking spirits. While Livesey's time-delimited foray was ultimately lasting and was followed by a lifelong pledge of total abstinence, membership records from other temperance organizations reveal that such perpetual pledges were often more symbolic than practical. For many who took the pledge of the Irish Total Abstinence Society headed by Father Theobald Mathew, the vow was less of a binding commitment than a declaration of hopeful intent (Bretherton 1991). Records from Finnish temperance organizations that required lifelong pledges of total abstinence tellingly uncover patterns of expelling – and subsequently readmitting – their members for drinking (Sulkunen 1990).

In other contexts, temperance was less of an objective and more of a means of political and social campaigning. From the 1870s, alcohol boycotts or 'drinking strikes' were used in Finland as a form of radical protest among factory workers who used their abstinence to withhold economic resources from the trade and taxation of alcohol. The practice spread and gained popularity, such that in 1898 approximately 70,000 Finnish workers pledged to drink no distilled alcohol for at least a year (Sulkunen 1990). Members of the German Social Democratic Party similarly called for an open-ended schnapps boycott – in favour of drinking beer – in 1909 as a form of protest against new taxation regimes and as a way to elevate the socialist cause (Roberts 1982). The strikes and boycotts had high rates of attrition, which highlighted the practical concern of feasibility for groups that would seek to use abstinence or temperance as a means for achieving other objectives. Roberts (1982) maintains that the German boycott, which was officially called off in 1912, was neither politically effective nor influential in changing drinking behaviours. Sulkunen (1990), nonetheless, argues that the precedents of episodic sobriety proved central in the development of nationalism and political consciousness for an expanding working class in Finland.

Finland would have several subsequent and arguably more successful experiences with temporary sobriety. In 1942, a movement for a Dry January (Raitis Tammikuu) was endorsed by parliamentary Speaker Väinö Hakkila in support of the Continuation War against the Soviet Union. Scientific temperance campaigners had long decried the economic wastefulness of drinking (Dingle 1977), and the short-term measure was meant to redirect both grain and funds to the war effort. While the practice fell out of favour in the post-war years, it was revived in 1974 by United Paper Mills as an industrial campaign for a Dry February (Raitis Helmikuu). The intent was neither political nor patriotic but, rather, a means to counter workplace intoxication and improve safety in the industrial setting. Management fashioned it as an annual event that pitted factories against each other in a friendly competition of adherence, and the practice endured until 1990 (Vismanen 2009). Both of these month-long campaigns foreshadow contemporary TSIs in not only their form but also insofar as they are explicitly linked to productivity and elements of competition. Given Finland's long-standing experimentation with episodic temperance, it is hardly surprising that TSIs originated in the Nordic state.

While episodic temperance is far from the most recognizable facet of the temperance movement, it has been one of the most influential as far as TSIs are concerned. TSIs have frequently used the shorter durations as part of their pitch to participants. Like Raitis Tammikuu, organizers of the Défi 28 jours confessed to choosing the shortest month of the year as a way to lower perceived barriers to participation (Vismanen 2009; Chouinard and Théorêt-Poupart 2013). The strategy of inviting time-delimited participation with the hope of a longer-term impact nonetheless features prominently, especially for socially oriented TSIs. The 'What Is Dry January?' page on the Alcohol Change UK website notes 'A month off is a great chance to get us all thinking about our drinking, so we can make healthier and happier decisions when it comes to alcohol year-round' (Alcohol Change UK 2020b). So as not to be missed, the page features three separate mentions of the relationship between the official month-long run of the campaign and anticipated year-long effects. The *Try Dry* guidebook also features a foreword by British comedian Lee Mack that details how a short trial of abstinence led to his ongoing sobriety, a story echoed by the volume's author (Booker 2019).

Moderating expectations to meet the perceived capacity in the target audience, a move that speaks to the operational pragmatism of philanthropic TSIs in particular, recognizes the limitations of lifelong pledges of abstinence that would often end shortly after they were made. Just as temperance organizations made an uneasy peace with those who made repeated efforts at teetotalism, TSIs have persevered in taking whatever commitment they can. The restrictions and severe economic downturn that resulted from the Covid-19 pandemic in 2020 prompted Dry July to introduce a 'Dry-ish' option of two or three weeks because 'We get it. 2020 has been challenging' (Dry July Foundation 2020). Go Sober similarly advertised 'Sober(ish)' options of twenty-one or fourteen days because '2020 has already been quite the challenge'. The option to abbreviate the period of commitment attests to a willingness to compromise on the part of campaign operators, as these shorter campaigns also allow those who may have missed the start of the campaign to participate without feeling as though they had missed their chance. This was especially true for Dry July in 2020, as 1 July inaugurated a much-anticipated easing of Covid-19–related restrictions on licensed premises in many Australian jurisdictions. Would-be participants were able to benefit from a return to the sociality afforded by the hospitality industry but still take part in the fundraiser. Even the more socially oriented TSIs have been more accommodating of abridged or modified forms of participation. In 2020 the Défi 28 jours created three tiers of participation: gold for the month-long commitment, silver for weekends without alcohol (totalling thirteen days) and weekdays without alcohol (totalling sixteen days) (Fondation Jean Lapointe 2020). Public commitments nonetheless continue to be mobilized as a way to motivate compliance (Katzev and Wang 1994) and to capitalize on any opportunity for fundraising.

Temperate exemplification

Past temperance movements, especially those of the suasionist variety, have traditionally relied on examples to galvanize adherents, spread their messages and influence behaviours. Room maintains that 'education and example' were the means by which the temperance movement 'sought to build a sober society' (2015: 44). As expressed in the Anglo-American Protestant revivalist tradition, one's personal example furnished a means for others to see the efficacy of self-improvement 'in order to show others the correct path' (Eriksen 1990: 82). As TSIs generally work towards helping participants cultivate a vaguely healthier, more responsible or simply a changed relationship to drinking and alcohol, they are less prescriptive about their assertions of what is and is not 'correct'. As subsequent chapters will illustrate, they rely on examples to do much of their educative work, and in this too, they draw inspiration from earlier temperance movements.

Temperance cultures, especially those that favoured total abstinence, relied heavily on the negative or counterexample of the perpetual inebriate. Portrayals of the drunkard, a staple of temperance literature, illustrations and theatre, were paradigmatic – stereotypical even – in the ways in which they represented the drinker and their inevitable slide into destitution (Lender and Karnchanapee 1977). This always tragic figure was the epitome of what a life that involved alcohol could become for any who imbibed, as differences between the moderate drinker (or even those who consumed only wine or beer) and the inebriate were purely of degree and not of kind. With the core condition of exemplarity – instantiation – fulfilled, any commonality could become the basis for the intervention.

Armed with the negative example, the task of the temperance campaigner was then only to expose a degree of similitude between the drinker yet to be convinced of the necessity for reform and their tragic example, for: 'If a person comes to see himself as disrespectable and immoral due to his drinking, he may be persuaded to change his behaviour' (Yeomans 2011: 48). Valverde contends that this slippery slope model continues to underpin the popular vernacular of pseudo-medical and self-help 'diagnostic tools' for alcoholism, where members of the public are asked to assess their identification with various facets of paradigmatic alcoholic behaviours (Valverde 1998: 24). Even the World Health Organization's Alcohol Use Disorders Identification Test (AUDIT) employs similar strategies in quantifying risks based on the frequency of alcohol-related behaviours.

Although it may be the negative examples that are best remembered, temperance cultures also provided positive models for imitation. Yeomans (2011) notes how suasionist advertisements for temperance-aligned goods (such as hot chocolate and non-alcoholic beverages) used what we now refer to as lifestyle advertising, a genre that evidences the power of temperate examples. Advertisements of this kind used the interplay of person, setting and product to inspire a desire for the lifestyle depicted and for the product as a means to achieve it (Leiss et al. 2005: 194). The product, and by extension the larger temperance movement, became an imitable model that would allow access to the prosperous, healthful lifestyles depicted.

Conclusion

Neo-temperance initiatives are akin to the temperance movements of the past in far more than just their outward endorsement of moderate drinking, non-drinking or 'clean' living (Engs 2000). Social and economic circumstances made demonstrable behaviours projects of self-fashioning that could be mobilized as a way to evince one's alignment to respectable sectors of society, notably those that portrayed themselves as civic-minded and redressing rather than contributing to social problems. These problems were principally those of law and order but also of health, household economics and productivity.

TSIs, as a particular type of neo-temperance, overtly draw on certain forms of temperance and temperance logics. TSIs, for instance, most closely resemble the drinking strikes and other forms of episodic temperance that occurred in Finland at various points in the twentieth century. Discourses of health, economics and productivity, which animated temperance speeches, tracts and literature, are also prominent in TSIs, but they are individualized in the contemporary context and tend more towards personal than familial or societal objectives. The ways that temperance movements have enshrined both illustrative and normative examples have also been adopted by TSIs. As with the earlier movements for moderation, abstinence and/or prohibition, positive and negative examples were essential to educate and influence drinking behaviour. The remainder of this volume documents in greater detail how TSIs have organized themselves around the creation and deployment of examples to achieve their stated objectives.

5

Embodiment and affect

TSIs as pedagogues

By the time proponents of teetotalism were in the ascendency within the temperance movement, abstinence was regarded as qualitatively similar to moderation – the former being merely a superlative or exemplary form of moderation (Levine 1978; Yeomans 2013). Socially oriented TSIs in particular rely on this premise – of abstinence being (only) an exemplary form of moderation – to sensitize people to the ways in which their own personal abstinent example can be a way to learn to drink moderately and responsibly and to respect the choices of others who choose not to drink (as much). These TSIs rely on a period of sober embodiment to realize their didactic objectives as public pedagogies of moderation that serve the health and social objectives of the TSIs, participants and societies more generally.

Although TSIs serve many objectives, including within official frameworks to address alcohol consumption at a population level, this chapter focuses on what might be framed as their health education aims. Health education is understood as a broad and varied set of strategies to influence both individuals and their social environments in order to improve health behaviour and enhance health and quality of life (Glanz et al. 2008: 11). Health education has its roots in patient-care settings, schools and communities, and is centred on two key principles:

(1) That there is a reciprocity of interaction between individuals, their behaviours and their environments.
(2) That these influences play out at multiple levels.

Regardless of their social or philanthropic orientation or their context, the very structure and organization of TSIs are oriented towards producing conditions that allow for the emergence of examples that can function pedagogically for the purposes of health education.

The imitable examples of others are important to the success of TSIs as popular lifestyle campaigns or movements, yet it is the self-generated example of the participant – the actions of a current self, engaged in an experiment or test of will or discipline that will provide a model for a future self – that has the greatest pedagogical impact. Whether understood in terms of embodied learning (Stolz 2015), mindfulness (Shusterman 2008) or body pedagogics (Shilling 2017), participants are brought into a deliberate and potentially novel state – sobriety – and are encouraged to attune themselves to that experience to better understand alcohol's embodied effects and drinking's role as a cultural practice that is called to be carefully managed and navigated.

This chapter examines ways in which the outward- and inward-facing sober embodiment of TSIs creates examples that serve informally didactive purposes relating to health, which is understood broadly in terms of physiology, psychology and environment. The analysis begins with the roots of TSIs and considers the much-publicized examples of founders and early adopters. These stories of grassroots initiative establish the necessary conditions of commonality between the exemplar (the founder) and the class (prospective participants) needed to define an outward-facing example. They are accordingly important for understanding TSIs as lifestyle movements predicated on another's example, albeit an example that eschews any basis in superior morality, health consciousness or generosity and is instead premised on ease of imitability.

The analysis then shifts from outward or interpersonal exemplarity to a more inward focus where participants learn from examples generated via their own embodied practices. First is an exploration of how processes of discovery enable participants to employ experimental strategies to construct defined personal exemplars – a past drinking self and a present non-drinking self. In consciously embodying these two identified personas, participants are able to ascertain both the embodied and practical effects of alcohol consumption. Second is an analysis of the inherent temporality of normative examples and their role in developing self-efficacy, specifically around navigating alcogenic environments. The chapter concludes with a widening of the lens, specifically about how a participant's embodied experience enables deeper understandings of the entrenched social and cultural role of alcohol, insights that facilitate experiential empathy with non-drinkers.

One person's imitable example

TSIs, like any modern and media-savvy social movement, craft and curate their narratives about their vision or mission, their impact and their history. In these

Embodiment and Affect

self-presentations, tales about the origins of the campaign are a common theme. These stories often feature as elements of official websites, as part of media releases or as commentary, and are remarkably similar for their emphasis on the grassroots nature of the campaign and the ordinariness of the founders. As discussed earlier, these stories serve an important role in differentiating TSIs from the implied moralism of temperance and the (unfair but still real) stigma of abstinence (Cheers et al. 2020). Relatedly, they also establish the founders and their commitment to eschew alcohol for a short period not as exception but as an utterly imitable example that fellow ordinary people could and should take up. Far from simply being a colourful backstory or human-interest aspect of TSIs, these origin stories are part of their pedagogy. They position TSIs within an emergent tradition of lifestyle movements, which prioritize personal action, often in ways understood as simple or mundane lifestyle choices, as a means for larger cultural or social change.

Haenfler, Johnson and Jones's (2012) work on lifestyle movements defines and maps this class of initiatives, which includes temperance and neo-temperance, as well as movements including vegetarian/veganism, voluntary simplicity, green living and purity pledges. Their analysis highlights the role of both localized or personal influence and prefigurative politics. Prefigurative politics is a 'principle of direct action, of directly implementing the changes one seeks' (Leach 2013); it is commonly understood via the aphorism of 'being the change one wants to see in the world'. In their estimation, lifestyle movements succeed by (a) having people enact the larger change they seek to effect and (b) spreading the philosophy or ideology through practice.

While anyone can enact change for these purposes and can use informal social networks (both direct and mediated) to broaden the reach of the movement, lifestyle movements often highlight the role of 'cultural entrepreneurs' – authors of guidebooks, podcasters, bloggers, YouTubers, social media influencers or otherwise well-connected individuals adept at mass self-communication – as particularly influential figures. Implicit in this analysis is the role of exemplarity, including among peers and local role models, in driving what might be described as a ripple effect that converts 'nonadeherents to adherent and adherents to participants' (Haenfler et al. 2012: 11).

Origin stories in TSIs celebrate the role of the cultural entrepreneur but do so in a way that emphasizes the mundanity of their initiative rather than its exceptionality. TSIs, wherever they occur, are positioned as homegrown solutions to local circumstances or even personal concerns. They are enacted by relatable individuals whose success was in simply convincing those around them to support their cause, whether via donation or by following their example. The example in question had a particular form – a month of abstinence – but couched in the lesson was a pedagogy that also helped to destigmatize abstinence and moderate drinking. In contrast to the temperance tales of decades past where it was the rehabilitated drunkard who provided the example to others (Lender and Karnchanapee 1977), the founder provides an example that proves that episodic abstinence as a form of moderation is neither a slippery slope to becoming a teetotaller in societies that still value the social affordances of drinking nor a futile exercise in terms of either philanthropic or social outcomes.

A quick survey of origin stories helps to establish the hallmarks of the genre in relation to the imitability of the founders' example. FebFast (2009: 2) reports that their campaign was dreamed up at a barbeque, an Australian summertime tradition, as people were already starting to feel the accumulation of the celebratory season. The founder, Fiona Healy, and a friend joined forces in an endeavour to raise $900 for a local charity. Dry January (2017) cites its origin as the personal health project of Emily Robinson, who gave up drinking for the month of January in 2011 to help her train for a long-distance run. Dry July traces its origin to Brett Macdonald, Phil Grove and Kenny McGilvary, when a health scare and a family member's cancer diagnosis prompted the trio to raise money to support the under-resourced oncology unit of their local hospital (Dry July 2009). Macdonald, however, speaks of earlier (admittedly short-lived) challenges among the trio to see who could go the longest without drinking (Macdonald 2018). The Défi 28 jours is on record as the brainchild of two friends, who used Facebook to encourage a group challenge to abstain from alcohol (Chouinard and Théorêt-Poupart 2013). The pair embarked on what was effectively a dare to their friends with the promise of hosting a boozy party to toast the end of their sobriety. While these individuals are credited with launching TSIs as organizations that have raised millions of dollars for charity and altered drinking culture and practices for thousands of participants, the origin stories regularly downplay these outcomes as stemming from the achievement of these cultural entrepreneurs. These narratives are more often excavated from annual reports or come up in longer form explanations, such as interviews and histories of the initiatives.

The genre instead insists on the utter ordinariness of the TSI founders as a way to establish commonality with the largest possible pool of participants. According to these stories, these cultural entrepreneurs attend barbecues, use social media to enrol their friends into their projects, suffer through health scares, struggle with (overly) ambitious exercise commitments, start new jobs, engage their friends in slightly outrageous dares, are self-deprecating about their levels of willpower and plan overindulgent parties. These seemingly tangential details are included precisely because they provide the salient information required for prospective participants to find points of commonality between themselves and the founders. The would-be TSI participant is meant to identify with the pre-campaign founders, not with the spokespeople they have become.

The origin stories also speak to broader cultural norms and provide would-be participants with something of a script for their own navigation of changing drinking behaviours. For instance, they highlight largely uncontroversial reasons to cut back on drinking or engage in a philanthropic project: recognizing a need for restraint after a period of excess, a commitment to fitness and an impetus to donate to a cause to which one has a personal connection. They also make clear that the founders drank – by their own admission sometimes to excess – and did not inherently consider alcohol to be a social ill like temperance campaigns did. Quite the contrary, the founders are positioned as part of the majority of the population in their respective national contexts that drink but do not believe themselves to have an overall troubled relationship with alcohol (Garnett et al. 2015). Moreover, the founders began their practice of temporary sobriety not with an objective to change the broader drinking culture – a strategy that recalls the temperance movement and other lifestyle movements engaging in prefigurative politics – but simply to fulfil personal objectives where alcohol was either an impediment or a means to an end. Casting the founders as 'Joe or Jane Sixpack' (Young 2011) situates them within a large class, but one from which they can – and given the success of their initiatives, did – emerge as exemplars.

The participant and observer comments on the Facebook event page for the Défi 28 jours provide an insight into how people reacted to the founders' example. The page documents the self-deprecating comments of the first participants (founders and others) as they eagerly await their celebration. Jokes about mineral water tasting sessions (akin to wine tastings), near fruitless searches for dealcoholized wine to celebrate Valentine's Day, dry vacations and keeping oneself busy with sex and/or exercise confirm for the small initial audience that the founders were challenged by their commitment but were fundamentally unchanged by the campaign. For all to see, they retained their sense of humour, love of dinners with wine, celebrations of alcohol-centric rituals and passions of many sorts, even if they temporarily moderated their alcohol consumption. They also fitted neatly back into their pre-TSI social lives without alienating friends or romantic partners.

As relayed in the origin stories, the founders' exemplarity owes little to their views on alcohol, health and philanthropy. Indeed, the image of the founders as ordinary, which is to say not having (at least publicly) become teetotallers, health 'fanatics' or philanthropic pioneers, is important. Cheers et al. (2020) note that both adult drinkers and non-drinkers still see abstainers as potential threats to fun, social connection and a favourable sense of self (for drinkers). As a result, origin stories tend to keep the focus on founders as almost accidental cultural entrepreneurs rather than converts to a cause. To use Throsby's (2018) typology of abstainers (developed in reference to sugar, not alcohol), they are experimental or charitable rather than (off-puttingly) evangelical.

Keeping TSI founders relatable is important when thinking about TSIs as a public pedagogy of lifestyle because, recalling the importance of a concordance between a self-narrative and an example that may be imitated, prospective participants must be able to align their self-narrative with that example if it is to be emulated. In Warnick's formulation, 'those perceptions of human action that provoke imitation are those that are classified in a way so as to be not incompatible with the narrative senses of self' (Warnick 2008: 73) of those who would be induced to imitate. In short, a prospective participant must be able to see a commonality of both intent and ability to fulfil the commitment, or at least not see themselves as too dissimilar from the example to imitate it. The importance of commonality between the example and the potential imitators is reflected in the fact that most TSIs in the Anglophone world began among groups of friends. The founders and the first adopters already knew each other and had enough in common in terms of obviously shared interests, values and circumstances to be friends.

Where there is no personal connection between the TSI founders and participants, the basis for commonality needed for the example to be imitated rests on vaguer notions, such as a shared cultural ethos with respect to health and/or altruism. A large majority of TSI participants feel that they are somewhat health conscious and many also consider themselves to be charitable (Robert 2016b). These self-characterizations allow the founder's example and the campaigns that have modelled themselves to support the founder's story as archetypal to be, at least abstractly, influential. By contrast, TSIs can struggle to find an audience when the example is seen as unrelatable. Such is the problem in France, where the local version of Dry January is largely regarded as a contrived English solution, binge sobriety, to an English problem, binge drinking, that is at odds with the lay perception that 'French' drinking is not problematic (Robert 2014).

The self-narratives of prospective participants may include elements of unrealized desire for moderation, productivity, fitness, philanthropy or even preparation for a major undertaking but not – a trait shared with the founders

Embodiment and Affect

83

– an aspiration for abstinence. Frequent FebFast participant David explains his rationale for first taking part:

> I had a personal trainer at the time – trying to lose weight – and in January she said, why don't you, because alcohol is your downfall (because I like a glass of red wine). She said, why don't you try giving up alcohol during February because it's a short month and just see how you go, it's only four weeks. I thought, okay, I'll do it.

Similar themes are echoed by others when recounting their original inspiration to undertake their first (and subsequent) TSIs:

> For me it was to improve my health, save some money and raise funds for a cause that I really believe in. – Leisl

> You know, over Christmas time, [you] tend to start drinking a little bit more than usual as it is a holiday, so I thought it would be an opportunity to have a break, obviously, give my body a break. . . . Then also – my best friend's brother had some issues related to drugs, so we did it in support for him. This year too was different; we're trying to have more children. But it was a way of getting ready and planning for that. Yeah, lots of reasons. – Fiona

The founder's entrepreneurial example, which is predicated on simply being first not atypical or exemplary in the superlative sense of the word, is one that aligns with the prospective participants' self-narratives.

Where lifestyle movements grow through snowballing (Cherry 2015), participants in turn become examples for others: 'lifestyle movements speak to an imagined positive exemplar, one typically found within reach of those who make the right lifestyle choices' (Wexler et al. 2017: 6). Commonality, or at least a lack of obvious dissimilarity, as theories of imitative exemplarity maintain, is nonetheless required for actions to become examples: 'To serve its purpose, an example must somehow fall within the social reach of its follower; some link must enable identification sufficient for mimesis to be thinkable' (Noyes 2016: 78). Natalie explained that she hoped to be an example for her friends but was doubtful about her ability to inspire others to take up the challenge or to change, in part because she already had a reputation for being a light drinker. By contrast, Thomas, a football-loving IT consultant who had completed FebFast for five consecutive years, proved to be an effective vector for the example of TSIs to reach a wider audience. For five years, he had been recruiting first-timers from work to join him, but his strategy was dependent upon neither 'preaching' nor 'standing on his chair'.

TSIs, however, need not rely on invitations for examples to inspire participation. Adam highlights the role of mass self-communication and proximal examples as influential in his decision to attempt a TSI:

> Things like Shave for Cancer, FebFast and Dry July and all those kinds of things, I think they permeate the popular culture particularly on things like social media because you do witness that people are actually doing them. You do become, maybe unconsciously, aware that these things are actually occurring by the fact that you're just reading people's feeds or you're seeing what your peer group is actually doing.

TSI founders being perceived to be (or indeed remaining) 'normal' despite the temporary alteration of their habits, and having lifestyles and lifestyle objectives in common with a peer group of prospective participants, is essential to them being recognized as imitable examples. Where campaigns are patent imports from other contexts, as Dry Feb is in Canada or Dry January is in Switzerland, participants (rather than founders) are responsible for facilitating the identification (and their identifiability) with the larger population.

Learning with, about and through embodiment

One reason the founders of TSIs, and indeed the cultural entrepreneurs behind many lifestyle movements, are imitable is because the body is semiotically rich and its practices can be outwardly demonstrative (Featherstone 2000; Shilling 2005). Imitative learning of embodied acts, as Noble and Watkins (2003) illustrate, in some ways depends on the observation and replication of models; we learn how to do by watching others. Recent and increased attention to the role of embodiment in public pedagogy has sought to explain the processes by which we learn with, about and through our embodiment, including how we create and learn from examples.

Learning from the body is a form of public pedagogy that is, more often than not, predicated on discovery. Accordingly, public pedagogies are framed less and less as linear processes of knowledge transmission – teaching – than they are as 'possibilities for experiential, and often unspoken methods of embodied and emplaced knowing' (Fors and Pink 2017: 2). This less didactic notion of public pedagogies leaves space for discovery, which is to say that the 'lesson' can become apparent, and indeed be variable depending on the individual or the context, rather than being a declared objective or learning intention from the outset. The pedagogies of embodied discovery are most prominently considered in terms of quantification and data (Lupton 2016; Swan 2013; Pantzar and Ruckenstein 2015), but such processes can and do revolve around qualitative indices, causal relationships and affective states, as these are frequently closer and more accessible to our unmediated experience of our embodiment.

As an inwardly focused process, whether learning about one's body or learning how to use one's body in particular ways, what is often required in embodied learning can nonetheless be difficult to effect: 'While in one sense the body is the most abiding and inescapable presence in our lives, it is also essentially characterized by absence. That is, one's own body is rarely the thematic object of experience' (Leder 1990: 1). In the absence of pain, dysfunction or concerted attention, our bodies do not draw our own attention to themselves. As pedagogic examples, especially for the self, they lack expressive reference because they do not draw attention to that which they exemplify. Strategies must accordingly be employed to render the body a pedagogic example for oneself.

Elgin (1993) argues that for the sake of creating a referentially telling or significant example, we can contrive scenarios that are capable of fulfilling a demonstrative or didactic purpose. Defamiliarization, a process that 'heightens awareness of things that are so obvious that we routinely ignore them' (Elgin 1993: 403), is one such strategy, for it is the accompanying processes of resensitization or attunement – rediscovery – that give new meaning to the readily apparent and make accessible that which may be submerged. Leder (1990: 44) maintains that 'strategies of reflective observation', including those occasioned by intersubjective consciousness of ourselves (ibid., 98), are part of a set of techniques that can allow for greater knowledge or awareness of even those parts of the body, such as internal organs, that most elude our attention. Fors and Pink venture that such experiments, including when aided by technologies of various sorts, are often about creating 'new routes for the user's already-existing embodied knowledge to develop' (Fors and Pink 2017: 3) rather than only generating new information, per se. Following Dewey's explanations, these processes, whether simple reflective observation or more elaborate (including technologically mediated) options, are how anoetic knowledge – what may be sensed or felt but not necessarily realized – is made noetic, which is to say available as an object of cognition (Garrison 2015).

TSIs are structured and managed in such a way that they defamiliarize routines and guide reflective observation; they prompt noesis from anoesis. While they may not have originated with such pedagogical intent (a month is a ready unit of time in which to try something new, not necessarily a calibrated timeframe for personal experimentation), they have come to be framed as time-delimited experiments that render the seemingly banal – both within and outside participants' bodies – unfamiliar. It is this newly unfamiliar body that is capable of revealing new information or ways of knowing, in short the way to learn by discovering a new example. TSIs have accordingly evolved to produce new embodied examples that, if only for a short time, allow greater access to and awareness of the body, its processes and states in relation to alcohol. As exemplary periods of moderation that are carefully delimited, TSIs defamiliarize prior periods of moderate consumption or abstinence by sensitizing participants to both the anticipated effects of alcohol (impacts on sleep, caloric density, etc.) and by allowing them to discover others for themselves. TSIs thus function and are understood by participants – and increasingly by the organizations themselves – as periods of self-experimentation. These experiments yield information about the (embodied) self but also about alcohol as a chemical compound, a cultural object, the locus of practice and tradition, and a commodity.

Operating as a small-n or $n = 1$ experiment, TSIs involve establishing a personal baseline and observing the effects of an intervention, such as withdrawing and introducing a stimulus (Dugard et al. 2012; Kazdin 1982). The baseline, pharmacologically speaking, involves the body being free of a compound (such as alcohol) and its lingering effects, a condition that may require some time to establish (Atkinson et al. 2012).[1] For most TSI participants and behavioural researchers, however, the baseline is the pre-intervention or 'normal' state that is subsequently compared to the post-intervention measures (de Visser et al. 2016). These comparisons produce information that is especially relevant to the objectives of socially oriented TSIs. This is because practices that provide a framework in which to convert impersonal or abstract knowledge into personalized or felt knowledge (Newby-Clark et al. 2002) add an affective element to what are often highly rationalist decision-making paradigms about drinking behaviour (MacDonald and Zanna 1998; Thompson et al. 1995) that do not adequately account for non-rational but highly pertinent factors such as pleasure and sociability (Keane 2000; O'Malley and Valverde 2004; Heath 2012). The objective is often to test the individualized applicability of general knowledge or normative advice, in essence to see if one is a good example of a hypothesized phenomenon (Nafus and Sherman 2014).

The notion of TSIs as experiments comes from the participants themselves. Many consciously adopt the language of experimentation to describe their experience. Rebecca notes, 'It's almost like a social experiment on yourself to be able to go out and not drink alcohol.' Others, like Brad, are not as overt with their choice of descriptors but implicitly characterize their TSI participation as a way to test hypotheses, for instance, about their health and their alcohol consumption.

> To be perfectly honest with you I've been feeling rat-shit. My alcohol consumption has increased or had increased steadily over the years up to the point where I was actually drinking mid-week as well. Now before taking up FebFast I was putting a lot of my lack of energy and what I felt were some health concerns down to probably my alcohol consumption. So, I thought 'Well, why not?' so I put my hand up and just [did] it.

Rebecca focused on the social aspects of alcohol and abstinence, while Brad considered its physiological effects. The month-long duration allowed them to experience most routine facets of their lives without any influence from alcohol – a meaningful variation from a behavioural baseline – and establish an alcohol-free pharmacological baseline after which alcohol was eventually reintroduced. While far from scientifically rigorous insofar as other changes (a new relationship for Rebecca and the commencement of a fitness routine for Brad) would have complicated any effects that could be attributed exclusively to sobriety, both Rebecca and Brad ascribed considerable influence to their newly abstinent behaviour and became far more conscious of alcohol's effects.

In line with the claims TSIs make about their salutary effects (FebFast 2013), independent evaluations (Hillgrove and Thomson 2012) and even common health advice (National Health and Medical Research Council 2015), many participants confirm the personal applicability of hypotheses around alcohol and weight, sleep and energy levels. In most cases, these discoveries come as a surprise to the participants, nearly all of whom had post-secondary qualifications and considered themselves health conscious or at least knowledgeable about general health advice. Despite their education and apparent belief in many other aspects of medical advice widely circulating in the Australian context (concerning matters such as diet, exercise, smoking and sun exposure), participants frequently used terms such as 'shocked' and 'amazed' to convey the impact of their new understandings of alcohol's realities.

David's summation of the effects of his participation is quite typical in that it mirrors the discourse about common benefits:

> I can't remember exactly how much I lost, but I certainly did lose weight. I think I slept better. You know, I certainly woke up better because my drink of choice is red wine and a few glasses of that and you can wake up the next morning a bit,

88   *Alcohol, Binge Sobriety and Exemplary Abstinence*

> not hung over but a bit lethargic. . . . Yeah, but when I stopped drinking then I
> had a bit more energy.

As a seven-time FebFast participant who had also engaged in independent periods of abstinence, these commonplace findings should not have come as a surprise. David, nonetheless, relayed them with a sense of wonder that suggested that this once novel information had been forgotten only to be recalled or rediscovered anew through periods of resensitization.

Seeing for oneself the personal relevance of arguably commonplace knowledge was a way to employ processes of discovery and rediscovery to deepen understanding of alcohol as a substance and its social and cultural role. Abstaining and losing weight, for instance, impressed upon many participants that alcohol is a caloric beverage that had surreptitiously been adding, both directly and indirectly, to their waistlines for years. While most participants would have been abstractly aware of it, those who mentioned it always did so when referencing the results of their experiment; it was always a lesson that had been learnt, not knowledge they had long possessed and used to inform their choices. Jillian, for instance, noted her tendency to eat or snack less – notably skipping an additional, often unhealthy, late-night meal – when she refrained from drinking. Rebecca confessed that she became aware of the hidden sugars in the wine she had been consuming on most days. The experience of losing weight through sobriety allowed participants to experience and thus concretize their tacit or anoetic knowledge of just how much drinking added to their overall caloric intake. Alcohol thus came to be understood, noetically, as a liquid food, a reality that in the Australian context is often overshadowed owing to a popular and public health discourse that has emphasized alcohol's status as a drug and not, as is the case in many parts of Mediterranean Europe in particular, a food (Gual 2007).

Participants also found the TSI instrumental in making unanticipated discoveries about the physiological effects of their alcohol consumption. Deliberate sobriety, for instance, led numerous participants to note connections between drinking and facets of their embodiment – allergic reactions, migraines, eczema – that they had not expected to be affected by what was for many moderate drinking, at least in their own estimation. This deliberate sober selfhood was, moreover, distinct from any actual past or perceived sober selfhood (such as pregnancy and during travel to dry locations) that might have been experienced in the past. Janelle volunteered the following:

> I get really bad allergies and stuff as well and so I get eczema and all that stuff
> and I found that that was a lot better when I wasn't drinking as well, which was

intense to realise that maybe, you know, [I've] been going around to all these different doctors trying to find a solution for it for years and I'm like, 'oh maybe just stop drinking'.

What is striking about this statement, as with David's commentary on the more predictable outcomes, is her surprise; the condition that had caused her to seek out medical advice and intervention on numerous occasions ('all these different doctors') and for a prolonged period of time was linked to her alcohol consumption. The TSI therefore proved to be a diagnostic tool akin to a medically supervised elimination diet.

While participants tend to be guided chiefly by the structure of TSIs to re-establish a pharmacological baseline or to contrast their behavioural baseline to their exceptionally moderate state, organizers nudge them to consider certain embodied examples. In the 2014 campaign, FebFast staff would send a weekly text message timed for 'beer-o'clock – 4 pm Friday afternoon – and sent from various body parts' including the heart and liver (Emanuel 2014). These attempts at humour were memorable and informative for participants like Rick insofar as they facilitated a connection between abstaining from alcohol and likely bodily effects:

> It can be a little bit corny too when you'll get this random SMS . . . but you might get one day, some weird message saying: 'From your liver'.
>
> 'From my what?' Then you read it and you go, 'Oh that's FebFast.'
>
> Then, week two it's, 'Your lungs are loving you' or something. Or 'Your kidneys are . . .'

Sent from normally silent viscera, these text messages reinforce the broader discourse of FebFast's health benefits. They draw participants' focus inward to the 'depth organs' whose processes and reactions, including to what is consumed, are obscured by their hidden location, their inarticulateness (they emit few perceptible sensations as part of normal functioning) and the 'spatiotemporal lacunae' they engender, which make it difficult to connect actions to bodily reactions (Leder 1990: 42–4). While few accustomed to Western paradigms of medicine would be able to sense their liver or appreciate their body's inflammatory response (without blood tests and medical imaging), the messages prompt participants to scrutinize or at least consider their bodies in a way that they likely would not have, absent the prompt. For instance, Rick had not made the connection between his lungs and alcohol before receiving the text message.

Where most people have no baseline sense of their hepatic function but might well grasp behavioural or more apparent improvements (sleep, complexion, weight, energy) as a result of not drinking, participants are open to the suggestion that their vital organs would be reaping similar benefits thanks to the assumption that our surface embodiment functions as an externalization of visceral health (Leder 1990: 43). Alcohol Free for 40 encourages participants' thinking in this vein, as they counsel them to take a close-up photo of their face to show the detail of their skin and eyes before the campaign and then again at regular intervals throughout. These photos provide the surface evidence of the more clinical measures (complete blood count, comprehensive metabolic panel, lipid panel, gamma glutamyl transferase, vitamin B12 and folate panel, high-sensitivity C-reactive protein and sedimentation rate) that participants are also encouraged to have recorded pre- and post-participation (Kimball 2020).

Beyond the physiological, TSIs use the example of disuse to allow participants to discover more about alcohol's resource implications, such as its impact on personal finances and its environmental costs. Where price is an effective way to control alcohol sales and consumption owing to the elasticity of demand (Wagenaar et al. 2009), the relatively middle- to upper-middle-class demographics of those who tend to be the participant base for TSIs are not (or are no longer) used to seeing cost as a strictly limiting factor for their drinking. They had thus lost sight of alcohol as a commodity. Upon noting that they saved money during the campaigns, many became newly aware of alcohol as an expense or an impost on their disposable income. Where they were able to reallocate the funds they had previously spent on alcohol (and expenses related to a night of drinking, such as a late-night snack and/or taxi fare to return home) to other purchases, they deepened their understanding of alcohol's impact on their finances. In cases such as Brad's, where the post-campaign resumption of drinking entailed a shift away from quantity ('rubbish beer') towards quality (single malt whisky), alcohol also took on new gradations in value more linked to taste and status (maturity, class, import versus domestic production).

Adam observed that his volume of household waste, specifically the volume of wine and beer bottles to be recycled, appreciably decreased when he stopped drinking. The drop in his domestic alcohol consumption made him aware of alcohol as a highly packaged good with environmental impacts. While scholars and those working within the alcohol industry (especially outside of contexts that favour spirits) have been keenly aware of this reality for some time (Amienyo et al. 2014; Arcese et al. 2012), the environmental impacts of Adam's personal alcohol consumption had escaped his notice for more than twenty years. This was true even though he considered himself as a responsible environmental citizen who diligently sorted his recycling.

Where alcohol is thoroughly but imperceptibly implicated in many aspects of an individual's life, it is easy to lose sight of just what this ubiquitous substance is: caloric foodstuff, drug provoking an inflammatory response, commodity of variable value and highly packaged product. Where its reality is shaped by practice and its use entails both embodied and material effects (Mol 2002), disuse proves just as consequential. Changes to normal circumstances and intensified attention on a (new) period of sobriety allow the experience to be considered with renewed attention that sets aside the familiarity of daily practice and circumstances. This period, acting as a contrived experiment, nonetheless facilitates access to these normally hidden or unnoticed realities, making them more graspable illustrations in a pedagogy of discovering for oneself.

An example for a future self

In his pioneering work on self-efficacy, Albert Bandura (1977) proposed that the greatest predictor of someone having the confidence that they would be able to overcome a behavioural challenge, and then to do so, was being able to draw on examples or models of their own earlier behaviour. These 'performance accomplishments' were more consequential than the vicarious experience of emulating or extrapolating based on another's example, persuasion or emotional strategies in the process of learning to overcome one's internal resistance or hesitation.

As discussed briefly in Chapter 2, normative examples have an inherent temporality; a past or present instantiation can serve as a model for one that is yet to be realized. Philosophers, anthropologists, psychologists and even literary critics suggest that people are routinely looking to the examples set by others to help them shape their own present and future actions and thus, indirectly, their sense of self. In that vein, Timothy Hampton argues that 'The history of exemplarity is . . . on one level, a history of figurations of the self' (Hampton 1990: xi). Nowhere is imitability more likely, however, than in looking to one's own personal history to find examples for a future self.

Bandura's work (which focused on phobias) has inspired subsequent studies in relation to addictive behaviours, including alcohol consumption. Reclaiming the identity and replicating the behaviours of an anterior, pre-addicted self has accordingly been proposed as an addiction recovery strategy (Kim and Wohl 2015). Outside of a treatment and recovery context, which arguably applies to a minority of cases, Bandura's findings have inspired the notion of drink refusal self-efficacy, an individual's belief that they will be able to resist or decline the offer of a drink (Young et al. 1991; Oei and Jardim 2007). Recent investigations into Dry January report higher levels of post-campaign drink refusal self-efficacy among participants than in the general population (de Visser and Piper 2020). Researchers attribute this in part to the forms of persuasive and emotional encouragements offered via email and other direct messaging (de Visser and Nicholls 2020) and to the prior attempt (but not necessarily completion) of a TSI (de Visser et al. 2016).

As might be expected of time-delimited campaigns, TSIs are strongly oriented to questions of temporality, especially as they concern a participant's future self. Yeomans argues that Dry January participation, and by extension participation in many (but not all) other TSIs, is a process of ethical self-formation that rejects the premise of traditional public health interventions that prioritize sacrifices in the present for the benefit of a future self:

> Dry January is not, therefore, about denying yourself drink but enjoying abstinence; it is not about prudently planning for your bodily future but perceiving that healthful embodied practices promote wellbeing and happiness *in the present too*. The self does not need to be disciplined so much as it needs to be reformed or replaced with a 'new me' or 'new you'. (Yeomans 2019: 465, my emphasis)

While Yeomans explicitly counters the subordination of the present to the future, especially given the social orientation of Dry January, more implicit is the way in which the participant's new, dry, present self is likely to serve as a model for their future self. This facet of the experience is nonetheless central to ways in which TSIs foster the self-efficacy that leads to the reduced alcohol consumption that is frequently observed post-campaign.

Rebecca's account of sober dating is particularly illustrative of the way an enjoyable experience of sobriety and/or moderation creates a performance accomplishment – an imitable example – in the present for the future:

> This is the first time I've ever, ever, ever dated someone sober, which again is a little bit embarrassing. But – yes, it's – I'm really proud of myself that I did it and that I could do it. . . . I know that I can get through conversations. I can get through a date. I can get through an evening. I can get through a dinner and a social event without the alcohol.

Her description of the success in the past (I did it) leads to an implicit future (I could do it) that is supported by numerous statements about present capacity (I

Embodiment and Affect

93

can) that are, in turn, based on actions performed successfully (unexpectedly so) while sober.

Rebecca's insistence on having broken with her old patterns speaks to a common discourse in TSIs – that of habits. TSIs often tout themselves as targeting habits to play into the popular mythology of a habit requiring twenty-one days to either break or form. The 'Why Do Dry January?' section of the Alcohol Change webpage raises the question of habits quite sympathetically:

> Dry January is the perfect training ground for helping you cut down from February onwards! Cutting down permanently is, for many people, very hard, because habits are hard to break. Dry January is an excellent way of learning what your habits are and how to break them, enabling you to cut down longer-term. You can think of it as a bootcamp for drinking self-control! (Alcohol Change UK 2020c)

Appearing under the heading 'What about When the Month Is Done?', the advice and its position on the page project the reader into a post-campaign frame when the difficult task of breaking a habit would have already been accomplished. There is accordingly a measure of success and thus self-efficacy that is already attributed to the reader, who is still (likely) only a prospective participant.

The imputed automaticity of habits is nonetheless countered, even in this case, by an emphasis on reflective behaviour, learning and training. These notions, especially the analogy of a military boot camp, underscore the discipline and effort required to change and the building up of self-efficacy as a process akin to the development of strength or fitness. Booker (2019) even structures the 'mental preparation' section of her advice to prospective participants around a reflective exercise based on a self-identified challenge previously overcome and the 'skills' that were important in that success that could be applied to a TSI.

Acknowledging the challenges of a sober month from the outset serves two purposes. On the one hand, it allows participants to recognize their capacity to complete the challenge, potentially even allowing them to access anew 'the sense of accomplishment, empowerment and even partial transcendence experience by those who survive and prosper within such pedagogic regimes' (Shilling 2007: 14). On the other hand, the reminders about the challenge and effort required by TSIs provide a framework for pre-emptively translating 'unsuccessful' TSI participation (i.e. non-completion) into a valuable undertaking with merit in its own right. While a non-finisher is not necessarily an exemplary TSI participant, they may still be an imitable example for their future self.

As in many areas of self-improvement, advice on how to effect this change to habits, even in the short term, abounds. In addition to the annual spate of magazine and newspaper articles and breakfast television segments providing strategies for succeeding in whichever TSI attracts local attention, TSIs have officially (Booker 2019) and unofficially (Glass 2016; Sheinbaum 2020) generated books full of tips, tricks and strategies for going a month without drinking. Framing temporary sobriety as a skill that can be mastered through practice and coaching moves moderation away from the earlier temperance discourses that linked abstinence or moderation with character towards an outwardly demonstrable behaviour that can be measured in terms of progress towards a goal. A TSI participant who has gone the month without drinking is therefore one who has already rehearsed and put into practice the strategies needed to not drink (as much).

Through sober eyes

The focused example created by temporary sobriety educates via illustrative examples, as it demonstrates to both participants and observers, that alcohol consumption has outwardly observable and inwardly appreciable effects. This example also works normatively through time, providing subsequently imitable examples of conduct for participants. Seeing oneself, one's relationships and the material conditions of one's existence through sober eyes is an important and indeed the most touted aspect of TSIs' public pedagogy. There are nonetheless intersubjective aspects to TSI participation where the example of sober socializing and embodiment demonstrates what it feels like to experience something different. Such experiences are not always reassuring or entirely comfortable for participants, in part because they prompt consideration of those who were previously excluded from consideration. In this framing, TSIs allow for both a fresh perspective on oneself in relation to others and use embodied examples to generate empathy for others.

While more of an incidental learning than a key selling point, TSI participation can put participants' relationships with one other and their environment in a new light. They do so by creating opportunities to experience non-drinking in contexts where consuming alcohol is the norm. Generating both experiential and reflective understanding of the social and cultural prominence of alcohol and the nature of interactions (between people and indeed between people and objects) in alcogenic environments is found to foster empathy for abstainers and habitual non-drinkers: those with medical conditions, those who refrain for religious or cultural reasons, those in recovery or those who abstain simply as a matter of personal preference. This in turn leads participants to modify their expectations of and behaviour towards light drinkers or abstainers in subsequent interactions, for the presumption of consuming alcohol is contested thanks to the exemplarity and its affordances engendered by the campaign.

The weeks-long duration of TSIs and their scheduling outside of months associated with prolonged holidays (December or the summer months) mean that participants typically go about living their normal lives while engaged in the challenge. They take part in both routine (work/study, sleep, exercise) and more event-based or infrequent activities (weekend socializing, special events, holidays) while deliberately sober. Participants will be called upon to go about their business in both environments mostly within their control (their home, for instance) and in settings where choices (such as whether both alcoholic and non-alcoholic beverages will be served or whether one can be alone) are made by others. While these are not novel events or circumstances, participants must navigate these settings and activities in an adapted manner, one that may entail differences of both an embodied and cognitive nature (Shilling 2017), that can allow for pedagogic discovery of learning from these new examples.

Rebecca, a near-daily and relatively heavy drinker, found herself dating and beginning a new romantic relationship while taking part in a TSI. While other participants expressed dismay and even feigned horror at the thought of trying to date a new partner while sober, the challenge of the experience was especially revealing for Rebecca. By her own admission, the TSI allowed her to (re)discover states and capabilities that had been largely forgotten and to challenge received wisdom about the role alcohol plays in interpersonal interactions that she had always upheld as applicable to her.

Like many people, Rebecca had used alcohol as both a 'social lubricant' and 'liquid courage' for the typically anxiety-producing first (and other early) dates. Recounting the experience of starting to see a new partner while undertaking FebFast, though, she was overcome with emotion: 'It really did open my eyes that, oh my god, normally I would be drunk by the third date – normally drunk on the first date with a guy – and potentially sleeping with him too on the first date and then mucking everything up.' Her insistence on the normalcy of being drunk and the unsuccessful outcomes highlight her realization that she had been using alcohol to attenuate her stress around dating. She reflected that she used to drink heavily on dates to ease the disquiet that stemmed from anxieties about being judged, appraised and sexually objectified – facets of the experience that routinely make dating awkward. Yet by reflecting on the different outcome as a result of a different embodied and emotional state, she also became aware that alcohol, when consumed to the point that it resulted in drunkenness, may have been a contributor to the awkwardness and unsuccessful outcomes she had experienced up to that point.

Her awareness of her default behaviour (of drinking to the point of intoxication) though came about only once 'forced' by the TSI to date in a starkly different state. The deliberately sober date would be one where both instantiation and expressive reference in the example were structurally assured, but the matter of what was being referenced – the quality of the experience – was still to be determined. As it eventuated, the experience of putting herself in such a situation without being able to drink disproved her tacit hypothesis that she would feel judged by her partner for transgressing social norms (the expectation that she would drink) and would be unstable without 'the crutch' of alcohol. The date proved to be a success, and approximately a month post-TSI, the romance had blossomed. Rebecca also reported that she remained virtually alcohol free, drinking only very moderately and infrequently, and quite giddily recounted that physical intimacy when sober was a more sexually fulfilling experience. The sober example she created, in part thanks to the timing of the TSI and her carrying on with activities as planned, both countered her previous experiences (for the better) and gave her a new, self-generated model to emulate once the strictures of the campaign were removed.

In contrast to the introspective or solipsistic discoveries, including about one's health, that TSIs commonly provoke, Rebecca's insight, with regard to alcohol, was also relational; from emotion to an intersubjective phenomenology during physical intimacy, various facets of sober and drunken embodiment took on interpersonal dimensions. While arguably an especially revealing scenario or limit-case, Leder (1990) contends that our general sense of our own embodiment, including its processes and the acts that affect it, is always intersubjective. Rebecca's account is thus merely an overt example of a situation that prompts greater awareness of how others see us, and how we may see ourselves, as either sober or under the influence of alcohol. In her case, a successful sober dating experience – one more successful than her previous attempts while drinking heavily – changed her opinions both about herself (her physical attractiveness, her personality, her appeal as a partner) and about alcohol's role as a hindrance rather than a facilitator of successful romantic encounters. Granted, her views on alcohol may have shifted had her date not gone as well as it did, for the highly contingent nature of socially complex cultural practices such as dating and sexual relations can compromise any pretence of objective discovery.

Stepping back from the specifics of Rebecca's encounters, her case demonstrates the potential for learning from example by having to engage with a full range of life events while choosing to be abstinent. The 'forced' experience provides erstwhile unreflective drinkers with insight into the experiences of abstainers. The ability to see through different eyes and fully experience the world at the level of feelings, affect and sensation provides what Boisserie-Lacroix and Inchingolo call phenomenal insight, a precursor to experiential empathy:

> We call *experiential empathy* the very dimension of empathy in virtue of which the empathizer is led to pay attention to the phenomenal aspect that accompanies the mental states of the agent with whom she empathizes. In this sense, empathy does not only aim at providing us with insight into the reasons that motivate the behavior of the agent being interpreted. It also aims at providing us with a dive into the very felt experience that accompanies them. (Boisserie-Lacroix and Inchingolo 2019: 12)

Recognizing the variability of perception and feeling, they concede that similarity of experienced circumstances will not necessarily generate an empathetic response based on identical or even comparable feelings. Still, the possibility of experiential empathy is that it 'provides insight into other people's mental lives' (ibid., 21), including where feeling and thought intersect with and stem from a different way of being in the world.

TSIs, especially those that support or are otherwise linked to drug and alcohol treatment programmes, are often reluctant to publicize the potential empathetic link with abstainers, specifically those who abstain as part of their ongoing recovery from addiction. This is not to say that empathetic motives are absent among participants, but organizers of causes that could be considered unpopular or stigmatized (Body and Breeze 2016) are often less inclined than other embodied philanthropy organizations to promote identification between the giving public and their beneficiaries.[2] Moderation Management (2016a), an organization that promotes a moderation-based alcohol dependency programme as an alternative to the abstinence-centric Alcoholics Anonymous, uses its Drynuary campaign as a fundraiser but bases its larger programme upon an initial month of sobriety. Drynuary, however, is unique in officially promoting a link between the TSI's structure and its therapeutic potential. More often, TSIs implicitly – and arguably quite problematically – reinforce the differentiated subject positions of the alcoholic or addict and the entrepreneurial subjects whose abstention is a project of distinction and self-differentiation.

TSI participants have nonetheless made the empathetic connections between going dry and recovery from addiction for themselves. Early Défi 28 jours participant and blogger Anne-Lise (2014) relates the campaign's form to its cause by observing that the length of the campaign corresponds to the length of a stay in rehab: '28 jours c'est aussi le temps d'un séjour à la maison de Fondation Jean Lapointe. On peut donc plus facilement imaginer ce que vivent les personnes qui décident de régler leurs problèmes avec l'alcool' (28 days is also the length of a stay at the facility for the Fondation Jean Lapointe. So you can more readily imagine what people who are trying to resolve their alcohol issues experience). The first 28 days of sobriety, regardless of their motivation, are made (at least in this very simplistic formulation) experientially similar. FebFast participant Thomas is more restrained in his empathetic considerations but maintains that the campaign affords him 'a minor glimpse into the dependencies society has on alcohol. It grounds to me to think that a lot of people do have difficulties.' He points to elements of the TSI experience such as cravings, breaking the association between drinking and other enjoyable activities (such as watching sports), and the curious – and sometimes probing – questions from others about his rationale for not drinking as the concrete experiences and practices that afford him phenomenal insight into what he perceives are the social experiences of those who are or were dependent on alcohol.

Irrespective of their philanthropic status, TSIs that have a strong social orientation seek to overturn common understandings of abstinence or sobriety as abnormal and potentially subject to pity. Instead, they seek to promote a destigmatized view, one more akin to that in societies with higher overall rates of abstinence and without TSIs, where non-drinking is cast as equal to or a preferable alternative, and is decoupled from stigmatized identities. This objective is most commonly fulfilled by forcing participants to undertake all the experiences they normally would while abstaining, a process that facilitates the generation of a degree of experiential empathy for abstainers. This is especially so in relation to social and cultural assumptions about alcohol, its overall prominence and, generally, the relative abnormality of abstinence in the contexts in which TSIs operate.

TSI participants report that one of their chief insights from taking part is the incongruence of not drinking during celebrations or other rituals such as funeral wakes. What Heath (2012) refers to as 'drinking occasions', birthdays, anniversaries, Valentine's Day, weddings, major sporting finals or championships

Embodiment and Affect 99

(e.g. the American Super Bowl, the Australian Rules Football Grand Final) and Mardi Gras, were all identified by TSI participants or commentators either as barriers to electing to going or staying dry. Of the approximately 50 per cent of interviewed participants who purchased temporary reprieves to allow them to imbibe, the majority did so because of a celebration. Lori, who purchased a pass to allow her to drink at her sister's wedding, reflected on what she perceived to be the absurdity of the situation, which is nonetheless rooted in centuries of tradition: 'That got me thinking, why do I need to show that I'm celebrating with someone by having a drink?' Liesl, whose month of abstinence ended with a bachelorette/hen's weekend and being chauffeured around vineyards, commented on the way certain occasions were wholly structured around alcohol consumption. She noted that she drank far less than she would have normally and also far less than her friends expected she would – a fact that was made clear to her through their frequent (and nagging) commentary on her moderate intake.

A number of participants spoke of the attention, often quite negative, that abstaining attracts in a culture that embraces alcohol as cohesive and, given Australia's conspicuously professed rejection of social hierarchies, a social equalizer. David relayed one acquaintance's hostile reception to his participation, which caused him to suspect that his friend may have felt implicitly judged about his own alcohol consumption. Many others reported reactions that were similar in spirit, albeit not as severe, with the temporary abstainer's motives being questioned. This was certainly the case for those acquaintances who knew the participants to be frequent or heavy drinkers. Some participants nonetheless noted that even first meetings in which they opted not to drink alcohol attracted quizzical looks and probing of their motives. Participants who extended their sobriety beyond the recognized timeframe or who undertook a self-directed period of abstinence modelled on a TSI were particularly attuned to such reactions, as their own temporary sobriety lacked the sanctioned philanthropic or organizational excuse TSIs could provide. The imputed judgement of others was thus an important intersubjective element in participants' sense-making of their changed behaviour.

The unease that resulted from abstaining, a state that was relatively novel for both participants and those who knew them, saw participants employ strategies to deflect attention from their changed consumption. David made a point of having a glass or bottle of a non-alcoholic beverage in hand when at the pub in order to blend in. Natalie's strategies involved more elaborate camouflage and management of both the interpersonal and material elements of drinking practice (Hargreaves 2011). To avoid arousing suspicion, she would ask for a non-alcoholic drink to be served in a glass normally used to serve alcohol. For her, having a Coke served in the same smaller glass that would normally be used for a rum and Coke was a way to disguise her abstinence and avoid probing questions. The objects became a locus for scrutiny, and the materiality of non-consumption accordingly came to figure prominently in how participants understand (and understand how to comfortably enact) abstinence or temperance.

Experiential empathy for abstainers came not just through the querying of the choice not to drink and attention to the practices of not drinking but also via a renewed sense of how it feels to be sober in a context where others are in various states of inebriety. When Oliver relayed his experience of being among the only sober adults at a wake, he described it as 'a really unpleasant experience to see how stupid your family is when they're drunk. I mean not at all unpleasant when you're drunk with them but really unpleasant when you're sober.' This experience was compounded when he imparted that after years of repeated TSI participation, his friends had quit inviting him to the pub while he was dry. Rather than being disappointed by the lack of invitations, though, he was thankful to not have to turn them down because 'if you're the only sober person in a group of drunk people it's not that much fun'. Occupying a different embodied and social position, participants came to realize that being the (only) sober person was an eminently empathizible position and one that they would go to great pains to avoid, either by absenting themselves when they chose not to drink (so much) or, counter to any health education aims, by pacing their own consumption to keep up with the group's level of inebriety.

Once committed to the TSI as a participant, the pledge of temporary sobriety provides opportunity to create richly illustrative examples of what it is like to navigate the many facets of one's normal life without alcohol. Through this experience, participants become more aware of their interactions with others who may not be drinking and their assumptions (as people who drink) that adults will consume alcohol to mark special occasions, to ease anxiety in social situations and to blend in and to alleviate the scrutiny or annoyance of being conspicuously sober.

Participants were less likely to link these new insights (or to frame these insights as a determining factor) in any changed alcohol consumption going forward. What had consciously changed for many, however, was the way they approached abstinence or moderate drinking. They reported being less questioning and more accepting of others' choices to not drink or to drink only very lightly. A choice to not drink no longer elicited the same level of curiosity (arguably suspicion) as it once did; or at the least, it no longer prompted them to request an explanation or an excuse of those not drinking. Aware of how conspicuous they felt – and in some cases were made to feel – their behaviour towards others rather than their own personal consumption was what contributed to changing the drinking culture's default presumption away from one of drinking unless there is an intervening circumstance.

Conclusion

The didacticism of TSIs as socially oriented, health education campaigns owes much to the demonstrability and the affective, embodied and intersubjective resonance of the examples participants produce. These examples have been outwardly demonstrative and have inspired imitation, as the frequent celebration of the founder's story confirms. These stories break with many of the assumed volitionally didactic models of exemplarity, insofar as they do not celebrate the loftiness of the exemplar and their worthiness of imitation. Rather these tales highlight some of the subtler mechanisms of public pedagogy that are predicated on simple, temporary and utterly imitable changes to actions, the hallmarks of many lifestyle movements as practices. Founders and participants are discursively rendered as close to prospective participants as possible so that the participant's potential to not just change their drinking behaviour in the short term but in turn be exemplary – for self and others – is made a legitimate and even likely possibility.

Outward exemplarity notwithstanding, it is the instructiveness of many forms of inward exemplarity – which are facilitated by the structure, organization and discourse surrounding TSIs – that participants identify as being especially compelling. A compulsory period of sobriety, understood as superlative moderation, is the main pedagogical frame and instrument of TSIs' pedagogies of health and social interaction. Working to promote both felt and reasoned knowledge derived from personal experimentation and experience, TSIs use the participant's embodied example to become a lived object lesson for self and for others. Future moderation as a lesser degree of abstinence and the strategies and skills needed to support it in context are accordingly very much within participant's demonstrated capability. By extension, the period of sobriety in the present or immediate past becomes an imitable example for a future self and for others. The success of TSIs as public pedagogies and lifestyle movements concerned with not only personal health and habits but also the much-touted 'awareness' of the problems stemming from irresponsible drinking nonetheless hinges on amplifying the demonstrability of temporary sobriety.

6

Lifestyle heroism

Soberheroes and Dryathletes

As explored in Chapter 5, embodied examples can serve a number of internally and externally oriented didactic ends, especially as they relate to health education to facilitate behaviour change. A key ingredient in those pedagogic outcomes is the sheer demonstrability of the example, arguably producing a kind of 'lightbulb' or 'aha' moment in which realizations about drinking and alcohol come into sharper relief. While some examples may tend to this necessary function naturally, others benefit from a reinforcement of either the circumstances of exemplification or simply of the discourse of the ways in which they are exemplary. In Elgin's assessment, 'An exemplar refers to certain of its properties; it exhibits them, highlights them, shows them forth, makes them manifest' (Elgin 1993: 400). There is no stipulation that contrivance or scene-setting be avoided and attention can be, and often is, drawn to the example. Noyes's (2016) examination of examples, for instance, focuses on a number of planned acts that became exemplars not by chance but as calculated gestures.

TSIs, as temperance movements for the neo-liberal and networked age, employ a number of discursive, visual and technological strategies, often ones that reinforce fundraising objectives, to make moderation exemplary through a reinforcement of its visibility. Through their online and social media presence and in their suggestions to participants about how to be exemplary TSI participants, they draw attention to the act of temporary abstention, which is always seen as simply a more extreme and demonstrable form of moderation, and what it entails. In practical terms, participants who abstain for short (and increasingly shorter and non-consecutive) periods are both called upon and publicly lauded as exemplars, indeed heroes of personal responsibility, of self-sacrifice and of good citizenship. Such framings are present in both socially and philanthropically oriented TSIs, albeit with different inflections. Regardless of the nuance accorded by any particular campaign, though, the objective is to make the unremarkable practice of responsible drinking an act of moderation visible and praiseworthy. TSIs thereby allow participants to not only subscribe to the neo-liberal lifestyle imperatives of health and philanthropic engagement but to be seen to be doing so in a way that invites recognition and further reward for their exemplary behaviour.

This chapter analyses the ways TSIs create conditions and supply the tools for participants to fulfil – and to be seen to be fulfilling – the dictates of responsibility for self and for society that are increasingly required. Addressing the question of how and why TSIs seem to tap into a cultural ethos that allows them to thrive, it first recaps the neo-liberalization agendas that have seen health and well-being elevated from fringe concerns to dominant social imperatives. This preliminary section also outlines the widely accepted social need to adopt more responsible approaches to drinking, the challenges inherent in doing so and why demonstrable examples of moderation and responsible drinking are seen as necessary.

The analysis then turns to the ways in which these social and cultural currents of neo-liberalism, specifically its concerns with self-governance and private philanthropy, are enshrined in TSIs. The first argument focuses on the transformation of moderate drinking from an all but invisible social practice to compulsorily demonstrable raison d'être. It considers the discursive strategies of heroism, athleticism and martyrdom as performative moderation and the utility of such concepts in TSI branding and communications. In the second argument, I demonstrate that these strategies serve the agendas of the campaigns but can nonetheless have the paradoxical effect of pitting health objectives against those of philanthropy. The third and final argument addresses the role of both traditional and social media, important elements in the successful spread of TSIs, in making the banality of lifestyle visible and praiseworthy. Although closely intertwined with philanthropic objectives, this chapter focuses on health and social objectives, while the philanthropic aspects will be more fully considered in the next chapter.

The neo-liberal politics of obvious responsibility

The often-touted mantra for drinking in the post-temperance world is to 'drink responsibly'. Post-prohibition societies (and those whose temperance movements were never so influential as to drive this kind of legislative sanction) have increasingly employed the language of personal responsibility to influence drinking behaviour. Indeed, the exhortation towards responsible drinking has come from both governments and the alcohol industry, a situation that many have criticized as sending confusing messages (Barry and Goodson 2010; Smith et al. 2014; Wolburg 2005).[1] The push towards personal responsibility in alcohol consumption is nonetheless part of the neo-liberalization of these societies. And it is the permeation of neo-liberal discourses of responsibility and personal agency that allowed TSIs to find the fertile ground they needed to take root and that influenced the form they would take.

Neo-liberalism with regard to alcohol – and indeed many other facets of life that have public health implications – is characterized by 'a reluctance to impose socially oriented protections in favor of a generic rationality of economic growth. In other words, economic growth is given greater policy importance than social goals' (Lenucha and Thow 2019: 515). States with neo-liberal tendencies have been reluctant to constrain activities and trade in products that bring both direct and indirect economic benefits – through employment, contributions to an export economy, or taxation – even if these developments entail a potential cost. Instead, they have embraced paradoxes; at the level of policy they regulate as little as possible all the while seeking to mitigate the potential risks of the overall permissiveness by encouraging private, protective actions. In these contexts, citizens are increasingly called upon to act in ways that support particular social and economic objectives rather than to adhere to precise rules governing their conduct.

As a case in point, trading restrictions on drinking venues in Australian jurisdictions were lifted from the mid-1950s until the 1970s. This allowed for more alcohol sales, increased markets for alcohol producers and greater tax revenue for governments. At the same time, however, laws criminalizing drunk driving and workplace codes of conduct formalizing expectations that employees be sober while on the clock were introduced (Fitzgerald and Jordan 2009). These more targeted interventions relied on private organizations and, more importantly, individuals to judiciously exercise responsibility for their own conduct in accordance with the circumstances and outcome-based principles of social responsibility, such as professionalism and not endangering others. While still relying (in some instances) on the legal and regulatory apparatuses of the state, and thus disciplinary power, shifts towards the exercise of governmental power were also in train (Foucault 2000). Drinkers were not legally prevented from drinking as they saw fit but were duly engaged in 'processes of endless self-examination, self-care, and self-improvement' (Petersen 1996: 48–9) to ensure that their behaviours aligned with the objectives of both economics and public health and safety. So long as the behaviours were within these bounds, the state would not intervene.

As more evidence of the cumulative dangers of alcohol (along with tobacco, sugar, fast food, sedentary lifestyles, etc.) became available in the 1970s and 1980s, the definitions of responsibility shifted towards models of health and social welfare that were not just concerned with the prevention of accident and injury but also chronic disease. Practices that had previously been regarded as normal or even healthy, such as moderate alcohol consumption during pregnancy and daily drinking, were identified as areas of risk and became a focus for researchers to formulate new advice to the citizenry. The social and economic burden of non-communicable disease and illness stemming from 'lifestyle choices' increasingly became matters of economic and thus state concern. Petersen and Lupton (1996) contend that this shift to identifying risks to health in everyday life gave rise to a set of rationalities that (in the context of health) are understood as 'new public health': expert-guided but individually enacted risk-minimizing choices in everything from diet and physical activity to the use of protective equipment during sport and the consumption of tobacco and alcohol (see also Lupton 1995). New public health infused nearly every aspect of daily life. Schools, workplaces, popular entertainment and recreation became avenues for both formal and public pedagogies supporting health objectives, and these in turn became engines of economic activity, especially in areas such as health, fitness and 'wellness' (Pilzer 2002). Robert Crawford argues that 'healthism', understood as the achievement of well-being through the modification of lifestyle (Crawford 1980: 368), was the emergent super-value of the late twentieth century.

In tandem with amplifying their focus on disease prevention, neo-liberal societies have, since the late 1970s, increased their reliance on individuals and private entities (corporations and not-for-profit organizations) to fulfil functions that had previously been the purview of governments (Clarke 2005; Brown and Baker 2012). They outsourced aspects of health care, income support, rehabilitation and community cohesion to philanthropic and non-governmental organizations and entered into public–private partnerships instead of providing services as they previously did. This occurred at the same time as they charged individuals with doing all they could to reduce their likelihood of needing to access these costly and increasingly rationed or privatized services (Petersen 1996: 49; Crawford 1980: 379). Self-management, personal risk reduction and self-improvement – all oriented towards not becoming a burden on the state – therefore became hallmarks of good citizenship in societies that made a virtue of self-sufficiency. The net effect of neo-liberalism was therefore a simultaneous restriction of supply of state services, efforts to reduce demand for these services, and legal and political differentiation of those who could effectively manage their lifestyle risk and those who could not.

Propagating the tenets of new public health followed in the public–private model. Health education programmes were made the purview both state (public health agencies, schools) and non-state (popular entertainment, community organizations, commercial entities) actors. The objective was to spur individuals and private groups to engage in a 'mass voluntary commitment' (Dean 1999: 53) to enact not only a subject position but a lived experience that conforms to the ideal of 'responsibility'.

Noyes argues that neo-liberalism's driving impetus – 'individual responsibility for outcomes' – causes the social world to be constituted 'as a field of models and influences' for those outcomes (Noyes 2016: 85). In short, she argues that neo-liberalism is perpetuated by pedagogic examples. The principles and goals of responsibilization, especially for alcohol, have remained relatively constant since the waning of the temperance movement. They entail managing the behaviours of individuals in such a way that they align with and support the aims of government and its ancillary agencies such as public health departments (Foucault 2000: 341). Responsible drinking is therefore that which walks the line between supporting the commercial interests of the sectors that derive profit (or at least revenue) from alcohol, while keeping personal and social risk within acceptable thresholds (Room 2011, O'Malley and Valverde 2004). It minimizes risk to health and productivity and promotes behaviours that increase social cohesion, all the while reducing reliance on disciplinary powers, such as policing (Beck 2002, 2009) and cost-intensive treatment services. It entails drinkers knowing (and acting on) when it is appropriate to drink, knowing when to stop drinking, not drinking if one should avoid it altogether and remaining in control of oneself despite having imbibed.

The promotion of responsibility for health and responsible drinking in neo-liberal societies nonetheless presents two practical problems – problems to which TSIs as health education programmes have responded particularly well. On the one hand, responsibility has few intrinsic or obvious rewards, thus posing a challenge for motivating adherence – especially when the immediate rewards and pleasures of drinking are known and are more obvious (Keane 2009; de Visser and Smith 2007). On the other, the specifics of what it means to be a 'responsible drinker' are variable, calling for new pedagogic examples. Both of these problems, however, have a common solution: making responsibility, and responsible drinking in particular, a visible and demonstrable practice, a pedagogic example. This allows responsible drinking, in its changed and changing forms, to be demonstrable and thus imitable. At the same time, it allows particular forms of responsible drinking to become recognizable and thus worthy of social reward and recognition.

The first challenge is that responsibility for one's health within neo-liberal paradigms is hard to define and harder still to motivate in contexts where deferred gratification is often subordinated to immediate reward. Crawford's language of values and 'secular morality' is therefore not accidental. Like the Christian morality that was underpinned by the belief in intangible reward in the future or afterlife and social esteem in the present for adherence to the dictates of faith, healthism gave rise to belief in its own symbolic and deferred economies and exchanges. The prevailing social and economic conditions of the late twentieth century (and indeed those that have continued into the second and third decades of the twenty-first) mean that there is a little financial or structural reward, such as class mobility, for behaving responsibly and being healthy.[2] Where material rewards for responsibility are few (and arguably diminishing), attracting intangible but immediate rewards – plaudits, peer esteem and similar forms of minor recognition – gains in importance. Individuals who conform to the dictates of governmental power that have been enshrined as values benefit from the social kudos and accrue cultural capital (Bourdieu 1984). Scholars of modern temperance movements – which include not only restrictions on alcohol but also tobacco, sugar, animal products and drugs – thus consistently point to these secular and even scientific projects taking on overtures of virtue, morality and righteousness that were previously associated with religion (Wagner 1997; Engs 2000; Throsby 2018). For this recognition as a healthy, responsible citizen to happen, though, one must not only conform to the dictates of healthy living and responsibility but also be seen by others to be taking steps to live a healthy and responsible life. In short, healthism as a form of virtuous responsibility has to become demonstrable for the healthy to be recognized as exemplary citizens.

The second challenge of responsible drinking is one of shifting norms. Despite the continuity of objectives within the neo-liberal framework of exercising judgement and self-control over one's drinking, the specific practices and practicalities of being a 'responsible drinker' have changed. These changes call for new models, influences and examples if the public pedagogy of responsible drinking is to keep up with the times. For instance, much of what used to be thought of as unproblematic consumption – driving with blood alcohol concentrations in excess of 0.05 per cent, having more than four drinks in a sitting, counting 'drinks' according to the container in which they were served rather than in terms of standard measures of pure alcohol – has since been redefined as risky or even illegal (Yeomans 2013; Dufour 1999; Heath 2012). Of late, many governments have revised their guidelines and begun to insist that there is no such thing as 'safe' drinking (NHMRC 2009; NHS 2019), a still contested position that reverses a popular belief in the health benefits of moderate consumption, especially of particular forms of alcohol, such as red wine (Towers et al. 2018; Oppenheimer and Bayer 2020).[3] Societies have accordingly found themselves needing to redefine, at the level of both noetic and anoetic knowledge, what responsible drinking is in practice. They have also had to source or produce new examples to adjust to the changing lessons of their health education programmes.

Responsible drinking, as both a healthist project for which people expect social recognition and a collection of practices requiring concrete examples to imitate, calls for demonstrability. In a practical sense, however, responsible or moderate drinking poses a challenge in terms of public pedagogies and exemplarity. Unlike other, arguably more demonstrable, forms of responsible 'healthy' behaviours where one either performs a somewhat conspicuous action (e.g. working out, refusing to snack on sweets offered during a morning tea) or fails to draw attention to oneself for irresponsible behaviour (e.g. having the odour of cigarette smoke about oneself, being obviously impaired), moderate drinking does not lend itself to being a particularly didactic example. This is because, as an example, it attracts little attention and does not exhibit or make its central quality manifest; quite simply it lacks the demonstrability needed to be exemplary. This is especially so in comparison to the extremes of both irresponsible drinking and teetotalism.

The excesses of drunkenness, which have incited the press to cry scandal for centuries, are by far the more prominent examples of irresponsible alcohol consumption and act as overtly negative examples. From Hogarth's *Gin Lane* to the comedic *Hangover* movies and news footage of youth brawling or staggering the vomit-soaked streets of night-time districts, scene-stealing examples abound. Abstention, though, is also conspicuous, especially when compared to moderation in cultures where the majority of adults (and many adolescents) drink. It is still suspect at a popular level and occasions questions about belonging, as alcohol is still deeply enmeshed in rituals and practices of commensality, celebration and bonding (Douglas 1987; Wilson 2005). Abstinence presents itself as a water glass raised for a toast (considered to be an invitation to bad luck in many settings) or the 'uncouth' choice to accompany one's meal with tea (a perfectly normal practice in many parts of Asia) rather than wine or beer. It is also opting out of social gatherings at bars and pubs, a situation that literally makes abstainers conspicuous by their absence. Responsible drinking – to be recognized as such and emulated as an example within the context of health education – must therefore find a way to draw attention to itself as an imitable practice. It must take on a gestural quality, something that can render it as a kind of 'snapshot' (Noyes 2016).

Robin Room attempts to highlight exemplary, imitable figures who are paradigms of moderation. He compares the moderate drinker to Christian, the persecuted protagonist of Bunyan's allegory *Pilgrim's Progress*, to accentuate the performance of virtuous self-control required in moderate drinking: 'the modern pilgrim exercises and *demonstrates* his or her self-control and rationality in a new trial every day' (Room 2011: 146, emphasis added). In this formulation, the pilgrim's morality, which needs only be notable to God, has been replaced by a secular morality that has become a social obligation that must be evincible to the non-omniscient. Moderate or responsible drinking is accordingly made manifest so that the associated rewards and recognitions can be accorded and the moderate drinker upheld as an exemplar. Yet, the narrative form of the allegory affords, arguably indulges, a deliberateness of demonstrability and exemplarity that, while effective for those who engage with it, lacks the immediacy and signifying power of the images of drunkenness or even the small gestures of abstention. Moderation in Room's exposition must play out over time, while the extremes are almost instantly observable.

TSIs nonetheless respond particularly well to the challenge of making the unobtrusiveness and invisibility of moderate alcohol consumption and the banal figure of the responsible drinker both evident and praiseworthy. Following from Elgin's assertions that the circumstances may need to be engineered to produce an example, TSIs have turned 'the slow exemplarity of conduct' (Noyes 2016: 87) into a grand, highly demonstrable gesture. Their structure and targeting of potential participants, reinforced by their marketing and communications strategies (including their fundraising tactics), all solicit positive attention for the participant as an exemplar of the moderate or responsible drinker. This in turn serves the social (and philanthropic) objectives of the campaigns.

Amplified restraint

Individual motivations for TSI participants even within a single context or campaign are numerous, arguably idiosyncratic. Yet the ways in which these motivations are addressed by TSIs speak to an elevation of simple rationales. As formal organizations and as movements of people who fashion their own way of participating in the lifestyle movement, TSIs have developed particular patterns or models of *how* and *why* to temporarily abstain. Over time, these models have evolved to either amplify or impute laudable motivations, strategies that frame participants as exemplars of active intervention (on themselves), temporary restraint and overall moderation.

Before delving into the ways in which TSIs frame participants as praiseworthy paradigms of self-government and responsibility, it is worth considering the broad base from which these campaigns draw participants. TSIs are not designed to appeal to all but are devised to be particularly appealing to vast segments of the population. As previously noted, they actively discourage participation from those with alcohol dependencies and, by tacit omission, do not engage with those who consume alcohol very infrequently. In cultures such as Australia, New Zealand, Finland, the Netherlands, the UK and Canada, where the vast majority of the adult population consumes alcohol on a monthly or even weekly basis (WHO 2018), the pool of prospective participants is large, varied and anonymous. Yet, those who sign on to TSIs have generally been found to have riskier drinking behaviours than the population at large (de Visser et al. 2016: 287; Hillgrove and Thomson 2012: 13). TSIs accordingly found favour because a majority would consider that they could – although may not obviously want to – moderate their overall alcohol consumption. In the United States, where abstainers make up a larger share of the adult population, TSIs were championed early on by epicureans who identified as having strong lifestyle and/or professional interests in food and drink (Lew 2014; Ore 2015). The growing numbers who take up TSIs accordingly suggest they are in some way useful or beneficial to participants.

In line with the 'healthist' commandment of our era, one of the most common reasons for wanting to attempt a TSI is to look after one's health.[4] For some, there are very particular objectives that align with health advice that motivates participation. For instance, Fiona and her husband, heeding the now common advice that those looking to conceive would be prudent to avoid alcohol, signed up to FebFast in preparation for trying for another child. More often, though, participants embrace TSIs for reasons of generalized well-being rather than to address specific health concerns. Thomas notes, 'It was just after New Year's really and it was one of those things. I felt I needed a break from too much eating and too much alcohol.' Such comments are echoed by other participants, for TSIs are commonly perceived as a corrective to the excesses of the holiday period. For most, moderating alcohol and drinking behaviours comprises part of an unspecific project of health improvement, a situation that reflects wide acceptance that alcohol contributes to adverse overall health outcomes.

Participants' stated rationales for participation nod to the expectations of avoidance of risk and self-management in the neo-liberal context. However, they typically avoid mention of the buzzwords of responsibility and moderation. I argue that these terms, like the practices themselves, are too subtle for the highly demonstrative experience of TSIs. Rather than simply being a period of unobtrusive 'opting out', TSIs are instead understood as the demonstrable setting right of what had been allowed to drift, perhaps conspicuously, into irresponsibility. Even in the scholarly literature, TSIs are characterized in the more oppositional terms of resistance (Fry 2011) and anti-consumption (Cherrier and Gurrieri 2013). Participants, and some campaigns, accordingly prioritize the stronger language of self-initiated correctives or interventions, which are more visible, proactive and indeed dramatic, as a way to create examples for self and others and to champion the outward exemplarity of participants as self-managing, responsible individuals.

Participants, for instance, have taken up the discourse of lifestyle entrepreneurs in the health and wellness movement. The language of detoxing, a concept that nods to specious elements of the larger wellness industry (Dixon 2005), was particularly prominent, as evidenced by Rebecca's very typical summation: 'It's a chance to detox and get off the booze for a month.' Nearly half of the respondents – irrespective of the particular TSI (or formal TSI participation) or their pre-campaign level of consumption – used the word 'detox' to describe their experience. Where the detox discourse has recast dozens of previously innocuous substances and phenomena (e.g. sugar, blue light from electronic devices, refined carbohydrates, caffeine, plastics) as toxins and poisons, it elevates efforts to banish them from daily life and from the body to a sort of prolonged cleanse.

Less prominent, but still speaking to a self-initiated intervention, is the concept of the 'circuit breaker'. As Mark observed, 'Everyone's lives these days are too busy, stressful and all-consuming for us to not fall victim to some of our impulses and habits every now and then. I think the counterbalance to that is having a circuit breaker.' In this formulation, the passivity of 'falling victim' is countered by the participant's deliberate act to break the cycle of stress and self-medication through management of the self.

As organizations, TSIs reinforce this discourse of active and demonstrable abstinence, at least for a time. FebFast's logo is composed of the organization's name and the double vertical bar of the pause symbol, the caesura mark, that is universally employed on electronic devices. The website for the 2020 campaign also features a photo of someone holding a wine glass (containing red wine), with their hand placed over the mouth of the glass, as if to protect themselves from the contents. In the same year, Dry July and its affiliate organizations Go Sober and Dry Feb used a similar but simply drawn image to illustrate the core concept of 'going booze free' for the relevant month. In prior iterations, they featured people holding upturned, empty wine and beer glasses. Ocsober's logos have also featured wine and beer glasses. In one version they are simply crossed out with an X, and in another, they are surrounded by a dotted line with an attached pair of scissors, a prompt to 'cut out' the booze. These visual cues each in their own way signal that participants are not simply taking or leaving alcohol but are, rather, actively and demonstrably refusing or removing it. The imputed reversibility of some of these signifiers – pause rather than stop, a hand over the mouth of otherwise full glass – nonetheless signals that the need for abstention applies only during the designated period of the campaign.

While websites and logos communicate the proactive intent of temporary sobriety in the service of moderation, participants must also be assisted to evince the kind of mass exemplarity – the widespread cultural adoption of the practices of temporary sobriety in service of moderation – needed to affect the cultural shifts that define the objectives of lifestyle movements. Accordingly, TSIs and the regular commentary in the press that greet them promote, and sometimes stage, popular and repeated demonstrations of responsibility that help to normalize participation in the immediate and, for socially oriented TSIs in particular, beyond the duration of the campaign. This discourse highlights the period of extreme moderation to briefly but purposively render the inconspicuous act of moderation, given its temporarily accentuated form as performative abstinence, attention-getting and praiseworthy.

Dealcoholized beverages and mocktails are one of the ways that responsible drinking is made visible while at the same time supporting governmental and economically liberal rather than disciplinary approaches to alcohol. As TSIs have grown in popularity, the beverage and hospitality industries have begun to bemoan reduced earnings during dry months (Dubecki 2013). They, along with a number of TSIs themselves, have consequently advocated continuing to socialize as one normally would and promoted mocktails and non-alcoholic alternatives to traditional tipples, including non-alcoholic beers, wines and spirits (Bird 2019; Hooper 2020). These substitute beverages are often priced comparably to the alcoholic drinks they replace and, not coincidentally, are heavily promoted during local dry months. These strategies continue to emphasize consumption and also afford participants opportunities to showcase their restraint in social settings. An order for a mocktail or a non-alcoholic beer, for instance, is evidence – for the benefit of one's companions and the servers – of the participant's self-discipline and responsibility. It is still, however, a substitute alcoholic beverage, the choice of someone who would be likely to have the alcoholic version were they not choosing to be responsible.

For campaigns that allow purchasable reprieves (i.e. Leave Passes, Golden Tickets, Time-Out Passes), there is an additional opportunity for participants to perform both their commitment and self-control, all while bolstering their contributions to the TSI's philanthropic project. Rebecca describes how a friend offered her a time-out pass as a gift: 'One of my girlfriends was going to pay for the pass out for me. That was going to be her treat. She was going to pay for the pass out so I could go out and have a few drinks one night.' She proudly reports, though, that she refused and continued to abstain. In doing so, she accentuates how the proposal itself created an opportunity for a further and renewed show of her behaviour as a more responsible drinker, one who (with overtones of virtuousness) honours her commitments.

The small acts of demonstrated or imputed restraint that come via drink and reprieve refusal are widely celebrated by the TSIs themselves and by those close to the participants. Analysis by Bartram et al. reveals that the messaging employed across TSIs can vary, but that, despite the particularities of any given campaign, there is a strong orientation towards discourses of heroics, especially in reference to the classic narrative structure 'in which a hero receives a call to adventure . . . encounters temptations and trials, but is ultimately rewarded with a boon or treasure. The hero returns to the ordinary world, transformed by the experience, and uses the treasure they have received to benefit the world' (Bartram et al. 2018: 81).[5] The narrative underpinning of heroism is here especially important, for it construes the quest (temporary sobriety) as a testing and intriguing phase of what is still a continuous formulation of self. There will be enduring transformative effects (responsible drinking), but these will fail to attract the same attention as the acts that vaulted the hero to notice.

The hyperbolic comparisons to heroes and the larger emphasis on positivity, the latter being common to both philanthropic and socially oriented campaigns, speak to neo-liberalism and new public health's emphasis on individual responsibility. There is nonetheless a collectivist orientation to the performance of responsibility that is overshadowed when TSIs *as lifestyle movements* are not in focus. The connection between fundraising and the collective ends of philanthropic engagement notwithstanding, TSIs create visibility for the prefigurative politics of the lifestyle movement, particularly at the level of changing problematic drinking cultures.

Official TSI rhetoric, especially in former temperance cultures, champions the efforts of participants to valiantly correct problematic drinking cultures. Ocsober, which raises funds for a school-based health education programme, was initially emphatic about its status as a corrective solution – both formally and informally educational – to the problems of youth and binge drinking: 'We decided that it's time that Australians really put alcohol into perspective and recognised that, as a culture, it's something to be enjoyed but not abused, and to send a message to our kids and to be an example' (Fawsitt 2008). Where Australia's National Binge Drinking Strategy focused on youth drinking and targeted funds towards educational campaigns for parents of teens to help them inform their children about teen drinking (Government of Australia: Department of Health 2013), the focus on young people and example setting directly links with national priorities. Not all TSIs are as obvious about the role model status of their participants, but the means to exemplify larger social and parental responsibility as personal restraint with alcohol are implicated in the very structure of the campaigns.

Go Sober's 'soberhero' (Go Sober 2016) branding for many years used the popular image of the superhero to recognize participants for both their changed behaviour and fundraising efforts. While earlier versions of the branding featured cartoon-like drawings of the 'soberheroes', the final outing of the strategy in 2019 had more lifelike representations of the heroes. The images were photos of people embellished with superimposed cartoon illustrations of superhero accessories – capes, belts, gauntlets, masks, diadems and boots – in fluorescent green and electric purple (Sober October UK 2020). The shift to mixed medium imagery better accentuates the dual identity of the superhero: ordinary, unassuming person in one instance; superhuman role model and saver of the day the next (Brownie and Graydon 2015). Unlike the superhero whose true identity must never be discovered, though, the soberhero must be simultaneously and outwardly both the role model and their everyday self.

The health entrepreneur, the performative abstainer, the detoxer and the soberhero are all demonstrative formulations of the typically invisible responsible drinker. These discourses and performances accentuate the active and socially valued role that participants play in managing their drinking and modelling conduct that aligns with increasing social demands around moderation and the management of one's health with risk-minimizing aims.

116   *Alcohol, Binge Sobriety and Exemplary Abstinence*

Frequently serving the dual objectives of social change and philanthropy, TSIs have also capitalized on the participant's presence and indeed performance of abstention and responsibility in alcogenic environments, such as pubs and bars, to bolster fundraising efforts.

Martyrdom or fundraising gimmick?

Accentuating the sense of personal accomplishment that comes from taking a responsible approach to one's health is a mainstay of both socially oriented and philanthropic TSIs. In campaigns with strong philanthropic orientations such as Dry July (and its international affiliates) and the later incarnations of Ocsober, there is nonetheless a countervailing discourse of passivity – of suffering through the trials of sobriety inflicted by oneself, by others and by circumstance in the name of moderation. In various yearly and national iterations of different TSIs, organizers have adopted visual and discursive strategies that accentuate the participant's misery as they forgo the pleasures that should normally be available to them for the sake of a good cause.

Not surprising for anyone who has witnessed the viral popularity and rampant fundraising success of the Ice Bucket Challenge (Sherman and Wedge 2017) are findings that confirm that people are more likely to engage in prosocial action, typically donating money, and to donate larger amounts to the cause, when the fundraisers are perceived to be sacrificing (Johnson 2018) or suffering (Olivola and Shafir 2013; Olivola 2011; Olivola and Shafir 2018). This holds true both for those who are fundraising (participants) and for those who are entreated to donate as sponsors or non-participants. TSIs with strong (but not necessarily exclusively) philanthropic objectives have accordingly amplified their portrayals of the sacrifice and pain required to abstain.

From the very outset, the name TSI organizers choose for their campaigns set expectations for participants and sponsors. In 2013 and 2014, the Défi 28 jours began as *Les 28 jours les plus longs de ta vie* (in French) and Soberary (in English). The initial moniker, at least in Quebec's dominant language of French, is unapologetic in its pitch: the undertaking will be twenty-eight days long but will feel longer. Perhaps an indication that the new initiative had overplayed its hand, responses were cynical. The thirty or so participants in the Facebook event were referred to in an online article as 'mean pseudo hipsters' who pretentiously publicized their undertaking (Nightlife.ca 2013), one the article's author noted they personally engaged in at least twice a year (presumably for reasons of health and wellness) without fanfare. As the campaign's social objectives grew in relative importance once the link with the Fondation Jean Lapointe was formalized, the name was revised to emphasize challenge without overstating the personal cost. Arguably, the torturous aspects of surviving a month without drinking were elided as the social objectives of normalizing moderate or non-drinking became more important for the now in-house fundraiser of a drug and alcohol treatment organization.

The strategy of drawing attention to one's sacrifice and amplifying its personal cost was echoed in the early iterations of Dry July, where the website featured famous (and sometimes misattributed) quotes about the joys and pleasures of beer and wine (Dry July 2013). It is, to be sure, a contradiction to read 'Beer is proof that God loves us and wants us to be happy' on a website for a neo-temperance organization. The published explanation of the Golden Ticket that year was similarly oriented towards forgone – and potentially briefly reclaimed – pleasures. The $25 exemption was described as 'a Wonka-esque pass to the magical kebab-scented world of a good night out'. The trope-laden descriptor alludes to both the magical indulgence of Willy Wonka and his storied chocolate factory (Dahl 1964) and a favourite Australian post-drinking snack: the kebab. If sobriety is about depriving oneself of happiness and sensual pleasures, the inherent logic here dictates that the sacrifice, as painful as it is, must be in service of something worthy.

Dry July's early rhetoric of sacrifice gestures tentatively towards a corollary notion in the logics of martyrdom: suffering. Pain, discomfort, endurance and effort – the more obvious, the better – are all worthy of reward, arguably one commensurate with the effort and toll. Dryathlon, which is similarly philanthropic in orientation, has pitched itself as a variant on one of the many fitness-based charity challenges, or 'thons', which simultaneously address neo-liberalism's individualization of both philanthropic and health obligations (King 2006). The product of a creative agency rather than a grassroots initiative (Bryant 2020), the campaign explicitly targeted younger men (but found an audience among women as well) and leveraged the notion of a test of strength, both physical and mental, to position participants as enduring a gruelling trial. Participants were dubbed 'dryathletes', a designation reinforced by a visual branding strategy in which participants are recognizable thanks to their (both ironic and iconic) pink athletic sweatbands (Dryathlon 2016a). Would-be dryathletes are similarly goaded into demonstrating their strength via advertisements featuring photos of a glass of cold beer and are asked to demonstrate their strength via the taunting question: 'Are you strong enough *not* to lift it?' (Bryant 2020).

Because Dryathlon typically runs at the same time as Dry January in the UK and must distinguish itself from other TSIs that are competing for both participants and donations (Birkwood 2014), it has been characteristically tongue-in-cheek about its effortful stance on responsible drinking.[6] Abstinence for this strongly philanthropic campaign is something to be endured, and participants, complete with their headbands, are often depicted looking at a frothy pint with exaggeratedly pained and longing expressions. The participant, down to the attention-getting signature colour of pink for a campaign that first targeted men, is marked to stand out, and their efforts are highlighted as exceptional, taxing and potentially even emasculating. The development of willpower as a focal point in the 2016 Dryathlon campaign (Dryathlon 2016b) dared or taunted would-be participants, especially those who scored poorly on the Willpower Test (a humorous online self-assessment), to prove both the calculator and the dubious among their social circles wrong. Responsible drinking, as exercised during the period of the TSI as abstinence, therefore requires a show of strength that encompasses the physical (resistance to the euphemistic bending of the elbow) and the mental, namely a show of willpower.

Dryathlon's Willpower Test highlights the strategic role that unlikely participants, notably those who drink heavily or those with little (acknowledged) willpower, play for TSIs with social and philanthropic objectives. First, the unlikely participant becomes a locus for fundraising, as the efforts of those who are perceived to be suffering for a cause are more likely to attract greater contributions from sponsors (Olivola and Shafir 2018). Second, a welcoming and even challenging or daring stance towards unlikely participants actively solicits participation from a group that may not have felt included by campaigns that prioritize messages of social responsibility. Discourses that instead accentuate challenge, effort or strength are able to engage participants 'where they are' relative to the social messages around responsible drinking rather than where organizers might like them to be. This not only helps TSIs to target those who may be at higher risk in terms of public health and overall drinking behaviour but also broadens the pool of possible participants to those less likely to be self-responsible. This is a way for socially oriented TSIs to reach a group that may be both highly resistant to change sought on other terms and one likely to benefit from the experience.

Extending the reach of TSIs to less-likely participants is of direct and tangible benefit to the philanthropic campaigns, especially those that charge registration fees, because having more participants multiplies the number of donors and fundraisers working in service of the campaign. Unlikely participants are also more apt to be those who can best showcase the advantages of moderation and abstention, including in unlikely places, such as bars and pubs. In so doing, they not only become examples who show change is possible for even recognized heavy or committed drinkers but also become exceptional vehicles for particular fundraising strategies.

As philanthropic TSIs are likely to derive greater financial benefit from the performance of suffering among unlikely participants, they have pioneered various schemes to monetize the demonstration of short-lived teetotal ways. An unlikely participant can be the subject of a wager, a strategy that works particularly well in contexts like Australia where gambling is nearly as enmeshed in the cultural fabric as drinking is. Brad, for instance, reported that some of his friends preferred not to donate to support his participation but accepted a large bet – with the winnings going to FebFast – if he succeeded in going the month without drinking. The amount ultimately donated was, in Brad's estimation, about twice what he would have expected his friends to contribute had they donated outright. Arguably, this fundraising tactic leverages the power of a counterexample turned example and uses the threat of personal financial penalty (a risk to further suffering) rather than just the implicit contract of philanthropy to enforce the participant's commitment.

A number of TSIs have promoted capitalizing upon the affordances of being atypically sober in an alcogenic environment, such as a pub or at a party. The designated driver service (Dry January 2016; Go Sober 2019; Cancer Research UK 2020c; Cowra Guardian 2014), where participants continue to socialize as they normally would, but provide their intoxicated companions with a ride home for a donation equivalent to what may have been spent on taxi fare, is perhaps one of the most common fundraising tactics. It has the added benefit of being particularly useful, and thus effective, outside of metropolitan areas with reliable public transit. Even small donations, though – the cost of a drink that would normally be offered as part of a round or a shout – are encouraged via the ability to use mobile donation technology to make a contribution to a participant's fundraising tally. Dryathlon created such a strategy with their 'Mine's a donation' initiative. The campaign promotes and indeed depends on engagement with the rituals of drinking culture but simply substitutes a monetary contribution – as little as a pound – for the drink (Chapman 2015). Thanks to their continued participation in the socially cohesive ritual of rounds or shouts (Adler 1991), participants are given the occasion to present the wallet-sized card and earn a donation. This strategy allows participants to reinforce social objectives and to exemplify the ways to change a facet of the drinking culture that has been particularly problematic from a public health perspective (Murphy et al. 2016). Participants, though, must still be notable exceptions in their circles for the strategy to be effective; a group of TSI participants in a bar each requesting donations from one another would be non-sensical.

Dryathlon positioning itself as a form of physical training, for all its advantages, nonetheless entails an element of risk insofar as what may be a Herculean feat for a novice may be accomplished far too easily for somebody who is well-conditioned. Indeed, this is the threat that all TSIs with a philanthropic objective face. Those who are not heavy drinkers, those who are known to be able to take or leave alcohol, and even those who undertake the TSI year after year must find ways to position their efforts as socially significant and their sacrifice as worthy of compensation. Both Oliver and David were seven-time FebFast participants and both conceded that fundraising under such circumstances was harder. Oliver noted that repeat participation had simultaneously made fundraising more difficult and less of a priority for him: 'Normally I try and raise five hundred or a thousand dollars but I did very little fundraising. I don't know why. I didn't really get into it. The other thing is, if you do this for a number of years people are less inclined to continue to give. They gave last time, that sort of thing.' His strategy instead was to be more of an evangelist than a martyr; he recruited more first-timers from his workplace and felt that he was bolstering the organization's twinned social and philanthropic objectives through them.

For David, fundraising remained a priority, and he would set a reasonably ambitious goal – upwards of $500 – for himself every year. In 2013, when he found that he was struggling to reach his target, he devised a new strategy: 'I did a special incentive during the last week where I told people I'd match their donations dollar for dollar.' He had concluded that forgoing alcohol was no longer seen as a donation-worthy cause. Yet, the double sacrifice of him paying not to drink, when one of the touted benefits of TSIs is the financial savings for participants, boosted his overall fundraising tally to $2,000. For both Oliver and David, the social responsibility around alcohol that was meant to be exemplified by their abstinence became utterly unremarkable for others, if not for themselves. Their strategies to make their period of abstinence exemplary accordingly shifted from accentuating personal suffering of an embodied or affective nature to devising ways to amplify the social and financial costs of their participation.

Lenten TSIs, which are well aligned to notions of sacrifice – albeit not for philanthropic objectives – are due special consideration. Campaigns such as IkPas, 40 Brez Alkohola and Alcohol Free for 40 are longer than standard month-long TSIs and are arguably aligned with established or at least historic cultural practices. These campaigns, however, are resolutely socially oriented, deal with their extended length matter-of-factly and eschew discourses of suffering and sacrifice. This is not to say, however, that the connection with Lent is dismissed. Alcohol Free for 40 founder Molly Kimball embraces the connection, insofar as southern Louisiana's cultural context provides legitimacy – even anonymity – for those who opt to go dry for forty days in New Orleans, a city famous (especially in the normally abstemious American South) for its nightlife and drinking culture.

It is worth noting that my research participants, all of whom took part in non-Lenten TSIs, who identified as Catholic or having grown up in a Christian household also failed to connect their contemporary philanthropically motivated sacrifice with those of their religious youth. Some were insistent that a Lenten sacrifice was unremarkable; Leisl noted that her prior sacrifices were largely compelled by her father, and many people she knew from her cultural community were making similar gestures. Forgoing alcohol for charity was, however, a personal choice – and a sacrifice – that she was proud to highlight as something above and beyond the practices of her faith.

The common image of a martyr is somebody who endures considerable suffering – even a torturous death – for their commitments. A martyr's influence stems from the example they set, specifically around their unwavering dedication. This principled stance would suggest that discourses of martyrdom, whether of sacrifice or suffering, would be strongest in socially oriented TSIs, which uphold responsible drinking as an aspiration and seek to model and instil that change at a societal level. In contravention of this logic, it has been philanthropic TSIs, with their fundraising schemes to monetize abstinence, that have embraced and amplified the image of the abstinent martyr. Socially oriented TSIs have instead sought to normalize and reinforce these lifestyle choices, albeit by using the same aspects of embodied exemplarity. Positive reinforcement for the first tentative steps towards greater responsibility – whether in service of social and cultural change, personal health or charitable engagement – nevertheless remains important to the pedagogy of TSIs.

Likeable lifestyle choices

The demonstrability of the participant's example and its potential to be (indeed objective of being) recognized as worthy of imitation by self and others is at the core of TSI strategy and arguably in lifestyle movements more generally.

Previously, meetings, events, conferences, newsletters, literature, posters, radio and even television have been instrumental in showcasing exemplars and propagating the activities of lifestyle movements (Tyrrell 1991; Haenfler 2019). The internet and social media have accelerated and intensified the ways in which examples are showcased to inspire adherence and imitation and to solicit endorsement (and also sometimes scorn) for participants' choices (Szto and Gray 2014; Maher et al. 2016). For TSIs, the rapid, repeated and calculated promotion of abstinence (and possibly the philanthropically motivated sacrifice) undertaken in the name of the campaign have afforded the performances of self-restraint, moderation and responsible drinking the essential visibility they typically lack. In being broadcast or disseminated in this way, social media has also provided participants with recognition and validation for their efforts that are important for the perpetuation of neo-liberal objectives of personal responsibility.

Information and communication technologies, social media, in particular, have inaugurated a revolution in the mechanisms of mobilization (Castells 2015). Although the effects are not universal, in many ways these technologies and platforms have made social action more accessible: 'The Internet creates its own venues and demand for action but also lowers the threshold for participation' (van Stekelengurg and Roggeband 2013: xv). Influence in movements is, in the contemporary context, no longer dependent on having access to official platforms such as temperance publications and conferences (Tyrrell 1991; Fahey 2006), and the pace and frequency of engagement can also accelerate. This means that more people can speak if not for, then at least in affiliation with, a movement and can more readily generate the impression of collectivity needed for mass exemplarity.

TSIs have relied heavily on the affordances of social media, but also of conventional print and broadcast media, to gain momentum. Alcohol Free for 40's very name, which is based on its #AlcoholFreefor40 hashtag, evinces the TSI's entanglement with social media. It was, however, founder and dietician Molly Kimball's regular column in New Orleans' main daily newspaper (itself a mostly online publication) that launched the campaign and redirected reader interest to the initiative's social media presence on Facebook, Twitter and Instagram. The Défi 28 jours began as a Facebook event that was shared among friends and onward to their larger networks (Chouinard and Théorêt-Poupart 2013). Of all the posts, the one that attracted the most 'likes' ($n = 27$) and comments, mostly of a mocking nature, was Chouinard's 2 February 2013 interview with the Concordia University radio station. The Facebook 'event' was nonetheless written up by online magazines and websites, publicity that helped to propel the nascent TSI from an undertaking within a friendship circle to a major fundraiser affiliated with a prominent charity. Radio also played a significant role in launching Dry July in 2008. Australian Broadcasting Corporation radio personality Adam Spencer heard of the plan to raise $3,000 to purchase a new television for a hospital waiting room. In publicly signing on to the challenge, fundraising and encouraging others to do the same, Spencer helped what would become the Dry July Foundation raise more than a quarter of a million dollars that year, far exceeding their goal (Dry July 2009; 2013).

For the period in which TSIs were fledgling and in many cases still private initiatives, the endorsement of the mainstream media conferred legitimacy, especially where fundraising was involved. The media provided a platform to publicize and widely disseminate the concept to reach a wider audience. Media celebrities with their own social media followings were accordingly recruited (especially during the early days of TSIs) to serve as official campaign ambassadors. Spencer, for instance, remains affiliated with Dry July and became the official 'patron' of the organization (Dry July 2014a). These ambassadors served as public role models, high-profile exemplars, of what the campaigns stood for and the behaviours – health-oriented and philanthropic – they championed.

While celebrities bring a concentration of attention and mainstream media reach when they embark upon a TSI, participants of all stripes are entreated to publicize their commitment to undertaking a period of sobriety. Jon Dean characterizes this broadcasting of one's involvement rather than just the commitment or donation itself as the result of 'social pressure to perform goodness in the right way' (Dean 2020: 64). To ensure that this promotion is done 'in the right way', TSIs employ marketing strategists and social media managers to produce collateral for participants to download, customize, upload and share themselves, which helps them to stay on-message and to be consistent with the image of participants – temporarily performative abstainers and overall responsible drinkers – that TSIs seek to promote.

Aligning one's motives for participation with those of the campaign establishes an important baseline of legitimacy. Kerry, for instance, dutifully used the text of a message Dry July sent to all participants in late June to email her friends and colleagues to announce her participation and to ask for donations. The message was customized to include her own rationale for participating (a memorial gesture for her father who had died of cancer many years earlier) and a link to her personal fundraising page. She also shared similar (but abbreviated) content on her Facebook page. Her focus on the way cancer had affected her aligned with the campaign's objectives and communicated the need for the recipients to support her efforts, and to acknowledge her motivations, with a donation.

Online promotion of participation has also been geared to keep attention focused on behaviours that risk becoming normalized or unremarkable. Noyes argues that 'attention is a scarce resource, and if you make a gesture when no one is looking, you cannot set an example' (Noyes 2016: 82). With an objective of maintaining the attention of a participant's circle and creating a fresh reason for participants to engage with them, Dryathalon produced a series of shareable digital badges (some with animation to override the stillness of text and image) that participants could post to their social media channels. These badges functioned as 'virtual conspicuous tokens of recognition' (Chell and Mortimer 2014) and included both earnest and expected messages – for having signed up or completing the campaign – and more humorous ones for points throughout the event to reinforce commitment, celebrate progress towards the goal and continue to command attention (Lansdown 2018). There is a badge for roughly every week of the campaign (seven days, halfway, seven days to go), with a concentration of collateral for the final days (both one and two days remaining). There are also badges decoupled from timing but focused on the affordances of sobriety (e.g. a right to be smug, saving friends from dubious online dating choices), which substitute the valued quality of humour for achievement in the world of shareable collateral and social media postings. The creative team behind the badges characterizes their function as 'egging on' participants in their fundraising efforts (Lansdown 2018).

From the participant's perspective broadcasting one's participation in a TSI can serve multiple purposes. In the first instance, and as was most obvious from Kerry's messages, the announcement was tied to her fundraising goal. It was a way for her to connect those in her network to the Dry July donation page while they were already online, thus removing one of the common logistical barriers to donation (Saxon and Wang 2014). Her declaration around her personal connection to the cause afforded her a way to more effectively engage in peer-to-peer fundraising, as donors could more directly link her engagement with an increasingly trendy fundraiser to a genuine and personal rather than an ostensibly self-congratulatory engagement with a cause. More in line with the social and health-related objectives, the message also served as a warning to let her friends, many of whom she would regularly connect with over a drink, know that she would be abstaining over the course of the month. Where she was hesitant about her ability to honour her commitment, the initial public announcement helped to pre-empt invitations to occasions that would normally revolve around drinking. Crucially, Kerry's announcement and subsequent ones of its kind, all posted to Facebook, garnered her considerable kudos from her circle of friends, family and colleagues. It is this third function that transformed her from unlikely abstainer to local exemplar of moderation and responsibility.

Kerry's posts about her TSI experience included both the sharing of official collateral supplied by Dry July that marked milestones and those of a more personal nature. One such post documents her attendance at an event with an open bar and her 'successful' but admittedly difficult choice to consume only non-alcoholic beverages. This post in particular attracted over a dozen 'like', 'love' and 'wow' reactions from her online friends and even more congratulatory and encouraging comments. Referring more to the philanthropic than the dual or more resolutely social objectives of TSIs, Dean characterizes such incidences of self-congratulation as '#humblebrags' stemming from the affordances of social media. The selective self-presentation via social media nonetheless applies equally to both contexts, as social media 'enables you to update the world on only those bits of your life that you want others to see, and with the options to frame exactly how you want them to see it' (Dean 2020: 51). Kerry's decision to publicize an occasion where she succeeded in abstaining despite temptation was not only self-congratulatory but an invitation – one that was obligingly taken up – for additional praise. By contrast, her use of a Golden Ticket during the same month was not mentioned on her social media feed. As purchasable reprieves are likely to attract suspicion and accusations of cheating, Kerry was selective about how she presented her experience of the campaign so as not to undermine the esteem she had cultivated through publicizing her exemplarily responsible, committed and self-sacrificing behaviour.

Where social medial users post about their involvement and accomplishments to solicit and receive praise and support from their networks, one's participation is a way to fashion a self that can be validated within the neo-liberal context that requires philanthropic and lifestyle choice (Rose and Miller 1992). Rogers Brubaker argues that social media, specifically its hyperconnectivity, its means to like and comment upon posts and the obvious quantification of sentiment that these forms of online endorsement provide, is 'an unprecedentedly powerful and pervasive infrastructure for governing through choices and for training people to be responsible choosers' (Brubaker 2020: 40). The training occurs via positive reinforcement: the kudos (rather than material rewards) upon which self-responsibilization depends. The facilitated exchange of virtual tokens and peer esteem makes social media's hyperconnectivity 'admirably well suited to engineering neo-liberal selves' (ibid. 41). It is worth noting that this style of engagement on a participant's existing social media channels (Facebook, Twitter, Instagram, etc.) is more typical of TSIs than in online abstinence support programmes or sober-curious movements such as Hello Sunday Morning, which provides a bespoke platform for blogging that facilitates a more introspective examination of the participant's relationship with alcohol and connects them to other participants rather than to their existing networks (Cherrier et al. 2017; Fry 2014; Carah et al. 2017).

As a signal to others that is meant to draw recognition, commendation and even emulation, announcements via social media about TSI participation recall the temperance pledges of old. Temperance pledges, especially in the more overtly religious rather than scientific temperance organizations, entailed a dual focus on both a prospective commitment and an atonement for past wrongdoing (Young 2006: 120). Although the immediacy and limited horizon of TSIs lack the full retrospective inclinations of temperance pledges, both forms of commitment communicate an individual's recognition of a need or a desire for 'improvement' and a new adherence to contemporary dictates of respectability, whether that be morality or the imperatives of health and/or philanthropy. This respectability via commitment confers esteem and advantage where public perception is deemed to be important (Lamme 2014).

Just as temperance pledges were often forgotten or overridden by intemperate action (Sulkunen 1990; Roberts 1982), commitments made on social media risk accusations of 'slacktivism': low-effort, low-commitment gestures of support, frequently conducted online, for a cause and often in lieu of more meaningful or effortful actions.[7] Those who make or celebrate modest commitments in such forums can also be accused of 'humblebragging', making ostensibly self-deprecating comments with the intent of drawing favourable attention to oneself. A satirical letter published on the popular American site Thrillist, for instance, takes aim at the smugness of Dry January participants: 'You have boldly gone where no man has gone before, to the Strange World of Completed Resolutions, only to return to overshare your Life Lessons with every moderate drinker, as if they were moon rocks, or alien skeletons, or something remotely interesting' (Gentile 2016). The letter concludes with a post-script, 'P.S. I saw you Instagram a beer on January 7th', that transforms the normally self-congratulatory medium for TSI participants into one that undermines the accomplishment and potential respectability of this fictional abstainer to instead portray them as a hypocrite.

Dryathlon has acquiesced to and ironically embraced these critiques. The 'One week dry, trying not to cry' and 'Dry as a bone: Soaking in smugness' badges (Lansdown 2018) allow participants to both flaunt their participation and earn their social validation within the neo-liberal frameworks of health and philanthropic imperatives. They nonetheless do so in a way that defuses foreseeable critiques (especially in Tory-led Britain) about participants having yielded wholesale to logics that remain associated with temperance, and in a more contemporary sense, social and financial conservatism. Proving themselves to have a sense of humour about sobriety while positioning themselves to receive the endorsements from their network, participants who opt to not take their efforts too seriously or to ascribe a still suspect moralism to them occupy an ideal position. They are able to participate in ways that fully construct them as an exemplar of healthist and philanthropic respectability but have the added benefit of showing their critical self-awareness of this status. This balanced position is crucial for TSIs and participants being, on the whole, applauded (but not too earnestly so) for their efforts.

The personal publicity and conspicuous tokens of recognition that TSIs supply are among the main features that differentiate them from self-directed dry months. While identical in structure and logic, especially when compared to socially oriented TSIs that have no official philanthropic activity, self-directed temporary abstainers are less likely to draw attention to themselves or their efforts. Their commitments lack the cover of philanthropy or an organized undertaking and accordingly risk being seen less as the joining of a legitimate movement than as a form of personal intervention that recalls the confessional tinge of the temperance pledge.

Liz, for one, noted that the publicity around Dry July and some joking reproaches from her adult children 'rang alarm bells' for her about her drinking. She decided to go dry for a month starting in September but downplayed her self-imposed sobriety. She kept her initiative from all but her immediate family, didn't publicize it on her social media accounts and didn't even mention it to close friends, whom she found herself avoiding so that she wouldn't need to explain her obviously changed behaviour. She saw her project as introspective and corrective and without links to a prefigurative politics of changed relationships to alcohol. She was very proud of having surpassed her initial commitment to thirty days of sobriety but relayed that she dared not confess to feeling as she did for fear that any pride in her accomplishment would be read as evidence of her being an alcoholic. Contrasting Liz's experience to that of participants in formal TSIs suggests these campaigns provide recognition and accepted scripts of heroism, sacrifice and effort for people, regardless of their actual level of responsibility to cast themselves as conspicuous and accepted examples of responsibility.

TSIs have used social media to help participants curate and publicize an online self that epitomizes the personal and social responsibility of the neo-liberal citizen. The dissemination of customizable content solicits recognition for participants that reinforces the legitimacy of their choices and assists them in meeting the objectives of the TSI, which are likely to be both philanthropic and behavioural. The visibility of mainstream social media and the affordances of both the platforms and supplied collateral help to create and propagate an image of the participant as an exemplary citizen: health-conscious, philanthropic, committed but also, and crucially in the temperance cultures in which TSIs thrive, good-natured. TSI participation accordingly entails some degree of willingness to, sometimes self-deprecatingly, recognize their performance of exemplarity.

Conclusion

TSI participants are performative episodic abstainers who, at least outwardly and thanks to partially contrived situations and discourses, fulfil the objectives of their campaigns. They continue to support the sectors of the economy that rely upon the drinks trade. Yet, through the highly demonstrative practice of temporary abstinence, they moderate their overall consumption. This allows them to champion the now social objectives of personal responsibility for health and private, philanthropic support for health and community services. In both their online and offline self-presentations, participants employ strategies – often with the guidance of the TSIs themselves – to draw attention to the socially valued exemplarity of their sober embodiment, their abstinent social presence and their self-sacrificing commitment to a worthwhile cause. Through their examples of extraordinary lifestyle choices, TSI participants demonstrate how moderation and responsible drinking can be carried out in practice among those who still (and still want to) consider themselves drinkers.

For TSI organizers, this demonstrability and the attendant quantifiability via donations and social media reach substantiates, albeit via proxy, a change in drinking cultures. This is to say that individual participation confirms a larger collective movement that in practice, if not in intent, changes society's relationship to alcohol. The demonstrability that serves certain TSI objectives, particularly philanthropy, is nonetheless a source of potential tension, both within and between TSIs.

7

Selfish philanthropists, selfish abstainers

TSIs are prime examples of abstention-based embodied philanthropy initiatives, taking their place alongside appearance (e.g. Movember, World's Greatest Shave) and activity-based (e.g. Steptember, charity run/marathon) campaigns. In such embodied undertakings, participants 'channel philanthropy through the body and its capacity to evidence philanthropic engagement' (Robert 2018: 1). The rise in these semiotically rich and highly participatory forms of philanthropic engagement owes to a shift in the sector, where 'people care a lot about the *means* of achieving altruistic goals' (Olivola 2011: 59, original emphasis). Philanthropic TSIs such as Dryathlon and Dry July and its affiliated campaigns are part of a larger decades-long trend within the philanthropic, charity or third sector towards more involved and visible forms of participation, engagement and fundraising.

The move towards more involved forms of philanthropy has seen donors invest in the process for allocating donations to particular causes or beneficiaries (Eikenberry 2009). For instance, donors have taken to evaluating the marketized and signalling dimensions of their engagement (Nickel and Eikenberry 2009; Wirgau et al. 2010; Frank 1996; Rogers 2014), and using data and impact tracking services to assess the effectiveness of their charitable contributions (MacAskill 2016). The donor's greater investment in and concern for the means and effects of philanthropy point to a multiplicity of objectives or mixed motives – both altruistic and non (and potentially but not necessarily at odds with one another) – that may be at play for participants and campaign organizers alike.

As part of a new generation of prosocial and charitable initiatives, TSIs have evolved in a context where donor and participant expectations about the nature and extent of their involvement have been accounted for in substantial and significant ways. Although each philanthropic TSI envisions and sometimes actively scripts exemplary forms of participation – how to approach donors, setting personal fundraising targets and ways to update sponsors on progress

– they have also evolved their views of ideal or exemplary participation as a result of participant behaviour and expectations. It is participants who have grappled with the philanthropic, health-related and pedagogical objectives of their TSI's suggested model of participation and have worked to hold these in personally and socially productive tension. The participant experience, which is of vital importance to TSIs that must satisfy cause and organizational awareness and fundraising objectives, has precipitated a shift towards greater uniformity among philanthropic TSIs, especially in English-speaking contexts.

Breaking from the usual scholarly focus on socially oriented campaigns, this chapter examines the specific challenges and affordances of philanthropic TSIs. Of central concern is the exemplary figure of the altruistic, philanthropic abstainer, a figure that for many participants proves an unrealistic ideal. It delves into official TSI discourse (instructions to participants, annual reports and operational practice) to understand how TSIs conceive of the participant serving the campaign's philanthropic objectives. These normative examples are contrasted with participant experiences, which reveal that questions about their motives for philanthropic engagement and expectations around fundraising are often experienced as burdens that taint their impressions of their efforts. The chapter concludes with a longitudinal examination of TSIs to demonstrate how philanthropic campaigns in particular have adapted their structure, activities and emphasis to participant expectations over time. I contend that they have, with varying degrees of success, remodelled themselves to meet their objectives and maintain a sense for participants, who come to these TSIs with expectations about their multiple objectives, that they are indeed 'doing good' by going dry.

The model of the philanthropic abstainer

Neo-liberalism's privatization of erstwhile public services has resulted in not only the outsourcing of functions to private or public–private organizations (Brown and Baker 2012) but also new roles, arguably obligations, for private entities to fund these services. The rise of high-profile and high net worth philanthrocapitalists (Bishop and Green 2015) or philanthropreneurs (Gordon et al. 2016) such as Bill and Melinda Gates or George Soros are well-documented features of the permeation of market logics into all facets of contemporary life.

The influence of neo-liberalism on smaller-scale instances of charitable giving by individuals has resulted in a much more fragmented critical landscape: analyses of marketized philanthropy with corporate social responsibility tie-ins

(Polonsky and Wood 2001; Nickel and Eikenberry 2009; Einstein 2012), self-organized philanthropic collectives (Eikenberry 2009; Karlan and McConnell 2014) and fundraising as part of an activity-based or embodied philanthropy initiative (Palmer and Dwyer 2019; Nettleton and Hardey 2006; Klawiter 1999). Samantha King (2006) was among the first to explicitly link the form of embodied philanthropic engagement, itself fulfilling neo-liberal objectives centred on health, with the new ethical imperative for private philanthropy and volunteerism, especially in the United States. Such trends are nonetheless apparent in the UK, Canada and Australia as well, both in regard to philanthropic TSIs and other embodied philanthropy initiatives.

The corporeal and sustained nature of embodied philanthropy creates limited parallels with other, better-studied forms of prosocial engagement, such as volunteering (donating one's time and talents), medical philanthropy (donating bodily tissues or fluids such as bone marrow or blood) and financial gifts. Its closest parallels, though, are event-style fundraisers using fitness or sports challenges (e.g. long-distance charity bike rides, marathons or 10-kilometre runs, and multiple-day walking tours). These initiatives use physical effort, often in the form of endurance events, as a basis for collecting monetary pledges or sponsorship, typically from the participant's social and professional networks. As with these better-known means for altruism, there are salient questions about the links between donor resources and capacity to give (Bekkers 2006; Meslin et al. 2008), the real extent of donor knowledge or sympathy for the cause (Body and Breeze 2016; Sulik 2011; King 2006), and the (perceived) benefits that come back to the donor in return for their support (Martin 1994) to consider.

From the perspective of charitable organizations, embodied philanthropy presents a number of advantages and opportunities, largely afforded by the multiple ways the participant's body can be pressed into prosocial engagement. When participants lend their bodies to the cause and do so in line with the guidance provided, they demonstrably exemplify the organization's values and support their objectives centring on three key areas: awareness of the cause, fundraising and support for the organization. As embodied exemplars who are already enmeshed in social networks (which are made up of individuals with whom they already have a great deal in common and whose self-narratives are more likely to be concordant), their philanthropic examples are more likely to be influential and imitable in their local contexts.

TSIs with a charitable component share these three aims and guide participants to conduct themselves in such a way that they will contribute to the organization meeting its tri-fold goals. Philanthropic TSIs actively promote awareness of and education about their cause. Depending on the cause supported, this may directly overlap with the necessary action of temporary sobriety, or it may be at arm's length from it. They also have an obvious need to raise funds via both donations and the recruitment of fundraisers. In an increasingly crowded philanthropic 'market' (including where other TSIs are direct competitors), philanthropic TSIs must also cultivate recognition and esteem of their 'brand' or organization if they are to achieve their other two goals. Because an abstinent body engaged in philanthropic action for the purposes of fundraising can simultaneously fulfil many of these needs, often without additional impost on the participant/fundraiser, embodied philanthropy allows for multiple instantiations (Mol 2002) of the same body and act. This potentially makes embodied philanthropy an efficient and effective form of prosocial engagement, including for reasons of public pedagogy. Still, TSIs and their previously noted challenges of lingering temperance stigma and demonstrability (among others) are potential barriers to achieving these objectives. The ways in which each of these aims is fulfilled in the specific context of TSIs are discussed here.

Awareness

Charities that organize fundraisers often seek to raise 'awareness' of their cause. As Sarah Moore (2008) argues in her analysis of 'ribbon culture', awareness takes many forms. In some cases relating to health-based causes, it supports public health aims and direct action, such as encouraging routine screening and alertness to symptoms to allow for early detection, treatment and the likelihood of improved health outcomes (Sulik 2011; Gardner 2006). In others, it alerts the public to the extent or urgency of a global need or one in the local community. Awareness may also seek to destigmatize an issue or those whom it affects, a facet of awareness-raising that aims to foster empathy for the eventual beneficiaries. Awareness may therefore operate at the level of increased knowledge, but it may also entail a behavioural corollary where that knowledge inspires particular actions.

For Jillian, FebFast participation helps to bring attention to what she sees as worthy but comparatively neglected causes.

> I like the idea . . . of where my money's going especially. . . . Please don't get me wrong, but look, there's a lot of things that are done about breast cancer. There's a lot of things that are done about (and god help me!) children with cancer and babies. There's a lot of things that are done for the elderly. There just doesn't

Selfish Philanthropists, Selfish Abstainers

seem to me, when I look at TV, radio advertising, there just doesn't seem to be anything on the youth. . . . I used to work in courts, in the magistrate's court, and I have worked for a number of years at the coroner's court. I see and have seen the end result of drugs, depression, alcohol and family violence. So for me this is sort of a little bit close to my heart and I just don't think there's enough done in the public arena to make people aware of what our youth are going through.

The TSI affords her an opportunity to champion a cause that is neither as prominent nor as socially accepted as some others, and one she sees as not receiving the social regard it is due. Her personal connection to the cause – a lived experience of what a failure to support young people in trouble can lead to – makes her the kind of 'cheerleader' that Body and Breeze (2016) argue is essential in promoting the efforts of charities linked to 'unpopular' causes.[1]

The means of raising awareness can vary, especially when related to the stage of maturity for a charity or event. Charity-related symbols, such as the pink ribbon signifying support for breast cancer that Jillian remarks upon, have become mythological in the sense of being almost ubiquitous highly legible cultural signs (Barthes 1991). They effectively short circuit the need to explain to raise awareness, for the simple act of displaying the ribbon – which is often purchased with a share of the proceeds going to a related charity – communicates the bearer's support for a well-known cause. The risk with these renowned symbols, however, is that they can become tokenistic, empty signifiers where the content of the educational or awareness-raising campaign recedes (Moore 2008). In the case of emergent movements or those that lack an unambiguous symbol, awareness-raising beyond the individual participant or adherent requires more effort, often in the form of an explanation. When that occurs, participants or bearers of the symbol, if they are to be successful in raising awareness, are required to become unofficial spokespeople for the causes they support, for they must justify what they are doing and why.

For TSIs, awareness objectives are mostly served by performative acts and accompanying explanations centred on drink refusal, as well as by soliciting donations. As discussed in the previous chapter, these are the facets of TSI participation that participants are coached to engineer or use to maximum pedagogic effect in terms of lifestyle and social objectives, but doing so is also important for a campaign's more philanthropic aims. Vi, for instance, explains how she sees awareness-raising for FebFast's beneficiary organization taking place in practice:

> I know because of me doing it there's a couple of hundred people that are more aware of it now. That's probably the same for most people. When you think about the amount of people that you socialise with over a month, the amount of people that you work with over a month and you come into contact [with] over a month . . . of them none of them knew what it [FebFast] was last year. So I was able to tell them what it was about. . . . There's a hundred more people that are aware of the campaign. Or probably 200. Whether any of those 200 chose to do it this year, who knows, but they're definitely aware that there's [*sic*] campaigns out there and maybe it made them think . . . in their own little private corner about their drinking habits for a while.

For her, the mere fact of communicating her temporary abstinence, whether in response to a forgone and conspicuous opportunity to drink with others that is called out or questioned or as a follow-up to a sponsorship request, is likely to elicit the need for an explanation. This invites discussion about the TSIs' and/or her own social and philanthropic objectives and rationales. Owing to the overlap between the cause being supported (YSAS) and the form her participation must take (temporary abstinence), Vi's response reveals some slippage between awareness of the specific cause and the larger health and social aims of FebFast as a campaign that balances social objectives (changing individual and societal relationships with alcohol) and philanthropic goals.

Fundraising

The second major objective for philanthropic TSIs, one that often prevails over questions of awareness – especially now that TSIs have become established – is fundraising. The annual reports of philanthropic TSIs routinely document numbers of participants and the total funds raised as key performance indicators, as the yield per participant and the overall number of fundraisers is determinant of the overall sum that can be raised. TSIs pursue both of these objectives and provide ample suggestions and materials to bolster the result of participants' efforts.

Team participation, whether official or unofficial, has been a long-standing plank of TSI strategy, especially for campaigns with a highly philanthropic orientation. This strategy employs snowball-style recruitment to increase the number of individual fundraisers enlisted. Both Lori and Suzanne, for instance, signed up for a TSI as part of a family team, Lori with her parents and siblings, Suzanne with her partner and adolescent children (who abstained from sugar and non-work-related screen time given that they were not of legal drinking

Selfish Philanthropists, Selfish Abstainers 135

age). Where social tie-ins to charity events are a way to build lasting connection to a cause (Goodwin et al. 2017), team participation – which offers opportunities for mutual support, encouragement for reaching a shared goal and moderate in-group competition – is an asset. The competitive social aspect is further reinforced through campaign-sponsored leader boards and top-ten lists of individual and team fundraisers. Those who top the rankings are held up as models for those with more modest fundraising tallies.

Team participation also helps participants avoid a major source of temptation – the ritual post-work or post-game drinks – while still leaving access to important potential donors within other personal networks (such as family and friends, or colleagues) able to be approached for financial support. These relationships are important because the proven determinant of relational altruism (Scharf and Smith 2016) dictates that people are more likely to donate when solicited to do so by someone they know – and know well – because they wish to support that person's endeavours, perhaps even more so than their desire to support a worthy cause or beneficiaries.

Increasing the yield from each participant has been a more complex undertaking for TSIs, with campaigns having developed approaches that have varied in terms of their efficacy. As discussed in Chapter 6, cultivating scenarios that position participants as martyrs suffering for a cause is positively correlated with donation yields, both in relation to how much participants are willing to personally donate and in terms of non-participant (sponsor) donations. Consequently, TSIs have sought to reinforce for participants and sponsors alike the effort, sacrifice and suffering entailed in not drinking. This is especially so in social situations where one would expect the participant to imbibe and to enjoy doing so.

The exaggeration of effort that is characteristic of many philanthropic TSIs, however, is kept in tension with the need to attract participants, some of whom may be put off by the effort required. Jillian, for instance, relayed her husband's adamance that he would never personally take part in a TSI but would happily support the cause through donations. Evaluating the interplay of these two key variables, Olivola and Shafir observe that painful or effortful fundraisers 'more than make up' for the loss of participants who decline on account of difficulty 'by stimulating larger contributions from those who do participate (not to mention their sponsors)' (Olivola and Shafir 2013: 102).

TSIs do not just put a price on 'suffering' through forgone pleasures and having to listen to increasingly inebriated conversations when they are the only sober person among drinkers. Arguably playing both sides and leaving no opportunity

136   *Alcohol, Binge Sobriety and Exemplary Abstinence*

to fundraise untapped, TSIs also monetize the pleasures of consumption. The purchasable reprieves that are a feature of many TSIs are a way for the campaigns to take advantage of both planned and unanticipated breaks in a participant's commitment to sobriety. The reprieves are a way for philanthropic TSIs to eliminate a potential barrier to participation among prospective participants and thus their fundraising potential. Thanks to the allowance, special occasions that one knows about in advance and that one may want to celebrate while consuming alcohol can still be accommodated.

Many participants (and members of the community at large) nonetheless regard these reprieves as cheating both the intended social or health outcomes of the initiatives and on the implicit philanthropic contract participants strike with their sponsors (see Chapter 8). To counter these imputations, philanthropic TSIs attempt to reinforce discourses of charity over cheating: 'A Golden Ticket gives a Dry July participant a night off their challenge. For a minimum cost of $25, their night off will still make a difference to the lives of people affected by cancer' (Dry July 2020). Where Dry July charges no registration fee, some participants may paradoxically make their only monetary contribution to an abstinence-based fundraiser via paying for permission to drink.

The most successful philanthropic TSIs have devised ways to raise funds from nearly every aspect of their operations. Model participants who succeed in abstaining as defiant figures in their social groups can reap the benefits of their martyrdom, while those who cannot go the full duration will still pay for their indulgence. Participants can also band together, pulling those who may have been less likely to sign up – and fundraise – on their own into the fold. By accounting for each of these scenarios in their structure and communications, philanthropic TSIs recognize that there can be many examples of how to complete the dry month and contribute to their cause.

Building a support base

The final major aim of TSIs as philanthropic undertakings is to generate support and adherence so that they can fulfil both their social and charitable objectives. With myriad community needs and a limit to the number of possible causes that can be supported with one's time, efforts and finances, charities compete not only against each other but against many other organizations and initiatives (Schmitz 2020). For philanthropic TSIs – in contrast to those whose objectives prioritize changing drinking cultures – not all projects of alcoholic abstention are equal.

Selfish Philanthropists, Selfish Abstainers 137

By virtue of their success, TSIs have generated their own competition in the form of imitators (Bennett and Savani 2011). Within a single national context, it is quite common to have several TSIs operate either at different points in the year or even at the same time. The UK, for instance, has both Dry January and Dryathlon operating during January, Go Sober running its main campaign in October, and both Dryathlon and Go Sober (both fundraising for major cancer charities) have more recently launched smaller-scale initiatives in September and March, respectively. Australia has done better in spreading out its dry months across the calendar (February, July and October), aligning them with different causes and in playing to concentrations of regional support for particular initiatives.[2]

The factors that influence support for one cause or another may speak to a potential donor's altruistic aims, for instance, the ratio of administrative costs or the effectiveness of the programmes supported (MacAskill 2016). Others, however, are likely to be more reflective of personal tastes, capacity and inclination: whether or not one has a personal connection to a cause, what is required to participate and whether that is within someone's capacity or will to contribute. Non-altruistic motivations for charity abound; they range from tax incentives to societal expectations to peer pressure.

Among the non-altruistic motivations for charity – and for donations to particular causes or fundraisers – are the positive affective states that result from both giving and from effortful tasks. Economist James Andreoni (1989, 1990) argues that we experience a 'warm glow' after having done something charitable, and it is this positive feeling that provides subsequent incentive to do so. Simply put, we tend to (and want to) feel good about doing something nice. There is also a sense of accomplishment that comes from succeeding in a challenging task. Success provides an affective 'high' of self-congratulation and can inspire people to feel good, even proud, about their effort.

In defiance of purely rationalist theories that would have us seek out the best return on investment in terms of effort for reward, trends have seen supporters and donors look for effortful and challenging, but arguably more meaningful, ways to support a cause. Rather than simply making a monetary contribution to a worthy cause, a gesture that takes little effort and should provide social kudos and the sought-after warm glow, donors are seeking out more engaged forms of commitment. Giving circles, for instance, involve participants in vetting processes and exacting deliberations about where to direct pooled contributions (Eikenberry 2009). Activity-based charity challenges often require not only a major effort to complete the event, but many also demand months of training to develop the requisite fitness. In such cases, the participant's reward is not only the warm glow but also tangible tokens of recognition: finisher's medals or T-shirts. Targeting this combination of feelings is relatively common, especially in embodied philanthropy and sporting charity challenges. A narrative of model participation, generally found in testimonials that serve as exemplars for future participants, may even identify these feelings as expected. These narratives reference such feelings and enshrine the positive affect as an anticipated reward for effortful participation.

In the case of philanthropic TSIs, the main non-altruistic motivations that attract support and participants are identical to those of their socially oriented counterparts: personal health and wellness and the kudos that come from being seen to be responsible. Regardless of their place on the spectrum of philanthropic or social orientation, TSIs openly appeal to participants by touting the health benefits of a month-long break from alcohol: the potential to shed excess festive or comfort-food induced weight; and improved sleep, energy levels, mental clarity and productivity are staples of TSI discourse and marketing. The ability to train or work out with greater intensity has also been promoted, often via testimonials (FebFast 2015; Dry January 2017; Macdonald 2018).

The benefits most often touted to entice participation tend to focus on outwardly observable effects that reinforce conventional ideas of attractiveness (e.g. weight loss, improved complexion) or healthy living. Early iterations of FebFast, for instance, celebrated these benefits in terms such as 'get beach hot!' (FebFast 2013) that intersected with more appearance- or style-motivated philanthropic initiatives such as Movember. The outward signs of benefit reinforce a public pedagogy based on an action with a positive outcome that is observable as an example for self and others. These signs, if commented upon, are also conducive to the awareness-raising conversation, albeit where awareness is centred more on the means of achieving the philanthropic ends than the cause itself.

Specific health-oriented but less readily observable claims are also common for TSIs. IkPas (2020) promotes emotional and psychological improvements while Tipaton Tammikuu (Ehkäisevän Päidetyön Järjestöverkosto 2020) reminds participants of the link between alcohol and mental health and suggests that a month away from alcohol can strengthen mental health capabilities, such as awareness, interpersonal skills and problem-solving. The Finnish TSI is also explicit about the connection between alcohol and immune function, noting that participants could strengthen their immune system by drinking less. As might be expected from Go Dry, the fundraiser for the American Liver Foundation

(2020), the cited health benefits focus on chronic disease prevention and hepatic function.

With their emphasis on self-improvement and personal benefit, which ranges from the epidemiologically verifiable to the purely affective, TSIs cater in obvious ways to mixed motives for philanthropy and, when taking the social objectives of TSIs into account as well, a larger sense of public good. Without imposing a totalizing definition of 'public good', Jane Mansbridge argues that philanthropic engagement has come to depend upon a 'nesting' of private benefits within initiatives that serve public ends. Within such scenarios, 'the motives of altruism and self-interest remain distinct, but the material benefits that meet self-interested desires or needs facilitate altruistic action' (Mansbridge 1998: 14).

If philanthropic TSIs share the same non-altruistic benefits as their socially oriented counterparts, it nonetheless begs the question of why participants – unless motivated by altruism – would choose a campaign that required them to fundraise or contribute a personal registration fee/donation. Asking for donations is, after all, a frequent source of discomfort or awkwardness for participants in charity events and embodied philanthropy (Filo et al. 2020). For some, there are practical reasons such as timing and critical mass to consider. A number of Australian participants noted that Dry January – despite not requiring or expecting fundraising – would be unrealistic given its timing in the heart of the southern summer. Kerry, a reasonably heavy drinker, noted a preference for the humour of Dry July and how the campaign's clear prioritization of philanthropy didn't make her feel bad about her regular drinking habits. Kate, whose first TSI experience was with Ocsober, declined to repeat it in favour of the more philanthropically oriented Dry July because her friends had opted for that particular TSI. The British context offers would-be participants a clearer choice between a socially oriented and philanthropic campaign, as Dry January and Dryathlon operate at the same time. In settings such as Canada and Australia, though, where philanthropic TSIs predominate, participants often grapple with the nesting of altruistic and non-altruistic objectives.

Confessions of selfish philanthropists

TSIs, especially those with a philanthropic component, are adept at holding the multiple objectives of their campaigns in productive tension. The common aims of awareness, fundraising and building a support base are well served by what is a relatively universal formula for embodied participation. Despite the multiple utilities to the organization and the campaign (to say nothing of the causes) that accrue through participation, TSI participants are often under the impression that they are not contributing as they should. Via their reflections on their perceived shortcomings, participants interpret TSI objectives and articulate their own views of what it means to engage in charitable or philanthropic projects, especially those of an embodied nature. Noting that exemplarity must be understood as such by an audience for its status as a model to be confirmed, participant commentary provides great insight into what 'exemplary philanthropic TSI participation' entails.

Across my interviews with TSI participants, the word 'selfish' became a curious and frequent refrain in the context of a discussion about motivations:

> So to me that is a concern, that I'm not raising enough money. Although I guess if there's 10,000 people each raising $100 then it's not too bad. But – okay, this really is honest – my prime reason for doing FebFast is for myself and not raising money. That is really selfish because here I am saying that I am selfless but I am selfish in that it's for me – it's a chance to detox and get off the booze for a month. – Rebecca

> Yeah, so that's why, it was purely selfish motivation that I felt – I really felt ill in a way, and unhealthy. – Brad

> I mean firstly it's for selfish reasons. Because I'm doing something good for my health. But it just seems to be – yeah so that's the main reason for doing it. It's like oh well, good, a month off. But then knowing that – I think throughout the month I felt like I contemplated more often what it must be like to be addicted to something. – Bethany

Without using the word itself, a number of participants also spoke to their primary motivations being health-related. Statements of this kind contrast participant behaviour with what these same participants perceive exemplary TSI participation to be. Whether explicit or implied, self-accusations always arose from a conflict between a belief that one should be raising money for or engaging sympathetically with the cause and personal motivations having to do with health or productivity.

There are several possibilities to explain how participants come to believe in compulsory philanthropy or fundraising. Following the managerial mantra that 'whatever is measured is what matters', the tracking and publicizing of the fundraising tally may tacitly communicate that the primary objective for the

Selfish Philanthropists, Selfish Abstainers

TSIs themselves is financial. By comparison, other possible measures – drinks not consumed, kilos shed, hours of additional sleep – would be hard to quantify, potentially inaccurate given the tendency of heavier drinkers to under-report their consumption and rarely of significance except for the individual. As such, these tallies do not figure in official TSI discourse.

Some event-style fundraisers also require a minimum contribution or fundraising tally per participant. It is not uncommon, for instance, for charity places in major marathons or dedicated fitness charity challenges to require a substantial fundraising tally from the participant, lest their spot be forfeited (Edwards and Kreshel 2008). While TSIs do not set similar conditions of participation, the ubiquity of the practice in embodied philanthropy circles may foster a transfer of ideas from one context to its analogues.

Participants' inwardly directed accusations do not tend to centre on a failure to achieve a particular fundraising outcome but, rather, focus on their own motives. Curiously, their self-criticism holds, irrespective of the amount of money raised. Rebecca, for instance, was sheepish about having only raised $95 (in addition to her registration fee of $25). By contrast, Bethany raised several hundred dollars, and Brad succeeded in raising approximately $600. Where FebFast organizers observed that roughly a quarter of participants that year did no fundraising and contributed only their registration fee to charity, these participants' contributions are far from negligible. Indeed, for comparison, participants in the 2011 campaign, which was analysed by Hillgrove and Thomson (2012), would have been in the top 10 per cent of fundraisers had they raised $600. Participants nonetheless weighed their philanthropic outcomes against their intent and concluded that their efforts and overall tallies were paltry.

The feelings of selfishness for having not raised much money were especially acute for those who decided to fundraise as part of a team. Lori was part of a team of five, consisting mostly of her family, and reported on both her team's fundraising tally and her own contributions to that total: 'My team raised $800. But me personally, I only raised $75 (I think it was). I was doing it for more purely selfish reasons. Health reasons [more] than the actual cause, which I think a lot of people do.' Extracting her own tally from that of her team and comparing their respective contributions led her to feel as though she was not an equitable contributor, especially as a third of her total came from her buying a leave pass for her sister's wedding. Her self-impugning therefore encompasses two sources of guilt. On the one hand, there is a feeling of letting down her team via an unequal contribution: the behavioural economic concept of freeriding

(Olson 1965). On the other, she identifies a 'cheater's' reason (a time-out pass) as the source of a significant share of her meagre tally.

Informal TSI participants (those who followed the TSI model but were in no way affiliated with a formal campaign), such as Liz and Alan, represent an appropriation of the ostensibly philanthropic TSI for purely personal reasons. For these participants, the focus is solely on themselves, their health and their relationship with alcohol. While Liz was clear that her decision to go sober for a month was based on the timing of her realization that she wanted and needed to do something about her drinking, Alan chose to be sober in August because there would still be a 'tail' of people who had done Dry July extending their sobriety, but there would be no expectation for him to fundraise. Where he found the idea of fundraising to be off-putting and was thus a deterrent for him going dry for July, there was still a recognition that collective and charitable action provided a legitimating excuse. Rather than freeriding in a conventional way (simply choosing not to fundraise but participating under the banner of the philanthropic endeavour), he opted to benefit from the social legitimation of the TSI in a manner once removed. Unlike the 'selfish' donors and fundraisers described above, however, neither Liz nor Alan expressed feelings of falling short of expectations for not raising any money or linking their abstinence to a cause. It is unclear if independently organized dry months would be conceived of in the same way in non-Australian contexts where purely socially oriented TSIs are either more common or are the only model available.

Dean argues that philanthropic engagement carries a symbolic power, 'an automatic assumption of goodness' (Dean 2020: 3), that can be both positive and negative. In contrast to the 'warm glow' that donors experience for carrying out altruistic acts, the 'good glow' of philanthropy is an outward symbol for others that one both *is* and *is doing* good. The ascribed demonstrability of charity positions the donor, volunteer or participant as a laudable, selfless figure. In many cases, this is precisely the outcome that both charities and supporters seek, as it offers the proverbial 'win-win' scenario. The symbolic power of charity can nevertheless lead people to misappropriate it by freeriding. For TSI participants motivated by health or social objectives, the good glow of philanthropy takes on another negative inflection, as it is experienced as a burden that induces a sense of guilt or shame for deriving personal benefit from an act that is supposed to assist others. The fact that it is perceived as such speaks to a number of, in no way mutually exclusive, explanations.

First (and more generally), people outside the third sector still cling to a largely stereotyped and unrealistic expectation that altruism must be pure to be beneficial or effective. Mike Martin explores this tendency in depth, noting that 'the first whiff of self-interest evokes charges of hypocrisy' (Martin 1994: xi). He nonetheless argues that the combination of self-concern and altruism that is characteristic of 'mixed motives' for philanthropy is not only pervasive but 'also usually acceptable and even desirable' (ibid., 123). Many participants in philanthropic TSIs, especially where the local context provides no alternative to TSIs that have some philanthropic remit, nonetheless remain unaware or unconvinced of this view.

Second (and more particular to embodied philanthropy centring on fitness or abstention), participants' actions towards neo-liberal health and wellness imperatives are subordinated to the assumed obligation to fulfil 'civic duties' of the philanthropic kind. While health and wellness efforts can be construed as broadly prosocial contributions in their own right insofar as they are likely to lessen the demand on health and social services according to preventative health and risk logics, contributions of this kind are largely invisible and unquantifiable. By way of analogy, the popular recognition and structural prominence accorded to preventative health interventions such as proper sanitation and lifestyle have long paled in comparison to the celebrated status of 'silver bullets' or acute care interventions such as miracle drugs or life-saving surgeries (Marvasti and Stafford 2012). This is because acts or products that prevent people from falling ill, and thus presenting for care, not only fail to lend themselves to heroic narratives and press coverage but also resist quantification. As Robert Frank argues of 'drop in the bucket' gifts (Frank 1996: 136), contributions that cannot be accounted for in terms of impact produce little discernible benefit (i.e. good glow) for the donor. TSI participants are thus more likely to ignore any benefit their modified behaviour produces in terms of health (and even more so in relation to its role in effecting social change) and instead see only their lack of or modest fundraising as a failed obligation.

Third, philanthropy has implications for how participants conceive of themselves as individuals and as social actors. Radley and Kennedy (1995) contend that charitable involvement and donations are expressions of an individual's relationship to society as much as (if not more than) a personal act. The relational character of the philanthropic engagement is therefore of paramount importance. Extending on this work, Mohan and Breeze hypothesize that the actual nuance and complexity of these relations can often be overshadowed by the persistent fallacy that 'charity is viewed as something that exists for the benefit of "other people" rather than the reality that most of us are both donors and recipients' (Mohan and Breeze 2016: 14). This false dichotomy tying charitable involvement to an either/or identity position as giver *or* receiver of charity, argue Nettleton and Hardy, is exacerbated by medical charities that partner with sport or fitness charity fundraisers that layer further binaries onto embodied charitable participation through 'the spectacle of fit bodies generating funds for those with "needy" bodies' (Nettleton and Hardy 2006: 447). The generous and healthy in such scenarios give to those who need both charity and cure.

For TSIs with philanthropic components, the lines between donor and beneficiary, healthy and unhealthy, are both blurred and potentially stigmatized. Many become participants precisely because they seek to become healthful or more in control of their relationship with alcohol. Liz, Janelle and Brad, for instance, had all taken on the challenge of a TSI as a way to prove to themselves and others that they were still able to control their drinking and that they were not alcohol-dependent. Dryuary participants also knowingly commit to a moderation-based mutual/self-help initiative. Short of these more extreme cases, participants tend to draw from their TSI experience a realization that they can improve their relationship with alcohol, if only because of a temporary (such as a holiday-related) excess.

According to the still pervasive binaries of (health-related) philanthropy, these participants were not 'healthy', but they could still construe themselves as better off than others, including any beneficiaries of the charity their abstinence supports. The distinction between being the giver and the receiver of charity is therefore the only one that holds. It accordingly takes on proportionally greater importance for participants who can use it to buttress the identity position that participation itself weakens. If participants cannot be assured that they are healthy (not 'irresponsible' drinkers), they can at least gain confidence that they are charitable. By being charitable, they satisfy at least one of the conditions that warrants an assumption of goodness. Hence, philanthropy helps participants to protect their self-conception as 'good' and 'socially responsible'. When participants perceive themselves as failing a campaign's philanthropic objectives by not raising (enough) money, the self-judgement can be especially harsh, as it speaks to these questions of identity – as both good person and one in control of their relationship with alcohol – more than it does to a fundraising tally.

A context where concerns about not being sufficiently altruistic or charitable come into sharp relief concerns what to do with any financial savings from a dry month. Nearly all TSIs, philanthropic and socially oriented, trumpet financial savings as an incentive to go dry. They prompt participants and would-be participants to consider what they could do with the money not spent on alcohol.

Socially oriented TSIs openly celebrate the purely 'selfish' aspect of abstaining and licence reinvestment into one's other passions or desires, such as a dinner at a fancy restaurant or a trip. Alcohol Free for 40's sponsor, Oschner Health, links to a comprehensive article on the financial benefits of sobriety that encourages participants to 'reward themselves' with 'a standing massage appointment, new appliances, or a wardrobe upgrade' (Fuller 2021). The suggestion that temporary abstainers should spend their savings on non-essential items or small luxuries helps to differentiate TSIs from earlier temperance campaigns that deplored the resources (typically money that would go to support a family) that were wasted on alcohol and framed drink as that which robbed households of their necessities (Blainey 2000). It also points to the differentiated class emphasis of TSIs versus prior temperance campaigns, for TSI participants tend to be and address the middle class and preferences for allocating discretionary income to obvious markers of status.

For philanthropic TSIs, the question of what to do with the proceeds of sobriety is more vexed and a potential source of guilt. Participants interviewed as part of this study put their savings towards clothing, travel, a new television, paying down debt and enjoying fancier dining experiences than usual. Others simply lost track of the money they saved. Janelle confessed to being 'a bit slack' about her fundraising and to having little to show for any savings, as she found herself eating out more often. Mark was more philosophical when asked what he did with the money that he saved:

> This is the tension, the natural tension with something like a charity fundraiser. Part of it is for a community, holistic benefit so you support the cause. The second is a more selfish thing. I think everyone works on those two levels. So yeah, like anyone, kind of happy to enjoy some of the money saved myself, as well as the cause.

Mark's response is representative of an accepted but paradoxical truth within philanthropic TSIs. These initiatives regularly balance the financial benefit to others and the benefit to self, and participants find themselves weighing questions of how these savings are shared against the incentive for participation that savings provide.

TSI participants give an important insight into their experience and perception of what exemplary TSI participation, at least in the context of philanthropic campaigns, is meant to entail. While unaffiliated and purely socially oriented TSIs may be unaffected by expectations of fundraising, their philanthropic counterparts engender significant and sometimes disproportionate expectations about charitable contributions. Participants in these campaigns can show considerable affective but often less financial investment or effort in the exemplar of the self-sacrificing fundraiser. They nonetheless elevate the expectation of fundraising above other TSI objectives because fundraising is quantified and given prominence by the organizations as a measure of their – and their participants' – success.

Responsiveness and adaptation

Participant expectations, conditioned by normative examples of what is required for embodied philanthropy and participatory events such as TSIs, have influenced not only their experiences of the campaigns but the structure of the campaigns themselves. Their reckoning with the tensions between a TSI's philanthropic and social objectives has led to TSIs changing, both reflecting and catering to these expectancies. TSIs with previously strong social and pedagogical messages have acceded to an expectation of fundraising to either launch or become more emphatic with their fundraising efforts. Conversely, philanthropic TSIs have followed participants' 'selfishness' to reprioritize social and health objectives. While some of these shifts have been temporary, retrospectively conceived (typically when either fully or partially reversed) to be something of a misstep, there has nonetheless been a movement towards greater consistency of participant experience among TSIs.

Spurred by the success of some early philanthropic TSIs, a number of campaigns have increased their focus on fundraising. Dry July – which began as an unapologetically philanthropic undertaking – was the first transnational TSI, and its emphasis on fundraising largely sets the tone for similar campaigns in the English-speaking world. The other TSIs that launched in Australia in 2008, including FebFast which preceded it, nonetheless also had fundraising objectives. This is not entirely coincidental and suggests that a degree of philanthropic orientation was a baseline expectation for many contemporary TSIs.[3] With this expectation so firmly entrenched, a number of campaigns with a more dominant social orientation have acquiesced to the incorporation of a fundraising element.

The charitable implications of TSIs are most often analysed in terms of the implicit philanthropic contract between the participant and those who pledge money to support their abstaining. Qualitative studies tend to note that participants attribute a portion of their success in remaining sober throughout the month to the public commitment that they made and that was endorsed via pledged donations. Vi, for instance, acknowledged the commitment itself as a pact: 'I know you don't sign a contract but knowing I've signed on to do something, I'm not going to break that because that's just the way it goes. You don't do that. If you start something, you finish it.' Janelle was similarly cognizant of the way the commitment to the cause and those sponsoring her provided a framework of integrity that she leaned upon when tempted to drink: 'There was [*sic*] definitely moments . . . when it could have just been like, "I'll just have a sneaky drink and no one would know about it" and stuff but there's definitely – I don't know, there's definitely a pride thing and it's like an honour system.' Such experiences are common enough that Cherrier and Gurrieri (2013) have generalized the norm of exchange or accountability between participant and sponsors, but also between participants and the TSI organization which provides them with support. Their finding is also similar to the insight that participants in philanthropic endurance sporting events (such as marathons) use the charity and the good it will do, including for beneficiaries whose circumstances they may have come to better understand at an empathetic level, as a motivation to help them through the gruelling training and to complete the event itself (Bunds et al. 2016).

Findings based on quantitative data, which are not as influenced by a self-selection bias for successful participants, suggest that fundraising and a philanthropic connection may not be as impactful as suggested. In a larger-scale quantitative study, rates of successful completion of Dry January were not found to differ significantly between those who engaged in fundraising and those who did not (de Visser et al. 2016). A caveat to this finding, however, may be that Dry January has not traditionally emphasized fundraising, and its messaging has always centred on the benefit to oneself (Yeomans 2019), and to a lesser extent society as a whole, rather than on the beneficiaries of fundraising efforts or commitment to one's sponsors.

Still, Dry January has incorporated and increased its promotion of opportunities for philanthropy. While Alcohol Concern had always been a registered charity that encouraged donations from the public, they partnered with Virgin Money Giving in 2016 to allow participants to fundraise for a charity of their choice. Proceeds would be split between Alcohol Concern and the participant's nominated charity (May 2016). The organization has since moved away from formal association with high-profile online giving platforms, which have been criticized for the administrative charges they collect (Lepper 2018), and has instead opted to allow charities to associate with Dry July as a fundraiser in exchange for a set fee of either £100 or £1,000, commensurate with the charity's reported income (Alcohol Change UK 2020a). It is also worth noting that none of Alcohol Change UK's or Dry January's international partners or analogue programmes in France, Switzerland or the Netherlands, which tend to operate as the only TSI in their national contexts, incorporate this option for fundraising.

Addressing both participants and registered charities, the incorporation of a philanthropic element responds to community demand. Individuals and organizations see the dry month as a way to raise funds for causes they esteem, and Alcohol Change has been able to piggyback on this belief, even if its own core tenet prioritizes changed alcohol behaviours and attitudes over fundraising. The shift in practice suggests that despite early evidence that charitable involvement makes no meaningful difference to successful completion, there is a recognition that the possibility of altruism is meaningful for some of the already committed and/or that it may be a way to recruit additional participants, especially where they can direct the funds they raise to an organization other than Alcohol Change or, in light of competition from Dryathlon, Cancer Research UK. Where philanthropy is increasingly characterized by donors and/or fundraisers wanting a say in where and how their contributions are directed (Eikenberry 2009), Dry January has in some ways integrated even more flexibility than Dry July, where participants can choose which cancer treatment centre or local hospital will benefit from their fundraising efforts.

Dry January's partnerships with charities and its own fundraising efforts have remained secondary to its focus on public pedagogy and behaviour change, but this has not been the case for all socially oriented TSIs that pivoted towards philanthropy. Ocsober had been similarly oriented, but a significant cut to the government funding that supported Life Education (Doran 2017), the organization running Ocsober, meant that the 2017 campaign was reoriented to respond to new financial pressures. Philanthropy accordingly became a greater organizational impetus, and participants were asked to work towards a fundraising target of AU$700 (Life Education Australia 2017).

Fundraising targets of this kind are not unusual in event-based embodied philanthropy (e.g. marathon running, large-scale walks), which typically require significant logistical support and organization costs, and therefore set a target not as a suggestion but as a minimum contribution to secure a spot in limited capacity events. This strategy ensures commitment to and results for the cause but can engender exclusion, often along socio-economic lines. This is because one's networks (or one's own pockets) must be able to supply the necessary donations. While Ocsober participation was not limited in the same way, either logistically or as policy, the $700 target asked (but not required) of participants acted as an obstacle to participation. Where the TSI's principal messages were about the health benefits of forgoing alcohol and the social good that could come via Life Education's school-based programmes, the emphasis on fundraising was discordant with its larger communications strategy, as exemplified by its social media presence, which better aligned with participants' 'selfish' motivations around health and wellness.

Just as some socially oriented TSIs capitalized on the expected link between temporary sobriety and fundraising, philanthropic TSIs also found themselves reprioritizing what had previously been secondary concerns to better align with participant expectations. Health and wellness had from the outset been acknowledged as excellent incentives, or at the least outcomes, for participants. Yet philanthropic TSIs have over the years shifted their messaging and operations to acquiesce to the pull of the non-altruistic motivations for this particular brand of embodied philanthropy.

Dry July's original pitch was predicated on the idea of martyrdom: three friends, typical guys who enjoyed drinking, decided (in a bar) that they would raise money through their sacrifice. It is worth noting that Dry July does not levy a registration fee, a strategy concordant with the practice of socially oriented TSIs in that it lowers barriers to participation. In the context of an unabashed philanthropic TSI, however, it also signals that abstinence is, in and of itself, the participant's contribution to the cause. In the early years, the exemplary Dry July participant was one similar to the founders themselves: people who could exemplify the martyrdom of abstaining necessary for fundraising. In 2010, for instance, Australian celebrity chef and restaurateur Neil Perry was acclaimed as an ambassador and top fundraiser. The foundation's annual report touted not only the AU$28,000 fundraising total from a man who had access to some of the best wine cellars in the country, but the boost received by an AU$10,000 donation from businessman James Packer (Dry July Foundation 2011: 9), who admitted some years later to having battled alcohol addiction at the time.

As Dry July grew and more participants celebrated the health and wellness benefits they enjoyed as a result of participating, the organization amplified these less altruistic discourses. In 2013, the year that marked Dry July's fifth consecutive year of strong participant and revenue growth, wellness e-newsletters had become a popular part of the communication strategy. In 2014, a wellness 'micro-site' featuring tips for health, exercise, mindfulness and mocktail recipes was launched. Dry July had, to some extent, remodelled its notion of an exemplary participant from one who thoroughly enjoyed drinking but valiantly gave it up for a month in service of a cause to one who was focused on their health. While the micro-site was very popular with participants, the fundraising total that year slipped back to its 2012 levels (Dry July 2015b).

Dry July's 2015 campaign accordingly saw a reinvestment in fundraising efforts and a return to emphasizing the philanthropic work made possible by donations. The continued promotion of Golden Tickets, the new allowances for a shorter Dry-ish July and the renewed focus on the philanthropic objectives and outcomes via their communications to participants have continued to prioritize philanthropic activity as a focus and relegated the health outcomes to an incidental benefit. Earnest messaging about health and wellness has also been curtailed in favour of a return to the larrikinism that underpinned the earlier discourses centred on martyrdom and fundraising. The annual reports for 2017 and 2018 tellingly give pride of place (just below the mission and vision statements) to a noteworthy fact about the Foundation: 'We have Beer o'Clock on Fridays (but not in July)' (Dry July Foundation 2017: 3).

Following Dry July's retreat from the pole of health and a return to being a more philanthropic TSI, FebFast more decisively claimed the ground at the opposite end of the spectrum, a move that suggests a greater UK-style polarization of social and philanthropic TSIs in the Australian context. FebFast had always charged participants a registration fee, and this fee was an important source of revenue for the organization. Starting in 2019, however, registration fees were waived. This significant change was an acknowledgement that many of their participants were motivated by more 'selfish' rationales and that the registration fee was acting as a barrier to participation, ironically to support a cause that was fundamentally about eliminating drug and alcohol dependence. The decision to abandon the registration fee but still encourage fundraising redefines exemplary participation in this TSI to conform to participant preferences.

Conclusion

TSIs are exemplars of embodied philanthropy insofar as they are designed to simultaneously, but not always perfectly coherently, cater to a variety of participant motivations and campaign objectives. Performative non-drinking functions as the impetus for participants to solicit pledges on behalf of charitable endeavours and, in the process, to showcase themselves as charitably oriented individuals who are demonstrably committed to a worthwhile cause.

Philanthropy can nonetheless be a source of motivation for participants, who draw upon their quasi-public commitment and the implicit contract they have struck with their supporters to see them live up to the version of themselves they, ostensibly, committed to be.

The idealized image of the selfless philanthropist who puts their body, social life and enjoyment of normal activities on the line for charity nonetheless proves a burden for many participants. Even when successful in both the abstinence and philanthropic actions required by TSIs, they find themselves resisting the kudos of charity because they perceive themselves as gaining more from the experience than they give back, whether these gains are financial or purely the intangibles of health and personal challenge. TSIs must therefore calibrate their messaging and positioning to address both what motivates participants and what will fulfil campaign objectives. Efforts by TSIs to adjust their messaging and structure to accommodate either a greater or lesser focus on philanthropy have yielded mixed results. The dialogic nature of this process suggests that exemplars, even among TSIs, are not universal and just as easily weigh upon participants as they inspire them.

8

Unruly examples

Examples are at the core of TSIs' approach to public pedagogy. Instantiated and expressively referenced, the sober participant is a lesson to both others and a future self, inspiring imitation as a responsible, healthful, temperate (but not too temperate) and potentially even charitable figure. TSIs may be considered mass movements, whose participants serve as a collective example of how changes that had traditionally required regulatory intervention are possible as a popular cultural movement. Or at least that is the official story.

As TSI organizers can attest, the illustrative power of an example, or a rather a counterexample, can just as easily work against their objectives as it can serve them. A participant's affective and lived experience, regardless of whether they were successful, unsuccessful or too successful in completing their period of sobriety, can reinforce entrenched beliefs for the participants and for observers and perpetuate rather than dispel myths about both drinking and episodic abstinence. Depending on the relationship between someone's views and the outcome of their personal TSI experiment, the intended example of the philanthropic, self-responsibilizing drinker may never be realized and counterexamples may prove more instructive and persuasive. As such, these examples can be classified as unruly and, given the somewhat self-propagating nature of mass exemplarity in the age of social media and with the proliferation of niche media, become difficult examples to manage.

Many of the challenges and criticisms TSIs face stem from the impact of examples that do less than desired or more than intended. Based on anecdote and often confirming either the status quo or the apprehensions about what might happen, counterexamples tend to take on the status of myths or urban legends that may be at cross-purposes with the objectives, generally the socially oriented ones, of TSIs. As in many debates in allegedly 'post-truth' societies, the counterexample can prevail for participants and observers alike, even when contradicted by (sometimes large-scale) empirical research.

This chapter approaches the question of counterexamples, both ascribed and extant, through participants' interpretations of their experiences. Central to the investigation is the self-narrative component of imitation and learning by example, which accounts for why we are most likely to imitate examples that concord with our sense of ourselves or who we aspire to be. The exploration begins with the two most common critiques of TSIs – that they allow people with genuine alcohol dependencies to deny their problems and that they promote binge drinking – that have become the mainstay of cynical media commentary. These responses to TSIs tend to assume that TSIs reinforce a polarity of drinking behaviours over moderation rather than viewing temporary abstinence as a means to promote moderation. The role of counterexamples is then analysed at the level of participants, their own assumptions and hypotheses about drinking, temporary sobriety and the campaigns themselves, as well as the conclusions they and others draw based on their individualized example. While far from being common, these counterexamples can be disproportionately powerful, especially where TSIs are already seen as ineffective or antithetical to social norms or the objectives they purport to promote.

The power of the counterexample

Why are some examples of human behaviour more readily imitated than others? Why do violent movies or video games not inspire murder on a mass scale while celebrity fashion trends send millions of consumers to the shops to style themselves in accordance with the models? Warnick (2008) contends that the imitation of human examples, an outcome that can be deliberate or even seemingly involuntary, is fundamentally dependent on who we understand and experience ourselves to be. Deliberate imitation often speaks to consequentialism: simply that we seek to imitate when we value the outcomes. We willingly follow a chef's recipe and techniques to cook a dish that looks and tastes like theirs.

For the less deliberate forms of imitation, those that are more automatic and less rationally driven, Warnick posits that the relationship between an example and a narrative sense of self is what determines whether or not we will replicate the example. Drawing on the work of William James, as well as cognitive scientists and psychologists, he ventures: 'Those perceptions of human action that provoke imitation are those that are classified in a way so as to be non incompatible with the narrative senses of self and that exist within an enabling context that allows the imitation to take place' (Warnick 2008: 73). Nuancing the double negative, he argues that *unless* the example is incongruent with our narrative senses of self, we will default to imitation. In short, an example need not be overtly compatible with who we perceive ourselves to be for it to be imitated, almost unbidden.

The 'narrative senses of self' refers to who we tell ourselves we are and who we know ourselves to be, like, dislike, are capable of and so on, based on our personal experiences and values, as well as conditions such as cultural norms and regulations that we are conditioned to operate within. The resultant narrative senses (noting the plural) of self need not be unitary or coherent, as there can be different elements that come to the fore, and thus influence whether an example will hold sway or not, depending on the circumstances (Warnick 2008: 64). Just like the multiple instantiations of a body engaged in embodied philanthropy then, these different narratives of self often hang together loosely as part of a whole, unified but messy as it may be. There are nonetheless processes of sense-making that take place, both for subjects and for observers, where some elements of these narratives take priority over others.

Where background and cultural norms play a significant role in shaping narrative senses of self, examples that reinforce these practices are more likely to concord with common elements of the self-narratives in a given population. For instance, if the default position for adults in a society is to be amenable to drinking when an alcoholic beverage is offered, this expectation is likely to be part of a relatively common sense of self, and the example is liable to be imitated without much thought unless regulations (not drinking or drinking too much before driving), obligations (being sober while working) or convention (not drinking before noon) take precedence. Indeed, what we understand as being a 'social drinker' would likely have been learnt by example (imitating popular culture, parents, peers).[1] One's own experiences, those of a prior self, would also set an imitable example unless in some way contradicted, a situation that speaks to the persistence of habits and the pervasiveness of our own personal norms.

The premise of TSIs, whether socially oriented or philanthropic, is to have participants, first, purposefully defy the commonly accepted cultural norms of drinking and their own earlier examples. In doing so, they are then expected to reformulate their narrative senses of self in such a way that sobriety, temperance and self-sacrifice, all of which were adopted as part of the TSI experience, become imitable examples for the future. TSIs do not expect that participants will rewrite their self-narratives entirely, for instance, refashioning themselves as teetotallers, merely add to them such that the earlier version is tempered by their episodic temperance.

The prompt for this rewriting can be as the result of consequentialist reasoning, a calculation that one prioritizes the outcomes of reduced alcohol consumption and adjusts behaviour accordingly. This scenario would correspond to both the behaviours and the underpinning rationales of lifestyle movements, where there is hope for a sustained change. More often, however, the following of new examples comes as a kind of default or even a new habit, dimensions that speak to an automaticity of conduct that becomes evident only upon reflection. Most TSIs are agnostic about the means to achieve the ends of more responsible approaches to alcohol, and their websites are typically silent on how these results come about. Only in longer form explanations, such as Booker's (2019) companion guidebook to Dry January, are anything more than simplistic explanations offered. Socially oriented TSIs merely want participants to come to understand themselves and their relationship with alcohol in a changed manner, ideally one more oriented towards restraint.

Intent notwithstanding, the ideal of changed behaviour via recasting one's personal example is not always borne out by reality. If a TSI does not alter a participant's narrative senses of self or does not do so in ways that align with campaign objectives, a participant's lived but temporary example may reinforce views of drinking and alcohol that cleave to their personal or social status quo. The same process of exemplification underpinning TSIs can accordingly produce counterexamples just as – if not more – potent than the examples that align with a TSI's pedagogical aims.

The challenge for TSIs is to overcome the persistence of the status quo when it comes to drinking. This status quo owes to a number of elements, many of which are likely to be thoroughly entangled. There are well-documented affective dimensions, such as enjoyment, pleasure, comfort, solace and stress relief, involved in the consumption of alcohol. Elements of habit or ritual may also be at play, for instance, in after-work drinks or continuing to drink (rather than switching to a non-alcoholic option) if other members of a party are continuing to imbibe. Beliefs, however, are also important elements in the status quo of drinking. Many drinkers, including many of those in the present study, consider themselves to be moderate or responsible drinkers and thus don't see their consumption as requiring modification. Such beliefs tend to be based on both miscalculations about how much they drink (underestimation is rife) and whether those levels correspond with accepted – and epidemiological – definitions of moderation (Kneale and French 2015; Livingston and Callinan 2015). The task that TSIs set for themselves is therefore not an easy one, for the entrenched and largely unacknowledged influence of these factors is likely to result in a range of cognitive biases (confirmation, memory, attentional, approach biases, for instance) that make drinking behaviours and attitudes hard to shift in practice and equally as hard to acknowledge.

The unbidden nature of these cognitive biases means that they function as particularly tricky barriers to be overcome by those who seek deliberate ends, as they highlight the natural points of resistance that must be effectively countered in any process of change (Dawnay and Shah 2005). For instance, proponents of green living who seek to promote behaviour change work with the insights afforded by the theory of confirmation bias and its applications, to better understand the phenomenon and to reduce its practical implications on behaviours (Reidy et al. 2012), especially those which pertain to us directly (Nickerson 1998: 176). Where alcohol is woven into the social and cultural fabric of many societies and is an actor in instances of ritual, celebration, pleasure, stress relief, bonding and grief (among many others), there is an abundance of both personal and social expectation and belief to be overcome.

Research into the role of cognitive biases has found a psychological and behavioural impetus to favour what is already known or expected rather than to embrace change or contravening evidence, especially in relation to behaviours such as drinking that carry additional moral baggage thanks to subtle but lingering temperance affiliations (Wiers et al. 2015). We are therefore likely to persist with established behaviour and to downplay the effect of changes we do make if these changes challenge core understandings of our status quo, for instance, that we are moderate drinkers largely unaffected, at least in the day to day, by alcohol's drawbacks. However, recent experimental studies have begun to examine the effectiveness of cognitive bias modification training in changing drinking behaviours (van Deursen 2019). The findings suggest that interventions focused on those who are motivated to change their behaviour, who are abstinent at the time of the intervention and who have the greatest bias towards alcohol at the outset are those most likely to benefit and to drink less post-intervention (Karno 2018). Since TSIs satisfy a number of these conditions, future research may look to evaluate their influence not only on drinking behaviours but also on attitudes and beliefs about alcohol.

Media myths or publicized counterexamples?

In the years since TSIs first emerged as discernible phenomena, media outlets have become more accepting of them. They have transformed from quirky

158 *Alcohol, Binge Sobriety and Exemplary Abstinence*

human-interest stories to annual features with medical and social legitimacy, including official sponsorship from national public health authorities (this being especially common in the socially oriented TSIs of continental Europe). Despite the overall shift in tenor from TSIs being cast as fringe practices to mainstream movement with pedagogical intent, two common critiques of TSIs continue to feature prominently. These are cited as justification for labelling the initiatives as useless fads at best, potentially problematic pseudo-health campaigns at worst.

On the one hand, sceptics argue that TSIs function as an enabling excuse and provide legitimation for those who have alcohol dependency issues to deny their problems. Much like 'dry drunks' who address the outward behaviours of alcohol dependency but not the underlying mindsets that may occasion their excess consumption (Solberg 1970), binge sobriety is disputed as an answer to binge and other forms of problem drinking. On the other hand, there is an assumption that periods of sobriety licence and promote post-campaign binge drinking. What is often dubbed the 'rebound' is frequently cited as a reason to forgo the period of abstinence in favour of an altogether different approach to alcohol. The logic behind the scepticism stems from TSIs' reinforcement of an overall immoderate approach to alcohol, a sort of 'feast or famine' mentality. In both critiques, there is anecdotal evidence to support these much-publicized cautions. Evidence based upon salient counterexamples is, however, increasingly being displaced or qualified by more systematic analyses. Yet, the counterexamples remain influential among individuals and groups apprehensive about or resistant to TSIs as movements or forms of public pedagogy and still regularly feature as counterpoints in public debates about the utility of temporary sobriety in doing anything more than raising money for charity.

TSI participation among heavy or risky drinkers has emerged as something to be simultaneously celebrated and feared. If an initiative proves successful in helping someone to reduce their drinking, it is championed in terms of results in annual reports, website testimonials and other first-person accounts. The title of a column in the *Guardian Australia* (Alcorn 2019) – 'I was only going to give up alcohol for a month but I wasn't prepared for the impact it had' – is entirely typical of the genre. Such accounts often feature terms like 'wake-up call' and 'revelation' (Booker 2019) and therein are reminiscent of the religious revivals and discourses of American temperance movements associated with the third Great Awakening (Engs 2000). While generally positively received as validation for an individual's choice to drink less in the name of health or other valued objectives, these examples and the discourses that surround them can have the inverse pedagogical effect. As counterexamples, where the initial period of sobriety is framed as the first step towards a dry life or a slippery slope towards wowserism, they can deter potential participants. This tension, for instance, is one that mutual self-help group Moderation Management is at pains to address for a potential membership that is looking to the organization and its model as an alternative to the better-known total abstinence model of Alcoholics Anonymous.

If the opposite situation arises and the TSI has no effect for heavier drinkers, which is to say when their consumption bounces back to pre-campaign or greater levels, the TSI becomes a suspect model and the participant someone with a problem. Published opinion pieces, such as that by Chelsea Flood (2020), provide a counter to the typically optimistic first-person accounts of the immediate post-TSI period: 'Within a week my drinking was as troubling as it had been before the challenge,' she confesses. Such narratives link unfavourable outcomes with spurious motivations for attempting the TSI in the first place and seed fears that temporary abstinence campaigns are little more than a means for dependent drinkers to insulate themselves from legitimate concerns that they need to address their consumption over the longer term. The charge is that TSIs facilitate the very denial that keeps problem drinkers from seeking help to manage their dependency. The very concept of TSIs, based on the potential for counterexamples, is thus for some deeply suspect.

Hello Sunday Morning, a sober-curious organization that assists people to manage their alcohol consumption through a longer period of abstinence than TSIs, labels these concerns as being part of the 'dark side' of TSIs: 'It can gaslight a problem. By completing a month off the booze, you can fool yourself and others that all's well . . . nothing to see here . . . keep moving along ("I could not have lasted for a month off the grog if I had an actual problem with alcohol, surely?")' (Hello Sunday Morning 2019, ellipses in original). Parodying the thoughts or words of the person undertaking a dry month for what are framed as 'all the wrong reasons', the language serves as a warning to the reader. It uses the stark term of a form of emotional abuse centred on inciting delusional thinking to highlight the seriousness of the problem should the discourse sound too familiar.

Where TSIs are in part marketed as a tool to help people reassess or redefine their relationship with alcohol, it is hardly surprising that heavier drinkers are over-represented among participants compared to the general population (de Visser et al. 2016; Hillgrove and Thomson 2012). Janelle's motivations, for example, are emblematic of the concern:

I think there was a lot of me [that] wanted to prove that I could do it, I think. That was a big deal because, like I said, in my social group we probably would be drinking nearly every day so I was like 'oh – like, I wanted to know' – I wanted to make sure that I wasn't dependent on it. So to be able to get through the twenty-eight days was a really important thing.

In this summation of her rationale, the TSI was initially conceived as a high-stakes diagnostic whereby she would either pass (not alcohol-dependent) or fail (alcohol-dependent) based on whether she could get through the month. Reframed in terms of a public pedagogy of examples, the example she created through her participation would be one that would reveal of which class it – and by extension she – was emblematic. Her approach plays into critiques that TSIs do little to address all but the most extreme cases of problematic alcohol consumption because a pass, according to the imputed logic, would obviate any need to address what would still be considered high-risk drinking. Hepatologist Mark Wright's comments on Dry January are typical of this dissent insofar as he argues that a month of sobriety can be used as a 'decoy to justify drinking far too much in the festive season with increased intake for the rest of the year' (University Hospital Southampton 2018).

For as naive as Janelle's thinking about her relationship with alcohol may be, it represents a relatively extreme position on a spectrum of participant motivations, one shared only by Liz. For most, January, February and Lenten TSIs, in particular, are undertaken as correctives for overindulgent holiday seasons. These motivations are so ubiquitous that they form one of the punchlines in a satirical song 'Dry January Dan', when artist Tamar Broadbent (glibly voicing the titular participant) explains his rationale as 'I just hit it pretty hard over Christmas and I thought, why not give me body a rest' (Broadbent 2018). Earnest critics of TSIs nonetheless attribute the minority position of Manichean thinking about alcohol consumption to a much larger share of TSI participants. Such accusations have been levelled by groups representing both clinicians and those within the alcohol industry, albeit for different reasons.

The popular press, often eager for a different angle on what has become a rather familiar story when TSIs come around in yearly news cycles, has eagerly seized upon commentary critical or sceptical of the benefits of TSIs. In widely publicized statements that have since been reversed (to much less press interest), the British Liver Trust (BBC 2012) deemed a month of sobriety to be a grand but tokenistic gesture. For French agriculturalists and viticulturalists, in response to the government's planned backing of Dry January in France (Santi and Horel 2020), dry months represented yet another problematic English drinking tradition that was being imported, a feeble corrective for binge drinking, which was already conceived of as a 'foreign' phenomenon in both French alcohol advertising and the nation's public health discourse (Robert 2014). Critics who object to the 'all or nothing' approach they perceive TSIs to be advocating have instead touted moderation in the form of fewer drinks and fewer days where alcohol is consumed over binge sobriety as the way to promote a more responsible and sustainable approach to alcohol. In such positions, the idea that a short period of sobriety could be the means to effect an overall reduced consumption – the very notion ventured in the present volume – is dismissed outright.

The second widespread apprehension about TSIs – that they promote post-campaign binge drinking – is more common than those that focus on the dangers of using a TSI as a form of diagnostic for alcohol dependency. While underpinned by the same misgivings about all-or-nothing approaches, the post-campaign binge is a more relatable example and one with some basis in the qualitative evidence. According to the most extreme versions of the critique, hordes of parched participants await the striking of midnight at the conclusion of their period of sobriety to thirstily drink themselves into a stupor. Mainstream media, including the health, fitness and wellness press, routinely present pro and con style pieces on TSIs and propose arguments against TSIs that elevate the post-campaign binge to a taken-for-granted truth: 'In fact, many survivors of Dry January only undo their hard work, rewarding their valiant efforts by indulging in an almighty booze binge come February' (Downing 2019). In an alcoholic rendition of Newton's Third Law of Motion, weeks of sobriety are undone with an equal and opposite bender.

Lay sceptics could be forgiven for assuming that such behaviour is the norm among TSI participants, as the larrikinish origins of some of the most popular philanthropic TSIs boasted of boozy post-campaign celebrations. The first iteration of the Défi 28 jours was advertised with the premise that there would be an invitation-only party on the 1st of March for those who succeeded in staying dry for the month (Chouinard and Théorêt-Poupart 2013). An editorial about hometown TSI Dry July in the *Sydney Morning Herald* jokingly enumerated fictional 'reaction' months: 'For so many of us, Dryish July is followed by Alcohol August, Sloshed September, Overdo It October, No Idea What Went On Last Night November, Doo-doo-doo-doo-da-da-da-da December and Just Six Months to Dry July January' (Stokes 2014). An official counter-movement supporting the hospitality industry – Parched March – even sprang up in Sydney in the wake of the success of what were still (in terms of mainstream reach and influence) nascent TSIs (Carter 2014). These jokes and nominal counter campaigns were once predictable companions to TSI discourse. In more recent times, as TSIs have gained in legitimacy, in part thanks to the backing of the public health and medical establishments in various national and international contexts, the popular expectation of a post-campaign binge has been tempered. TSIs in this context are increasingly construed as a reset and an alteration rather than a mere pause on drinking patterns.

A possible reason for the shift away from an assumption of formal or exceedingly alcoholic post-campaign festivities is a greater awareness, including through personal or proximal example, that these are in fact not as common as the discourse suggests. Confirming the findings of large-scale quantitative studies (de Visser et al. 2016), a majority of participants interviewed did not mark the end of their dry months with atypically wet celebrations. Instead, the end of the campaign arrived with relatively little fanfare and the majority of participants waited until their next scheduled social event (generally the weekend following the end of the campaign) to resume drinking. David, whose preference had always been to drink at home after work, remarked that he had a single drink the day after his TSI ended but switched back to water once he had sampled the taste of the gin and tonic that he had been missing. The most common experience is that participants are in no particular rush to resume drinking and that they are more restrained when they do begin to imbibe afresh. As a repeat participant, David notes that he often winds up commencing the campaign from a similar baseline level of consumption, but that it generally takes him a much longer time – and the spur of the summer holiday festivities – to come back to those levels.

Where post-campaign celebrations did see participants snap back to their previous patterns of consumption, they are often reported as hangover-inducing reminders of what had temporarily been less painful mornings-after. Janelle's experience of wrapping up her month of sobriety is one that is repeated in some variation by a number of participants, and it complicates the myth of the post-TSI binge:

> JANELLE: I had something on that night so I went home and didn't do anything the first night. And then we all had a dinner planned for the 2nd of March. . . . We just spent so much money that night, just cocktails and heaps of food as well that we ate. But the bill was like half alcohol. Then we went out and everyone just got absolutely rip-roaring and smashed and I woke up and I felt atrocious the next day. . . . And I was just like, *this is awful. I have not felt like this for a month and I hate this.*
>
> FACILITATOR: Have you had any more of those nights since?

JANELLE: No, I went to a music festival. . . . There was a camping three-day music festival thing that we all go to every year. So we were all just like, *it's going to be like back on the wagon and back smashing it hard and stuff* but I don't know. . . . I think I drank a lot less at that than I normally do.

Her rendition of events, including a narration of her thinking about the experience, justifies the misgivings, as post-TSI binges (the night out, the music festival) are a real phenomenon.

Janelle's example is disproportionately powerful because (as conveyed) even the alleged counterexample is charged with an emotional or affective valence that makes the post-campaign binge a form of didactic example in its own right. Owing to the changed context from which the example of a typical night out arose, it was newly seen as expensive, 'atrocious' and 'awful'. Speaking of how such examples tend to take on mythological status when communicated via social media, which often come with photos and video, David Stukus explains that 'we all tend to recall the most negative or extreme examples of our past most vividly' (Stukus 2019: 66). For Janelle, the return to old ways so soon after a period of sobriety was rather extreme and, owing to the predictable effects of alcoholic overconsumption, unfavourable.

The second part of her anecdote, where she describes a more restrained approach to consumption at an event that normally invites excess, accordingly does not feature as prominently in her rendition of events. Similarly, her relaying that a month post-campaign what had been daily drinking was now mostly weekend drinking lacked the vividness of the big night out to celebrate the 2nd of March. The pendulum swung from prolific consumption to total sobriety and, one big night notwithstanding, ultimately moved within a more moderate range thereafter, as her post-campaign consumption had seen her give up mid-week drinking and drinking less (although not in a quantifiably distinct way) on weekends.

Janelle's bipartite answer to the question about how one breaks the alcohol fast provides a heavily qualified but also common counterexample, especially for first-time participants. What such (counter)examples reveal is that the myths about post-campaign binges are grounded in reality, but only in part of the story. Events that were postponed or scheduled for after the TSI period still see participants drink, often to a degree that local public health guidelines would qualify as a binge, but typically less than either they or their companions expected them to. This more restrained consumption is sometimes attributed to a decreased alcohol tolerance but is also typically framed as part of a choice or a

164   *Alcohol, Binge Sobriety and Exemplary Abstinence*

feeling that the participant simply did not want or care to consume as much as they once might have or others expected them to.

The counterexamples, like Janelle's, that (partially) reinforce the notion that TSIs promote extreme orientations to drinking paradoxically bolster the positions of two very different groups seeking different outcomes: those committed to moderation as both means *and* end and those who seek an excuse for not attempting a TSI. The first group draws from small segments of the public health and drug and alcohol treatment circles (Ward 2020; Hamilton and Gilmore 2016; Hamilton 2019). The second group of sceptics (not entirely distinct from the first) is more representative of the general population, and their views are made known via popular media, opinion pieces, blogs and social media. Emblematic of these positions are the views of the French agriculture minister, who declared of TSIs in November 2019: 'Je trouve ça aberrant. Je préfère la modération toute l'année, que l'interdiction et la prohibition un mois de l'année' (I find it absurd. I prefer moderation year round to interdictions and prohibition for one month of the year) (Guillaume 2019). The TSI-resistant, including those affiliated with segments of the alcohol industry (Graham 2012), are among the chief proponents of these discourses, and they have financial motivation for their position. As the TSI model has gained in popularity, however, it seems that more people are accepting that short-term abstinence – even if it gives rise to the occasional post-campaign binge (or going dry altogether) – can be an effective means to achieve an objective of moderating alcohol consumption overall or at least for a longer period.

Resistant examples

TSIs seek to raise awareness about not just the pitfalls of contemporary drinking cultures but also their own profile as a means to address personal relationships with alcohol while also raising money for charity. To do so, they rely on both the inwardly and outwardly oriented embodied example of participants. These examples are meant to be illustrative instantiations of a class; ergo TSI participants are posited as exemplars of temperance, moderation and civic commitment in service of personal responsibility for health and philanthropy. Participants are meant to be self-sacrificing, but not masochistically so, as the success of TSIs is contingent upon these examples being achievable and desirable. The experience is also meant to be instructive, and participants are expected to come away from it having learnt something about their local drinking cultures, the role of alcohol in their lives, alcohol's effects on health and well-being, the struggles of people who are alcohol-dependent and so on. The example of some participants – those who do not complete the TSI, those who 'complete' the TSI while still drinking heavily and those who do not engage with its pedagogical premise – nonetheless demonstrates different values or acts than those intended and thereby pose challenges for TSIs as organizations (or as subsidiaries of larger organizations) that, in the media-savvy ways of the contemporary era, aim to control their public image.

Reported intent to undertake a dry month, typically assessed via public opinion polls conducted online, is oft-repeated as evidence that TSIs are gaining in popularity. Intent to go dry in January, for instance, has been estimated to sit at between 14 and 16 per cent of the overall adult population in the United States and the United Kingdom (YouGov 2019, 2017), and lower at 11 per cent of the adult population who consume alcohol in France (YouGov France 2021). The gap between intent, commitment and completion is nonetheless likely to be significant, as the Hungarian example shows, only 1.19 per cent of those expressing interest wound up formally joining the TSI (Pados et al. 2020). Even among those who sign up, however, there are many who may manage a few days (or even longer) but who subsequently bow out. The popular hashtag #dryjanuaryfail, for instance, is evidence that an abandoned TSI is not only common but widely publicized as a self-deprecating badge of honour to rival the digital tokens of achievement.

In contrast to polls about intent, which require only a yes or no answer, or using social media data to track engagement with campaign sites, it is comparatively difficult to calculate the portion of TSI participants who undertake but do not complete a TSI. Individuals who do not complete their TSIs are less likely than those who complete the full period of sobriety to supply data to researchers and are therefore less likely to be included in formal research. A quantitative study of Dry January (de Visser et al. 2016) found that 64.1 per cent of formally registered participants, which was 3,791 people, signed on to the research. Eligibility, contingent upon completing all 3 of the surveys over the 6-month study period, subsequently fell to 857, of whom 549 were successful in abstaining for the full month. Where non-completion of the initiative is likely to account for an unwillingness to engage further with researchers, completion rates are likely to be significantly lower. Participants in many socially oriented TSIs and informal fasts, to say nothing of those who undertake their dry months independently but in parallel with recognized campaigns, are not required to register and are thus far less likely to engage with organizers. Tracking their completion or success rates is therefore even less certain. A 2020 YouGov survey in the UK found that 11 per cent of those who began a TSI (formal or informal) had abandoned it before the end of the month, and 35 per cent found themselves drinking but reframed their initial efforts to be abstinent as a new, unsanctioned, goal of drinking less. Slightly more than one in two participants remained alcohol free at month's end, although making it through the first fortnight proved the hardest part of the challenge (Nolsoe 2020).

Those who never commence their planned TSI or who abandon it nonetheless become powerful counterexamples for both themselves and others. Some participants, whether as an intention or as a fallback position, have permitted themselves an occasional drink (Aviles 2020), a strategy of do-it-yourself reprieves where none formally exist. Socially oriented TSIs without purchasable reprieves have even countered by rehabilitating failed attempts: 'A drier January is still something to be proud of, and your body will thank you!' (Alcohol Change UK 2020b). Participants' lapses demonstrate that drinking cultures and habits around alcohol are resistant to change – a view that TSIs are meant to dispel, not reinforce. By acquiescing to framing drinking less during the month as a still successful outcome, campaigns temper the effect of these negatively tinged counterexamples.

The official (or quasi-official) strategy of reframing 'dry-ish' months as successes to enable a sense of self-efficacy from efforts to abstain is largely supported by participants who have used purchasable reprieves. Thomas, who used a time-out pass when attending a wake, noted that he felt no ambivalence about drinking on the night and still characterized his commitment to the campaign and its objectives as strong, especially as a five-time participant. Bethany similarly justified her use of a pass as 'being within the guidelines' and prided herself on being 'very committed' to both the goal of abstinence and educating those who supported her in relation to the cause for which she was raising money. As a point of contrast, Jillian felt that her use of a pass was 'cheating' and resolved in future to either forgo the pass or emulate those, such as David, who slightly adjusted the dates of their month-long fast to accommodate events at either the start or the end of the month without compromising on the number of continuous days without alcohol.

The acceptance or repudiation of purchasable reprieves, or unofficial allowances where they are not available, is generally seen as working in the spirit of the TSI. Rare counterexamples, those judged to be out of sync with both the campaign's objectives and social expectations, nonetheless confound the imputed pedagogy of TSIs and risk becoming liabilities for the campaigns.

Unruly Examples 167

Repeat Dry July participant Himari presents one such case of an example that is not just counter to the TSI's objectives but is arguably unruly given her justification of her actions.

Himari had been an early adopter of the long-running Australian TSI Dry July, and she continued to take part annually. She recounted that – in contrast to the experience of many TSI participants – her drinking after each campaign quickly snapped back to its earlier levels, which she described as 'huge'. She noticed no appreciable differences in her sleep, productivity or overall health but found that her patterns of social interaction changed slightly and that she saved money. These differences to the typical experience aside, Himari considered herself to be an exemplary Dry July supporter owing to her long-standing participation, her regular success in raising several hundred dollars for charity and her sense of being part of the 'Dry July community'. She returned to the initiative year after year because of the warm glow from supporting a charity and rationalized that aside from the 'headaches at the beginning of the month' (likely symptoms of withdrawal) that she experienced as she gave up daily drinking, the campaign did her no harm.

What emerged from our conversation about how she found the experience (difficult) was that Golden Tickets were how she coped with the demands of the TSI. In her most recent undertaking, she had bought four of them to allow her to drink on the four weekends of the campaign. Like many participants making use of the reprieves, she put no limits on herself for the days for which she was on leave. In practice, her intent to imbibe as she normally did was somewhat frustrated because of temporarily reduced tolerance, which affected the amount she could comfortably consume in a sitting. She expressed no guilt or misgivings about the Golden Tickets, regardless of how many were purchased, as she considered them essential to the campaign's ability to attract participants and to its fundraising efforts. By contrast, she criticized non-participants and those who had recently refused to sponsor her as they had in previous years because they judged her drinking during July – in their reported estimation as 'cheating' – because they lacked knowledge of both how the Golden Tickets supported the philanthropic objectives and the rules of Dry July.

Himari's approach is emblematic of the fault strongly socially oriented TSIs, such as Dry January, accuse their philanthropic counterparts of promoting (Birkwood 2014). The common criticism is that reprieves make it more difficult for people to focus on and be more reflective about their drinking habits as they take a genuine break from alcohol. As Himari's example demonstrates, she did not appreciate a meaningful difference (or at least a positive one) between her normal and abstinent selves, likely because she never created the example – the expressively referenced instantiation – of moderation. Arguably because it never truly occurs, the period of sobriety fails to produce an illustrative example that could in turn generate imitation for Himari based on the consequentialist reasoning of feeling better as a result of not drinking (as much) and looking to replicate this behaviour to achieve these same effects.

Consequentialist reasoning aside, Himari's experience of the TSI does not alter her self-narratives around health or drinking. Despite repeated Dry July participation, she remains somebody who enjoys drinking heavily and frequently and, moreover, does not perceive alcohol to interfere with her life. Alcohol's status as a pleasure whose sacrifice is worthy of compensation, though, is confirmed. She could not generate the imitative example expected, but she did reinforce her self-narrative as a charitable and civic-minded individual willing to give up her own pleasures, on most days of the campaign, for a worthy cause. In terms of effects, Himari's consumption was among a small minority of TSI participants, and an even smaller pool of those who self-identified as successful participants, whose post-campaign consumption rebounded to equal or greater levels than before (de Visser et al. 2016).

Setting aside the internecine conflicts in the TSI community about the utility or liability of philanthropy in changing drinking behaviours among participants, participation that is reliant on the use of a number of reprieves also fails to cast the participant as an outwardly imitable example for others. This is true in terms of both changed drinking behaviour (they are not temporarily abstinent, responsible or learning about the benefits of moderation) and philanthropy (they are not truly self-sacrificing). An example like Himari's is therefore problematic for TSIs as campaigns with pedagogical, philanthropic and overall public relations objectives.

As with many lifestyle movements, TSI participants typically function as ambassadors or champions of the experience (Haenfler et al. 2012). Testimonials, whether published as part of official marketing strategies or simply shared among social circles, are important recruitment and pedagogical tools. Reports of the physiological, emotional, mental and material benefits previous participants experienced are what convince many to take part. Outwardly observable signs of improved health and well-being can also reinforce the abstinent example on which TSI organizers depend. As Himari reported no significant benefit from her TSI experience other than the positive feelings she felt for doing something charitable and saving some money, she could not position herself as an imitable example.

Unruly Examples

Even in terms of philanthropy, though, Himari's example was quite problematic, a facet of the experience that she reported but did not seem to grasp. She recounted that sponsors from previous years declined to support her philanthropic efforts in her most recent campaign, but she did not seem to comprehend (or be willing to convey) the reason for their withdrawal of support. It is nonetheless possible to interpret the previous sponsors' behaviour as a reaction to a perceived lack of integrity with regard to their implicit philanthropic contract. These people may have judged her as out of keeping with both their own values and the TSI's intent of a month without alcohol as a sacrifice worthy of compensation. This resulted in not just a tacit but indeed an unusual overt refusal of the request to sponsor the cause as a result of the individual fundraiser's action. The participant's refusal to honour the central premise of the campaign saw her operating, in all but a technical sense, outside of the rules and her friends refused the normally productive fundraising strategy of relational altruism.

Himari's atypical participation, reliant on purchasable reprieves, can also lead to suspicions about any health and awareness objectives, secondary though they might be, that a philanthropic TSI might purport to have. Where embodied philanthropy initiatives rely on the participant's embodiment to publicize their cause by appearing or living in a manner that is rebadged as philanthropic, she instead came to exemplify the limit-case of the tension between the means and the ends of philanthropic TSIs.

Where TSI participants do succeed in temporarily abstaining, the meanings they attribute to the experience and the lessons they derive from it may not concord with what TSI organizers, especially those with a strong social orientation, expect. These alternative interpretations can result in public pedagogies that are at odds, either in whole or in part, with the intent of organizers. Brad's account of what he got out of his TSI participation is illustrative of such cases.

Brad had reluctantly signed on to FebFast after several years of pressure from his wife and colleagues, a group of whom had been taking part in the campaign as a sort of office challenge and were enthusiastic proponents of its health benefits. Brad ultimately relented when he found himself feeling generally unwell and hypothesized that a break from alcohol could help – even though he routinely asserted that he enjoyed drinking and saw no issues with his consumption. Indeed, Brad was at pains to stress that he did not see the point of TSIs as anything but fundraisers. He persistently and vociferously insinuated, often peppering his discourse with cursing, that those who were pushing him to sign up encouraged teetotalism, that TSIs were the purview of abstainers

170   *Alcohol, Binge Sobriety and Exemplary Abstinence*

or those involved in providing rehab services, and were out of step with the mainstream of Australian culture. The only non-philanthropic use he saw for TSIs was for helping those who had a problem with alcohol to begin detoxing. Given the nature of his protests against TSIs, one could argue that Brad was motivated against finding a link between alcohol and his own ill-health, as it might imply that his drinking had in fact been detrimental and that alcohol was not the consequence-free consumable he claimed it to be.

A month after the official end of his TSI experience, Brad noted that he was drinking less frequently overall, had largely restrained his drinking to weekends and had swapped his previous tipple – 'rubbish beer' – for drinks that he enjoyed more, signalling that alcohol was still a source of enjoyment and pleasure, but was now more of a treat than the habit it had been before. He reported an overall improvement in his health – 'I'm feeling a hell of a lot better' – and attributed this to his general increase in physical activity and better diet (e.g. a homemade salad for lunch rather than takeaway). Brad's drinking behaviour in the post-TSI period undeniably reflects changes in his relationship with alcohol. In many ways Brad is a TSI success story, a shining example that would make for a great testimonial, insofar as it highlights changed attitudes, behaviours and outcomes without risking the dreaded accusations of wowserism. And yet, he vowed never to repeat the experience and would not advocate that others attempt it.

Reflecting on his period of abstinence and its outcomes, a fine example of the power of a short break from alcohol, Brad was reticent to attribute too much importance to temporary sobriety: 'I did, in reflection, feel that not all my problems are alcohol based; health and . . . but it [alcohol] might have been a contributing factor.' He came to recognize lower alcohol consumption as an element in his sense of well-being but was hesitant to accord it much influence, including in tracing its indirect effects. He did not, for instance, connect his new habit of going to the gym in the morning before work to the fact that eliminating mid-week drinking removed some major impediments to working out, namely sleeping later and feeling low on energy upon waking.

His protests about TSIs or his downplaying of their effects were most pronounced when rebutting the expectations of others who championed them as the benefits for undertaking a TSI and who urged him towards the campaign as a means to recognize the potential issues with his drinking:

> I did learn that, as I said earlier, that alcohol is actually not as big a problem as
> I may have thought – and my wife likes to point out. I don't think I've got an

alcohol problem. [sarcastically] My wife tells me all the time I've got a bloody alcohol problem.

Where many participants and touted testimonials point to discovering that alcohol is a problem of greater significance than they originally thought, Brad was at pains to make the opposite point. His self-narrative remained one of always having been in control of his drinking and of drinking because he enjoys it.

Analysing Brad's reactions, it is clear that the exemplarily temperate period in his regular drinking existence was instructive enough for him to change his habits and moderate his behaviour. He was, nonetheless, undeterred in his thinking that alcohol engendered baseless levels of concern, at both the individual and social level. The social objectives of the TSI were thus only partly fulfilled, as Brad's self-narrative as somebody who was in full control of his relationship with alcohol remained intact. If anything, he was more convinced that alcohol was a significant source of overreaction for others, especially those (like his wife) who did not drink. Remaining steadfast in his view that alcohol was not as harmful as people made it out to be was accordingly deeply enmeshed in relational processes of sense-making, including saving face in front of his spouse.

Brad's TSI experience, while completing the campaign and noting some positive outcomes, was largely a negative one that remained at odds with his sense of himself as being in control of his drinking and correct in his thinking. His willingness to draw upon his abstinent period as an example for his future drinking behaviour and reactions to non-drinkers is therefore limited, especially where consequentialist reasoning may be required to override the security of the status quo and inherent imitability of one's past examples.

Both Himari and Brad's experiences and their accounts of these are potentially problematic for TSIs as lifestyle movements with pedagogical intent. As campaigns, they rely not just on the embodied example of participants but on what they communicate and provide as evidence to others about the impact of their participation. For those who would see Himari drinking every weekend in July, just as she had in June and would continue to do in August, the TSI was ineffective. At worst, it was potentially dangerous, echoing the warnings of sceptics and confirming for her that she was in control of her drinking and that it was not of consequence, despite what she described as signs of withdrawal. Brad's behaviours, by contrast, were exemplary by TSI standards. He slept better, improved his relationship with his wife, lost weight, had more energy, saw lasting changes to his drinking post-campaign and even raised a considerable amount of money for the cause through inventive schemes to incentivize donations. His account of his TSI participation is nonetheless one that resists framing his pre-campaign drinking behaviour as meaningfully different from that post-campaign. While Himari's example is likely to be at odds with what many TSI organizers, especially of the socially oriented type, would expect and would hesitate to count her as constituting the mass exemplarity, it is Brad who repudiates his exemplary status within the TSI movement.

Conclusion

Apprehensions about TSIs and the examples they generate have inspired a reticence about the overall concept. 'When I did a 30-day challenge, this is what happened to me . . .' (Ward 2020) is an opening to myriad anecdotes that become evidence that can just as easily become the quotable testimonial organizers use in their marketing campaigns as it is the nightmare scenario to be quelled. Indeed, anecdotes and case studies, despite the caveats around non-generalizability that accompany them in scholarly circles, have become the popular basis for suspicion about TSIs. Whether real or imagined, commonplace or aberrant exceptions, counterexamples have emerged as something campaign organizers have to manage if TSIs are to act as public pedagogies.

It is nonetheless worth shifting the critical perspective on these anecdotes that speak to the existence and power of counterexamples from one focused on their reception to one concerned with their articulation. Community health perspectives advise that 'We need to understand the power of anecdotes to those who recount them: they are told specifically because they reveal something on which the teller has reflected and come to view as important, and others are expected to understand that importance' (Carlisle et al. 2007: 163). The anecdotes that reveal unruly examples are those that TSIs and their organizers, should they wish to more successfully engage with doubters, cynics and those most resistant to (but perhaps most likely to benefit from) the experience in future, will need to address.

Conclusion

'Unprecedented' might be the most overused word of 2020 and 2021. The Covid-19 pandemic has disrupted everything from global travel to the way we purchase items as basic as toilet paper. People worldwide, especially those living through months of lockdowns and the fraying of networks of services and supplies, have discovered for themselves what they are, both individually and collectively, capable of accomplishing and enduring in the name of shared responsibility for health and well-being. While the hope is that we will soon be able to revert to our pre-pandemic ways (a poignant sentiment for me, now two months into Sydney's highly restrictive second lockdown), these 'unprecedented' times and the discoveries of necessity they entail will likely leave behind a legacy of changed behaviours and attitudes borne of necessity. Videoconferencing, e-commerce, online learning, hybrid work arrangements, to say nothing of no longer using our bare hands to press lift buttons, are just some of the practices that are predicted to be forever changed thanks to our having had to adapt to new ways of working, consuming, learning, socializing and navigating the world.

Predictably, the pandemic has also changed the ways people drink and the questions scholars are asking about alcohol consumption as both a vector of epidemiological inquiry and a sociocultural practice. The pandemic's forced changes have rendered visible to individuals and societies more broadly some previously unseen or scarcely perceptible drinking practices. Nicholls and Conroy (2021) argue that these newly or now more visible phenomena are focusing attention on emergent (internet-enabled social drinking) or previously understudied (domestic consumption) phenomena.

By and large, TSIs continued to operate during the pandemic. While some TSIs organized by national public health bodies, such as the Danish Hvid Januar, did not run in 2021 owing to understandably changed priorities, most socially oriented and philanthropic campaigns proceeded as usual. Concerns about homebound lifestyles, boredom, loss of routine, social isolation, a lack of external accountability, depression and anxiety brought on by economic and other circumstances are feared to be causing people to drink more than they might otherwise (Koenig 2021), situations that suggest that TSIs are needed now more than before. However, some regarded TSIs as additional sources of pressure and potential stress for participants who may already be grappling with considerable challenges (Head 2021). Record fundraising tallies and participant numbers in 2020 and then again in 2021 for campaigns like Dry July (Dry July Foundation 2021) nonetheless suggest that TSIs were embraced either in spite of or more likely because of the pandemic. As with the much-hyped concerns about binge drinking and alcohol-fuelled violence that coincided with the rise of TSIs, the campaigns are yet again leveraging the opportunity for demonstrative individual control of drinking behaviours to respond to external circumstances.

Where the pandemic has heightened already strong neo-liberal discourses of individual responsibility for collective health outcomes, TSIs have duly emphasized the sense of accomplishment for control of drinking behaviours. The annual report for Dry July's 2020 campaign for the first time notes participants' 'sense of achievement' as the top reported benefit of participation (Dry July Foundation 2021: 25). This immediate and individualized sense of control stands in stark contrast to circumstances where many continue to feel that events are beyond their influence, and their personal actions in restricting their movements, getting vaccinated, wearing masks are, at best, drops in the bucket and, at worst, ineffective. As with prior temperance movements, the action to control alcohol consumption is more symbolic than of direct consequence for the issues at hand. Yet, it resonates with segments of society eager to use these demonstrative practices (and new forms of visibility such as TSI-branded virtual backgrounds for videoconferencing) to signal their responsibility for collective outcomes in relation to the virus through an analogous personal display of self-restraint with regard to alcohol. The temporal aspects of a pandemic that seems unending have similarly seen a hopeful investment in time-delimited change. The sense of accomplishment that comes from a sober month is increasingly framed as a tool for building resilience (Dry July Foundation 2021) and self-efficacy to withstand longer term, but still hopefully temporary change.

Covid-19, it seems, has seen TSIs transform from a type of lifestyle movement employing embodied public pedagogies to change collective drinking cultures into embodied pedagogies that leverage the power of changed drinking practices to help participants cope with more immediate and wider-scale challenges. In effect, the temporary abstinence demanded from TSI participants has become exemplary not just of moderation, the cornerstone of their functioning as neo-temperance initiatives, but also of short-term personal sacrifice in support of longer-term and collective endeavours.

Temporary sobriety: Neo-liberal neo-temperance

TSIs have always been orchestrated opportunities to both take and demonstrate responsibility for one's personal choices, specifically alcohol consumption, within frameworks of consumerism and entrepreneurial self-fashioning. They are, and have always been, paradigmatic neo-liberal endeavours, especially in regard to health and the new civic obligation towards compulsory philanthropy (King 2006). The short but transnational history of TSIs nevertheless reveals that as a collection of related initiatives, they have amplified these tendencies and not only, as evidenced by the mass exemplarity to which they gave rise, generated social and cultural change with regard to drinking cultures but have inspired new, embodied forms of public pedagogy and social movement learning.

TSIs are akin to older temperance movements, although the declared objective of TSIs has always been to promote moderation and responsible drinking rather than abstinence, prohibition or even anti-alcohol sentiment. In keeping with the consumer orientations of the present time, and as inventions of a twenty-first-century aspirational middle class, TSIs target individual consumption choices and increasingly seek to mitigate potential economic impacts from reduced consumption with alternative ways to consume, whether in the form of different categories of expenditure (travel, clothes, events) or simply through non-alcoholic beverage options. Temporary abstinence is framed as an amplified, performative form of moderation that serves socially pedagogic and, in some cases, philanthropic ends but always through the individual and the primacy of their choices. Where prior temperance movements sought social, cultural or even legal change and used modified individual conduct to show the benefits of and support for these objectives, TSIs subordinate and in many cases distance themselves from such aims. TSIs routinely construe themselves as instruments that support the individual's projects of ethical self-fashioning (Yeomans 2019) in relation to health, productivity and civic identity through support, encouragement and the social legitimacy of a coordinated campaign.

Philanthropic TSIs prioritize temporary abstinence as a basis for fundraising rather than as a trial period for a potentially enduring lifestyle choice. This model is more prevalent in Commonwealth countries than those of Continental Europe, which have stronger social safety nets, or (paradoxically) the United States, whose privatized healthcare system strongly incentivizes personal responsibility for health. Participants in these charitably oriented campaigns instead engage in the form of effortful and self-sacrificing contribution to a worthy cause that merits and, increasingly due to reduced public support for social services, needs private sponsorship. By virtue of the embodied demands of participation and the demands of self-promotion required for fundraising, those engaged are transformed – and transformed for all to see – from private donors to enterprising fundraisers who commit to an implied philanthropic contract where their abstinence is traded for pledges of financial support.

Not all TSIs, however, mobilize participants to use their sobriety to raise funds, a situation that has led to internecine competition in an increasingly marketized third sector about the best way to motivate temporary sobriety. Some operators of socially oriented TSIs and observers are critical, in a small minority of cases legitimately so, of the potential for the fundraising strategies of philanthropic TSIs to overtake the base premise and mechanism of the campaigns: an abstinent period of both pharmacological and behavioural significance. A focus on collecting donations, they argue, may also compromise the potential for a period of sobriety to bring about the awareness, social, health and pedagogical objectives that TSIs as organizations are increasingly being shown to afford participants. Owing to a lack of rigorous and large-scale studies assessing the impact of philanthropic tactics on the social objectives of TSIs, it is not yet clear if the concerns about philanthropic TSIs in comparison to their socially oriented counterparts likely owe more to rivalries and competition between campaigns than they do to verifiable evidence about outcomes.

The differences between campaigns notwithstanding, a thirty- or forty-day period of abstinence from alcohol is the bedrock of all TSIs. The sober self, embodied and experiencing most facets of daily life without alcohol, does not just experience a period of sobriety but, through the quarantining of the experience and the enactment of the most stringent form of moderation, becomes an instructive example for self and others. The temporarily abstinent body both instantiates and expressively references what moderation and responsible consumption entails. In this context, abstinence functions as a superlative, which is to say normatively exemplary, form of moderation. Yet abstinence by virtue of the attention focused on it as a result of the campaign also comes to be illustrative of how alcohol functions as a pharmacological compound, a commodity and a factor in all manner of relationships. Its benefits and drawbacks, affordances and opportunity costs are amplified, rendered observable and appreciable for the individual, those they interact with and, through reporting, study and commentary, for a larger social audience. This explicitly demonstrable form of moderation accordingly has the potential to become a didactic example, one that is lived, felt and experienced as a pedagogic lesson predicated on discovery twinned with subtle practices of health education, such as nudges and incitement to reflection.

Conclusion   177

By comparison to many other forms of education and pedagogy, the embodied nature of the example is especially instructive. TSI participants can experience the lessons – of alternative consumption, self-restraint, alcohol education – first-hand and therein derive and anchor both their knowledge and their capabilities in their own lived experience. In contemporary contexts where individual belief (about everything from climate change to epidemiology) and personal choice seem to trump scientific method, social norms and even laws, TSIs have popularized individualized pedagogies of discovery. The personal applicability of widely touted precepts about alcohol is allowed to be tested and either discarded or, more frequently, acknowledged as a kind of discovery or revelation. Even when backed by national public health bodies that are in other contexts refuting the popular primacy of individual anecdote over rigorously validated study, TSIs uphold the centrality of the individual. Moreover, in having practised the most extreme form of moderation, participants also come to have experience of and proven facility with more temperate approaches to alcohol. Drink refusal, for instance, becomes a practised and (ostensibly but imperfectly) rewarded action and the basis for self-efficacy on an ongoing basis. Sobriety may therefore be temporary, but moderation – the hope of public health and neo-temperance organizations – has the potential to be much longer lasting.

For as central as the individual is in TSIs, both in terms of practice and discourse, the campaigns have always relied upon the individual being socially situated in groups where the participant can be recognized a member – albeit an exemplary one – of a class. The effects of changed drinking habits, constituted as imitable exemplars, are accordingly expected to ripple outward, aided by technologies and practices of mass-self communication, such as social media platforms. Participants are encouraged, indeed expected and assisted through shareable digital collateral, to promote themselves as people who feel better, save money and look better as a result of their temporary sobriety. While arguably serving a campaign's future goals of recruitment and awareness-raising through consequentialist reasoning (i.e. that similar effects can come from comparable actions), the incitement to demonstrability also serves participants' self-fashioning objectives, for it publicly casts them as socially responsible exemplars who manifestly do good for others and for society through their own small (but still heroic) actions.

The history of many TSIs outlines that the campaigns originated as individualized responses to mostly personal but relatable circumstances. The highly entrepreneurial framings of the founder's story persist even though thousands of participants now sign up to TSIs and channel millions of dollars into the causes these organizations support. In these grassroots stories, the larger cultural framework of middle-class professionals in affluent liberal democracies using (anti-)consumption choices for the self-management of lifestyle, health and contributions to public services is unacknowledged. The proliferation of TSIs, often spearheaded by national public health organizations and health-related charities, nonetheless suggests that participants' own 'selfish' motivations, like those of the founders, are an effective means to bring about social and cultural change.

'Dry January' or its local analogue has become so well known as a phenomenon, if not so common a practice, that in many contexts it no longer warrants explanation. While TSIs initially framed themselves as a means for individuals to reassess and take control of their own relationships with alcohol with the goal of moderating their consumption, they have (as organizations) come to champion themselves as agents to change drinking cultures (and improve individual health, economic productivity, etc. in the process). Their numbers, especially of participants, are used as proof that a change in *society's* relationship with alcohol is already in progress. Far from just being self-congratulatory rhetoric (mostly on the part of socially oriented TSIs), this discourse is also taken up by those, such as the French viticultural lobby, who oppose the very premise of TSIs and suggest that this kind of mass, coordinated change to individual conduct (even in the short term) will lead to larger, economically devastating and socio-culturally disruptive change.

Assessments about whether TSIs have materially and/or enduringly changed drinking cultures at a population level have yet to confirm the results of impact reported among participants (Case et al. 2021). Moreover, some of the early critiques of TSIs – that they promote post-campaign binge drinking, that philanthropic campaigns sacrifice health outcomes for the sake of fundraising – have not fully held up. Participants, however, are not always the exemplary abstainers organizers would have them be; they short circuit the period of sobriety, fail to connect alcohol as a cause with its various effects and sometimes proclaim that they derive no notable benefit from the exercise. What is clear, however, is that as a form of participatory philanthropy and embodied health education campaign, TSIs have had a lasting impact.

As a means of changing habits and of raising awareness and funds, TSIs have become something of an example for other lifestyle movements, charities and behavioural-change initiatives. People are now encouraged to temporarily adopt a plant-based diet and lifestyle through Veganuary, a UK-based initiative that ran for the first time in January 2017 with the intent of raising awareness about veganism as a feasible lifestyle choice (Veganuary 2021). The Ration Challenge, where participants spend a week consuming only the rations provided to refugees through food aid programmes (unless they can fundraise enough to add meagre additions to their diet), emulates the self-sacrifice and experiential empathy that many philanthropic TSIs seek to cultivate in their participants (Act for Peace 2021). Even environmental change is bolstered by the activities of Plastic Free July (2021) which challenge participants to make short-term but hopefully more enduring changes to their consumption and use of single-use plastics by designating a period of intense but supported behaviour modification. The intent behind all these campaigns, as is the case with TSIs, is that participants will learn – either new forms of conduct or experiential empathy – from the new examples they create for themselves by taking part in the challenge. As per the TSI model, these temporary examples will in turn become not only instructive examples for their future selves but also for others.

While modern TSIs were not, by and large, conceived to promote widespread cultural change, experiential empathy or new consumer choices in the beverage industry, their core pedagogical principle of personalized learning through the generation and imitation of highly instructive examples has become a widely imitable and replicated model. Exemplary abstinence has accordingly led to the reduced consumption of not only alcohol but also meat, sugar, caffeine and plastics. More importantly though, exemplary abstinence of an embodied nature has emerged from highly neo-liberal contexts focused on individual optimization, personal responsibility for health and productivity to become a form of public pedagogy now also deliberately used by lifestyle movements and as a form of social movement learning.

Appendices

Appendix A: List of TSIs

40 Brez Alkohola (40 Days without Alcohol): Slovenian TSI taking place during Lent since 2005. Jointly sponsored by national medical and road safety organizations, the TSI focuses both on the personal decision to abstain and on the imperative to not offer alcohol to others. Participants are expected to normalize moderation by not labelling themselves participants or broadcasting their participation.

https://brezalkohola.si/

Alcohol Free for 40: Informal Lenten TSI initiated in 2014 as a local challenge to New Orleans and Baton Rouge area residents through the weekly diet and nutrition column of dietician Molly Kimball in NOLA.com, the major newspaper for Southern Louisiana. The TSI is timed to coincide with the end of the region's annual Carnival season and traditionally spanned the forty days of Lent, although a thirty-day version was piloted in 2019. There is no formal registration and no philanthropic objective, but a private social media presence allows participants to share their experiences. A partnership with a local hospital system encouraged participants to make a blood donation in return for pre- and post-campaign testing.

Big Easy Dryout: Now defunct philanthropic TSI operating in New Orleans during the month of March 2017. The initiative aimed to support small local charities as the beneficiaries of the fundraising efforts but, due to limited scale and operations, managed to support only one cause with a grant of approximately US$15,000.

https://bigeasydryout.causevox.com/

Défi 28 jours (28-day challenge): Begun as a challenge in 2013 among a group of friends in Montreal, Canada, as 'Soberary/Les 28 jours les plus longs de ta vie' (the longest 28 days of your life). In 2014 they began raising money for the

Fondation Jean Lapointe, a drug and alcohol treatment and education service. A formal affiliation with the beneficiary organization in 2015 saw the campaign become an in-house fundraiser for the foundation and a name change followed. Philanthropic objectives remain prominent, and participants continue to be charged a registration fee that doubles as a personal donation. Commitments to various arrangements of dry days (dry weekdays, dry weekends, a full dry month) were trialled in 2021.

https://www.defi28jours.com/

Défi de Janvier (January Challenge): The French version of Dry January that, despite the Gallic name, is more commonly referred to using the English *Dry January*. This TSI launched amid controversy in France in time for January 2020. Formally affiliated with Alcohol Change UK, more than two dozen French public health organizations sought to replicate the initiative's success and sought official government endorsement of the campaign from the French Ministry of Health. Late in 2019, however, the tentative official support was rescinded thanks to pressure from the agricultural and viticultural lobby.

https://dryjanuary.fr/

Dry Feb: Canadian spin-off of Dry July that is conducted in partnership with the Canadian Cancer Society. Launched in 2016, it is Canada's only national TSI.

https://www.dryfeb.ca/

Dry January: Socially oriented initiative of British not-for-profit Alcohol Change UK. Begun as a formal campaign in 2013, it continues to attract a proportionally small share of official participants, even without a registration fee, compared to unofficial adherents. While not obligatory, participants may make or collect donations for Alcohol Change itself or for charities which enter into partnership with Alcohol Change as a way to support both organizations at once. Owing to the public health and policy role of Alcohol Change UK and its openness to working with researchers, Dry January is one of the most studied and evaluated TSIs. Alcohol Change recently partnered with similar organizations in the Netherlands (2019), France (2020) and Switzerland (2021) to launch local versions of Dry January.

https://alcoholchange.org.uk/get-involved/campaigns/dry-january

Dry January (Switzerland): Launched in 2021 as an offshoot of Alcohol Change UK's Dry January and in partnership with three Swiss agencies: public social innovation fund Staatslabor; GREA, an addiction research consortium;

Appendices   183

and local and national arms of the Blue Cross, the largest national provider of drug and alcohol treatment services and addiction prevention education. The campaign operates in both French and German. Participation, and formal registration, is incentivized through prize draws with prizes provided by corporate sponsors.

https://dryjanuary.ch/

Dry January Feel Good February: Initiative of Drugs and Alcohol Northern Ireland begun in 2019; this TSI aims to prolong some or all of the social and health benefits of participation in a dry month by focusing on offering online and offline alcohol-free social events and supports.

https://drugsandalcoholni.info/campaigns/dryjanuary/

Dry July: Formally founded in Sydney, Australia, in 2008 in support of the cancer centre at the Prince of Wales Hospital, the initiative officially established itself as a national campaign in 2009 and created the Dry July Foundation to allocate the non-directed funds raised to projects supporting the treatment of adult cancers. Dry July expanded to New Zealand in 2012 with the founding of the Dry July NZ Trust. Further expansion, using the spin-off digital fundraising platform created by Dry July founder Brett Macdonald, ensued, in the UK in 2014 when Macmillan Cancer Support ran its first Go Sober for October challenge, and in Canada in 2016 with Dry Feb, supporting the Canadian Cancer Society. Dry July and its affiliate campaigns are principally philanthropic in orientation and have, in Australia, New Zealand and Canada, become the dominant TSIs in terms of both numbers of participants and funds raised. Despite having strong philanthropic objectives, no registration fee is charged.

https://www.dryjuly.com/

Dryathlon: A fundraising project of Cancer Research UK that formally launched in December 2012 in time for a first campaign in January 2013. Dryathlon employs humour and originally targeted a younger male demographic as a point of differentiation from the more socially oriented Dry January. This TSI has maintained a consistent focus, strategy and brand identity and continues to allow both free registration and reprieves in the form of a Tipple Tax.

https://www.cancerresearchuk.org/get-involved/do-your-own-fundraising/dryathlon

Drynuary: Name claimed – as early as 2007 – by popular American writer John Ore to describe a self-initiated and largely informal TSI.

Dryuary: TSI run by US–based mutual self-help group Moderation Management, this TSI launched to a broader audience in time for January 2015. Although nominally functioning as a fundraiser for the organization, its main function is to dovetail with Moderation Management's programme of initiating an intervention on one's drinking, beginning with a thirty-day break from alcohol. Participants seeking the benefits of the group's larger programme are encouraged to involve members of their circle in a collective challenge that destigmatizes their personal decision to abstain as part of a larger self-help strategy and recruits additional support from both their immediate social circle and online communities.

https://dryuary.org/wp/

FebFast: Formally launched in Melbourne in 2008 as a fundraiser for Youth Support and Advocacy Service (YSAS), an organization focused on the treatment of young people dealing with problems stemming from alcohol and other drugs in the Australian state of Victoria. In 2011, YSAS acquired the campaign and brand from founder Fiona Healy. In 2014, the February event diversified its offering of fundraising fasts to include sugar, caffeine and a 'digital detox'. Subsequent iterations in 2015 and 2016 allowed participants to select the timing of their own fasts or to nominate the habit or behaviour (smoking, swearing, selfies, fizzy drinks) they wished to break with a 'you pick' option. FebFast combines social and philanthropic objectives, but in 2019 abandoned its practice of charging a registration fee. It continues to offer participants the option of purchasing a reprieve.

FebFast New Zealand, in support of the New Zealand Drug Foundation, launched in 2011 and ran as an unaffiliated partner campaign of its Australian inspiration for five years. It ceased formal operations before the 2016 campaign.

https://febfast.org.au/

Go Dry: Philanthropic and socially oriented TSI sponsored by the American Liver Foundation, with a strong focus on personal health. First run in January 2019, it cited UK examples as inspiration. In 2021, it aligned its fundraising efforts with its health objectives by framing the donations and fundraising targets in terms of drinks not consumed (at the rate of $10 per drink).

https://alfgodry.org/

Go Sober: Fundraising TSI organized by UK-based Macmillan Cancer Support that began in 2014 in partnership with Dry July. Previously operating in October as a 'Go Sober for October' initiative, in 2021 a march campaign was organized under the banner of Sober March.

https://www.gosober.org.uk/

Hvid Januar (White January): Danish TSI sponsored by the Danish National Board of Health that was first run in 2018. The campaign's objectives are purely focused on health and social change. Owing to the sponsoring organization's central role in the Covid-19 pandemic response, the campaign did not run in 2021.

https://hvidjanuar.dk/

IkPas (I pass): Formally affiliated with Alcohol Change UK and inspired by Dry January, this Netherlands-based TSI commenced operations in 2019 and provides options for both a January fast and a Lenten TSI. It is run as an umbrella campaign sponsored by twenty-six local public and preventive health organizations, ten additional care institutions and a partnering organization focusing on healthcare for senior citizens.

https://ikpas.nl/

Lose the Booze: Socially and philanthropically oriented TSI in support of the British Columbia (Canada) Cancer Foundation. Begun in January 2015, the initiative predates the nationwide Dry Feb initiative. Participants can either register for $1 a day or choose to waive their registration fee in exchange for a commitment to raise a minimum of $50. Free passes are available for purchase.

https://losethebooze.ca/

No Alcohol April: Socially oriented TSI begun in Scotland in 2016 as a public awareness campaign. Sponsored by DRiNKLiNK, which focuses on supporting those who are affected by someone else's drinking, the campaign seeks to foster empathy for those struggling with alcohol dependency and encourages participants to enjoy any financial savings of abstinence for themselves.

https://drinklink.org/no-alcohol-april-30-day-challenge/

Ocsober: Australian TSI designed as an in-house fundraiser for Life Education, an organization widely known for Healthy Living school-based education programmes for youth. Begun in October 2008 with a dual focus on philanthropy and social objectives, the initiative has oscillated between these two poles in its framing and messaging from year to year. Participants paid a $25 registration fee and were able to purchase one- or two-day reprieves.

The TSI did not run in an official capacity in 2018 and has now ceased official operations.

https://www.lifeeducation.org.au/ocsober

On the Dry: Short-lived campaign of the Irish Heart Foundation that saw participants go dry from 2015 to 2017 and raise money for the charity. Participants paid a registration fee and could purchase an 'On the Sly' pass as a reprieve.

Septembris ei joo (Alcohol-free September): This socially oriented Estonian TSI first ran as a small-scale initiative in 2003. Having gained official support from the National Institute for Health Development and the European Social Fund, it relaunched as a larger national campaign in September 2017. Without fundraising or registration, it operates primarily as a media campaign.

https://septembriseijoo.alkoinfo.ee/

Sober Buddy Challenge: Initiative of Luxemburg's Cancer Foundation that had its first outing in 2021. The January-run social- and health-oriented TSI connects two participants (either somebody the participant chooses or a stranger they connect with once registered) via mobile or web-based apps. Participants are expected to check in with each other daily to offer support and report on progress.

https://www.sober-buddy.lu/

Sober March: 2021 relaunch of UK-based Go Sober, a previously October-run philanthropic TSI for Macmillan Cancer Support.

https://www.gosober.org.uk/

Suchej únor (Dry February): TSI founded in 2012 by the League of Open Men, a Czech men's mutual help group and NGO. Open to participants of all genders, the campaign focuses on the personal, familial and social benefits of a break from alcohol. Social media groups provide members with online connections to share their experiences, and the group collects donations and raises funds through sales of a companion book but does not entreat participants to engage in fundraising.

https://suchejunor.cz/

Száraz November (Dry November): Hungarian TSI first run in 2014 but popularized in 2016 and sponsored by the Kék Pont (Blue Point) Foundation, an organization providing multiple forms of service and support for users of alcohol and other drugs. The TSI focuses on social objectives and acts more as a participatory public awareness campaign than a formal initiative.

http://kekpont.hu/szaraz-november/

Tipaton Tammikuu (Dropless January): Begun in 2005 in Finland as a public health initiative of the Network for Preventive Substance Abuse Work. This socially oriented campaign does not have a philanthropic objective. Widely practised in informal ways, the idea of a dry January revived the mid-twentieth-century tradition of a politically motivated 'drinking strike' but shifted the orientation to a post-festive season focus on health, wellness and reducing alcohol consumption.

https://www.ept-verkosto.fi/tipaton/

Tournée minérale (Sparkling Round): TSI launched in February 2017 by the Belgian Cancer Foundation and transferred, in 2021, to two health promotion organizations (one Flemish, the other French). Although focused on health and social benefits without a fundraising component, the notion of a (fee-free) reprieve, a birthday wild card (joker d'anniversaire), was introduced in 2021 as a way to incentivize participation among those who would have otherwise been dissuaded.

https://www.tourneeminerale.be/nl

Appendix B: Methodology and participant profiles

At the time that my research into TSIs began in 2013, they were a relatively new phenomenon, one operating as a cultural trend and, perhaps, a transnational, social and public health movement with historical roots in the making. As my inquiries took shape, TSIs became increasingly popular, generated more public commentary and took root in new geographic and cultural contexts. In short, as the research was getting underway to understand these events, their nature and effects were also changing.

Research into emergent phenomena poses many challenges for the researcher, not least because the suitability of the methods envisaged as part of the research design is likely to change as the research problem is better understood. Hesse-Biber and Leavy argue that so-called emergent methods are apt for investigating novel or evolving phenomena precisely because the inquiry is guided by the researcher's 'hunch' about what is at play: 'many qualitative emergent methods bring the intuitive process – always an implicit component of qualitative research – to the forefront' (Hesse-Biber and Leavy 2008: 5). Kathy Charmaz further elucidates that 'Emergent methods are particularly well suited for studying uncharted, contingent, or dynamic phenomena' (Charmaz 2008: 155). Emergent methods are not so much methods in and of themselves as they are approaches – variations, adaptations and combinations – to more established methods. Emergent methods are also often used in research, such as cultural studies, that draws on many different disciplines, each with their own methodological conventions and underpinnings (Saukko 2003).

Cultural phenomena, especially those that involve an aspect of embodiment, are often interrogated using methods that can be understood as emergent. Indeed, Paula Saukko contends that cultural studies is a field that lends itself to combinations of traditional, most often qualitative methods that interrogate three often interrelated aspects of cultural phenomena: lived experience, texts and discourses, and social and global dimensions of reality (Saukko 2003: 12). My curiosity and nascent understanding of TSIs was informed by the multidisciplinary field of cultural studies, particularly as practised in Australia (Frow 2007), and my objective has been to understand TSIs from three main perspectives: those who participate, those who organize and structure them, and those who observe and may be affected at a distance.

The present study accordingly approached the novel phenomenon of TSIs with the objective of understanding them as objects and processes of cultural enquiry rooted in (a) empirical experiences, (b) texts and discourses and (c) underlying conditions and influences. While a cultural history (of sorts) could be presumed to begin with historical research, for instance, into temperance movements, the novelty of TSIs as a phenomenon lent itself to a more emergent method, which 'begins with the empirical world and builds an inductive understanding of it as events unfold and knowledge accrues' (Charmaz 2008: 155). The starting point for this enquiry was therefore the participant experience, which led to an examination of public-facing media and only subsequently organizer insights and historical enquiry. What began as a snapshot investigation into participant experiences, for instance, revealed that those who had been involved in many yearly iterations of the campaign were attuned to the ways organizers had shifted their discourses and communication strategies, which in turn affected their experience of the campaigns. Historical study therefore became an additional element of the project's overall methodology and opened new lines enquiry among both participants and organizers.

Although the overall methodological approach for the project was emergent in its combinations of methods and sequencing, it was underpinned by more conventional methods, such as interviews and discourse, textual and visual analysis, the particulars of which are elaborated here.

Participant experiences

Semi-structured interviews lasting between thirty and forty-five minutes were undertaken with twenty-three Australian TSI participants. Most ($n = 17$) had just recently taken part in the 2014 FebFast campaign, although the sample was rounded out with participants from Dry July ($n = 3$), Ocsober ($n = 1$) and self-directed, informal TSIs ($n = 2$). While slightly more than half ($n = 13$) had repeat experience of a TSI, most often returning to take part in the same campaign year after year, two participants had completed two or more different TSIs. All references to individual participants have been de-identified. See Table 1 for an overview of participant characteristics.

Working with a concentration of participants in a single TSI in a given year provided a consistent base of experience, as they all received the same communications (emails, text messages, website, phone calls) from the organizers. These participants were recruited from those who had completed the end-of-campaign survey (administered by the organizers) and noted that they would be willing to follow up or comment further upon their participation, either for FebFast or as part of independent research. FebFast organizers then facilitated recruitment by emailing these respondents general information about the study and passing along the researcher's contact details. Expressions of interest were made either directly to the researcher or via a response to FebFast that was forwarded on. These volunteers were subsequently given more comprehensive information about the study and provided written consent covering their participation and the use and dissemination of the information they supplied.

As is typical for inquiries of this nature, the sampling tends towards self-selection, which in turn may lead to somewhat biased conclusions (Costigan and Cox 2001). Participants in this study, who were able to be recruited because they had expressed willingness to invest more time into the TSI, are more likely to have found value in the experience than the larger pool of TSI participants, including those who quit before the month's end or who did not complete the organization's survey.

Participants recruited on the basis of their participation in other TSIs help to mitigate this potential selection bias among the larger sample. Participants

Table 1 Participant Profiles

	Pseudonym	Age	Gender	Occupation	Self-described drinking behaviour, pre-TSI	TSI
1	Bethany	37	F	Music therapist	Light drinker with infrequent binges	FebFast
2	Brad	34	M	Information technology	Daily drinker, heavier on weekends	FebFast
3	Rebecca*	45	F	Marketing	Heavy drinker	FebFast
4	Janelle	29	F	Marketing	Daily drinker, heavier on weekends	FebFast
5	David*	54	M	Television production	Daily drinker	FebFast
6	Natalie	26	F	Pharmacist	Light drinker	FebFast
7	Fiona*	32	F	Teacher	Moderate social drinker, mostly on weekends	FebFast
8	Adam	40	M	Publishing	Moderate social drinker	FebFast
9	Lori	30	F	Media manager	Moderate social drinker	FebFast
10	Liesl	28	F	Project manager	Moderate social drinker with infrequent binges	FebFast
11	Thomas*	44	M	Information technology	Moderate social drinker with occasional binges	FebFast
12	Mark*	29	M	Marketing	Moderate social drinker	FebFast
13	Alex*	33	M	Student	Moderate social drinker, mostly on weekends	FebFast
14	Jillian*	44	F	Public servant	Moderate social drinker	FebFast
15	Vi*	44	F	Social worker	Moderate social drinker	FebFast, Dry July, Ocsober
16	Oliver*	49	M	Management, technology	Moderate daily drinker	FebFast
17	Suzanne*	44	F	Office manager	Moderate social drinker	FebFast
18	Kerry*	55	F	Academic	Heavy social drinker	Dry July
19	Himari*	41	F	Office manager	Daily drinker, heavier on weekends	Dry July
20	Samantha	37	F	Researcher	Light drinker	Dry July
21	Kate*	32	F	Data analyst	Moderate social drinker with occasional binges	Ocsober, FebFast
22	Liz	58	F	Student	Daily drinker	Unaffiliated
23	Alan	40	M	Management, technology	Moderate social drinker	Unaffiliated

* indicates repeat TSI participation

in TSIs other than FebFast were recruited in response to calls for participants posted to social media and via direct introductions through the researcher's existing networks, including via self-nomination.

Given that the research objectives were not so much evaluative but rather to understand how participants experienced various facets of the TSI, even a self-selecting sample of this nature can highlight aspects of the experience that resonated with participants. Each participant was interviewed once, approximately a month after the campaign's end. This timing provided a reasonable opportunity, particularly for first-time TSI participants, for baseline behaviours to re-establish themselves, although it was not so far removed that participants' recollections of the subtleties of the campaign and their experiences thereof would be too difficult to recall. Subsequent interviews at a greater remove from the campaign's end would, admittedly, have allowed for a greater sense of the longevity of any changes to behaviour or the durability of changed perceptions, although this perspective was fortuitously provided by repeat participants and via participants who self-nominated as research participants with no distinct timing for their interview participation.

As the participant interviews were exploratory rather than focused on a narrow research question, the data was first coded to identify themes (Ryan and Bernard 2003). Principles of interpretive phenomenological analysis (Smith 1996), notably the concern for how individuals perceive and narrate their experiences, including of embodiment, were subsequently employed to deepen the analysis. Following the principles of contextualized analysis, which maintain that the way something is articulated is fundamental to its meaning and effects (Blommaert 2005), statements were considered with an eye to these more nuanced articulations of participant experiences. A second sweep of data collection would have allowed for more detailed follow-up questioning to probe themes unanticipated in the design of the original interview questions and prompts – including the framing of the TSIs as an experiment – although the flexibility of semi-structured interviews as an emergent research method was utilized to explore such topics as they arose.

The Australian context for this primary research is an important caveat on the generalizability of any conclusions. All participants took part in at least one Australian TSI and, even for the minority of participants ($n = 2$) who were not born or grew up in Australia, more than a decade of residence had steeped them in Australian drinking culture and its expectations, such as the acceptance of daytime drinking, the expectation of joining colleagues for post-work drinks and the exchange of drinks via the practice of buying rounds or 'shouts'.

The dominantly philanthropic nature of Australian TSIs, especially at the time that the interviews were undertaken, must also be considered. Participants, especially at the time, were more likely to be middle-class professionals who understood small acts of private philanthropy as part of the unspoken assumptions in Australian civil society, especially in their mostly secular contexts. They had all completed some form of tertiary study, a characteristic not as universally represented in the socially oriented TSIs in other contexts. As a group, they were thus more likely to reflect middle-class values and insecurities, have enough disposable income to not have to significantly limit their alcohol consumption due to lack of financial means and have good health literacy.

Organizer interviews

Subsequent to the participant interviews and preliminary coding, hour-long interviews were also conducted with members of the staff or organizers of two different TSIs, FebFast (Australia) and Alcohol Free for 40 (Louisiana, USA). This category of 'organizers' included formal leadership, campaign founders and media and communications staff. Interviews with FebFast organizers occurred during the same data collection period in 2014; that with Alcohol Free for 40 in 2017. As with participant interviews, the emergent nature of the enquiry allowed the interviews to be tailored to reflect the evolving nature of the TSI phenomenon, including where organizers of later-emerging campaigns may have been aware of antecedent TSIs and the small but growing body of scholarly research, and potentially devised their own campaigns or strategies with this knowledge in mind.

Published written and recorded third-party interviews (mostly limited to those available in English and French owing to my own linguistic limitations) with a number of other TSI organizers were also accessed and reviewed where these were available. This form of interview allowed access to a wider range of TSIs in different national contexts, as French, British, American, Finnish and Canadian campaigns were commented upon and local drinking contexts acknowledged.

As with the organizer interviews expressly conducted as part of this research, these interviews – including some with the same organizers – took place at a number of points between 2010 and 2021. They therefore provide insight into the changing public discourse those who serve as spokespeople for TSIs create. They also offer candid insight into the strategy underpinning particular initiatives, including the sometimes competitive relationship between different

TSIs. Organizer interviews with third parties, most often third-sector trade publications or forums, specifically speak to questions of strategy that may not always be apparent in materials aimed at the general public.

Discourse, textual and visual analysis of TSI publications and media

Official websites and social media pages act as the main public presence of TSIs and are the most common point of contact for members of the public and the organizations. These multimodal texts (including text, images, videos, interactives, etc.) present the carefully crafted dominant image of a TSI for any given yearly iteration and often include multiple perspectives: those of organizers, participants (in the form of curated testimonials), and in the case of philanthropic TSIs, the beneficiaries of the funds raised. A TSI's broader public communications – press releases, self-help books and media commentary – to participants and potential participants and direct electronic communications (emails, text messages, social media posts and notifications) to participants were also evaluated. Such materials have tended to be the focus of qualitative enquiries, typically systematic social media research, into TSIs (Yeomans 2019, Bartram et al. 2018). The methods employed in such studies, however, tend to examine a given yearly campaign and do not adopt a multi-year longitudinal approach.

Considering that the face of TSIs has tended to change from year to year, examining such materials over a decade reveals evolutions in the self-image TSIs present, especially in response to market-driven factors and events (not least the present Covid-19 pandemic) in the local or global context. Such perspectives are also gleaned from the semi-public documents, such as annual reports, that are a matter of public record for many charitable organizations but that are not widely circulated. Linguistic limitations have seen this evaluation principally carried out on English- and French-language sources.

Where TSI-produced and curated media tends to present an overwhelmingly favourable view of the initiatives, media commentary – including opinion columns, editorials, blogs, vlogs and podcasts – is a rich source of information on how TSIs are received in the larger cultural arenas in which they operate. Media sources frequently include participant perspectives but also encompass reactions to TSIs from those who have neither completed them nor attempted them. Such perspectives are often not considered in research that seeks to evaluate the impact of TSIs but are central considerations for understanding the campaigns as a cultural phenomenon, as they are often both representative of and important in shaping dissenting commentary.

Limitations

Now that TSIs are more established, are genuine international phenomena employing common discourses, images, operating principles and even web-enabled technologies, one could argue that the time for emergent methods is passed. In part, it is the work of this book to make this very case and to legitimate the investment in further research.

The next phase in TSI research will undoubtedly involve both more and more extensive case studies. The qualitative methods favoured by cultural studies, public health, marketing and communication scholars in Australia could provide nuanced understanding of TSIs in other contexts. The larger-scale quantitative studies that have afforded significant insights into the impact of UK-based TSIs might be replicated in both other Commonwealth countries that have much in common with the UK and in countries that have less in common in terms of drinking culture and social circumstances. More importantly, any future research should open up to more systematic comparative enquiries employing both qualitative and quantitative methods. International teams, attuned to aspects of local culture as much as to the subtleties of language, will be needed to determine if what is true of TSIs in one context also holds in others.

Notes

Chapter 1

1 For a sample of this research, see De Visser, R. O., Robinson, E., Smith, T., Cass, G. & Walmsley, M. 2017. 'The Growth of "Dry January": Promoting Participation and the Benefits of Participation', *European Journal of Public Health*, 27, 929–31; Cherrier, H. & Gurrieri, L. 2013. 'Anticonsumption Choices Performed in a Drinking Culture: Normative Struggles and Repairs', *Journal of Macromarketing*, 33, 232–44; Fry, M.-L. 2014. 'Case Study: Hello Sunday Morning! – Towards "Practices" of Responsible Drinking', in Brennan, L., Binney, W., Parker, L., Aleti, T. & Nguyen, D. (eds), *Social Marketing and Behaviour Change: Models, Theory and Applications*, Cheltenham, UK: Edward Elgar; Bartram, A., Hanson-Easey, S. & Eliott, J. 2018. 'Heroic Journeys Through Sobriety: How Temporary Alcohol Abstinence Campaigns Portray Participant Experiences', *International Journal of Drug Policy*, 55, 80–7.

2 My use of 'temperance movement' in the singular acknowledges the stereotype of temperance thinking and action as ill-fitting for the variety of temperance campaigns and ideologies that existed both within and across national borders.

3 Questions of public pedagogy will be addressed in greater detail in Chapter 1. For a selection of indicative sources on the topic, however, see Hickey-Moody, A., Savage, G. C. & Windle, J. 2010. 'Pedagogy Writ Large: Public, Popular And Cultural Pedagogies In Motion', *Critical Studies In Education*, 51, 227–36; Burdick, J. & Sandlin, J. A. 2013. 'Learning, Becoming, and the Unknowable: Conceptualisations, Mechanisms, and Process in Public Pedagogy Literature', *Curriculum Inquiry*, 43, 142–77; Sandlin, J. A., Schultz, B. D. & Burkick, J. 2011. 'Understanding, Mapping, and Exploring the Terrain of Public Pedagogy', in Sandlin, J. A., Schultz, B. D. & Burdick, J. (eds), *Handbook Of Public Pedagogy*, New York: Routledge; Watkins, M., Noble, G. & Driscoll, C. 2015. *Cultural Pedagogies and Human Conduct*, London: Routeledge.

4 See, in particular, Chapter 4 of Warnick, B. R. 2008. *Imitation and Education: A Philosophical Inquiry into Learning by Example*, Albany, NY: State University of New York Press.

Chapter 2

1 While there are important distinctions between these terms, often relating to the scholarly tradition from which they issue, I use public pedagogy (the most widely used of the designations) in a general rather than a particular sense. For an incisive explanation of these terminological distinctions, see the introduction to Flowers and Swan's *Food Pedagogies* (2015).

2 While not used in the specialist ways particular to education, the terms 'pedagogic', 'instructive' and 'didactic' are employed in a differentiated manner. The pedagogic is understood to be a source of instruction or guidance but allows for the possibility that such instruction may not have been formalized or intended. Something is understood to be instructive when there is intent in method, but not necessarily in the conclusions drawn. The didactic, in contrast, implies the purposeful transmission of particular knowledge.

3 Subsequent campaigns in 2018, running under the same tagline, continued to use the same rationale. The imagery accompanying the outdoor signage featured two photos, each one depicting two of three generations in a family with the child in the first image reproducing the parent's excessive consumption (a large, overfilled glass of wine, a collection of empty beer bottles) in the second image, where they are in the parental role. See DrinkWise Australia 2021.

4 The FebFast annual report from 2008 encapsulates both purposefully and subtly pedagogical facets. The mission statement, for instance, clearly stipulates a goal to 'educate and inform the public around issues associated with overuse of alcohol', but the vision is less forceful, citing a contribution 'to the Australian population's thinking and behaviour around alcohol consumption' (FebFast 2009: 2).

Chapter 3

1 While not officially part of TSIs, the popularity of the campaigns has led to some crossover, if in some cases temporary, with 'sober-curious' and mindful drinking groups and communities. Alcohol Concern's *Try Dry* (Booker 2019), for instance, identifies a number of such groups and includes them (and their UK contact details) as resources for those intending to complete either Dry January or a self-scheduled sober month.

2 The algorithms that tailor advertising content on social media platforms to mirror a user's search activity are also likely to reinforce the messages of sober sociality. Ads for non-alcoholic or dealcoholized spirits, wines and beers ensure that voluntary non-consumption of alcohol should not be linked with non-consumption overall.

3　The case of the Défi 28 jours and Dry Feb is not a straightforward case of rival TSIs operating in the same location. The former operates primarily in French at a local level (city extended to a province-wide remit), whereas the latter is a more recent introduction as a nationwide campaign that operates primarily in English. Thus while there is likely to be some overlap, especially given the bilingual character of Quebec's largest city, the TSIs effectively operate in two separate spheres.

4　Like TSIs, detox diets and cleanses involve highly visible practices of time-delimited retreat from normal sumptuary practices. For instance, many of these diets see participants replace solid food with juices, teas or other beverages for seven to ten days.

5　Many of the founders have nonetheless gone on to be genuine cultural entrepreneurs. Healy was appointed to the YSAS Board as FebFast grew in scale and the concept was eventually purchased by the organization. Robinson has co-authored research papers on Dry January's impact, and the founders of Dry July were able to pivot to full-time employment with the Dry July Foundation.

6　On the Dry ran its final campaign in January 2017. Since then, Dry January has been the unofficial Irish TSI.

7　The group had to change their name from Dry January to the Dry January Crew when the group was founded in 2018, likely owing to Alcohol Change UK's trademarking of the more generic term.

8　Throsby's analysis focused on the motivations of the abstainers themselves rather than the orientation or objectives of any sponsoring agency or organization.

9　Unofficial participation, arguably freeriding, is still a common practice even where there are no financial barriers to registration and official participation. Official and widely accessible social media activity and content allow unregistered participants to access many of the supports offered to registrants. Similarly, close contacts of participants may enlist 'sympathetic participants', such as partners and siblings, as unofficial participants who shadow the campaign. Heightened concerns about data security and privacy may also contribute to unofficial rather than registered participation.

Chapter 4

1　Temperance in other contexts was more aligned with working-class values. Finnish temperance was both primarily rural and working class (Sulkunen 1990), and in Germany, temperance was linked to socialism and workers' movements (Roberts 1982).

2　Heath (2012: 37) notes that adherents of temperance movements are uniquely outspoken about not only their choices but the choices of others: 'With respect to most realms of behavior, people who choose not to participate are generally indifferent when others do. But those who do not drink are often vocal, persistent, and influential in criticizing those who do, so the history of alcohol has been irregularly punctuated by prohibitions and restrictions, both legal and popular.'

3 So-called sober-curious organizations (Warrington 2018) are based on extended periods of abstinence and are seen as a way for adherents to experiment with sobriety as a lifestyle choice.

Chapter 5

1 The concept of 'detox', whether popular or clinical, is predicated on re-establishing a pharmacological baseline.

2 Empathy with the beneficiaries of an embodied philanthropy's charitable efforts is often one of the impetuses behind highly participatory forms of involvement (Robert 2018). The most publicized example, both as an unaffiliated action and in concert with initiatives such as the World's Greatest Shave, is shaving one's head in support of cancer-related causes, reflecting the common side effect of hair loss among those undergoing chemotherapy.

Chapter 6

1 The concept of 'responsible' drinking' in the UK is principally used by industry bodies and references vague behavioural definitions rather than the quantifiable measures preferred by medical and public health practitioners (Hessari and Petticrew 2017). This choice of phrasing, however, does not necessarily hold in all contexts. In Australia, many prominent politicians and government officials have adopted the rhetoric of 'responsible drinking' to differentiate between those who engage in violent or anti-social behaviour while under the influence from those who drink (whether very moderately or heavily), but who do not generate public disturbances. This popular use of the term has allowed 'responsible drinking' to be widely employed as an imperfect synonym of 'moderate drinking'.

2 The United States and its privatized healthcare system is a notable exception. The cost of insurance or treatment for the un/under insured means that one's economic circumstances can be severely affected by disease or illness.

3 Variations in definitions of moderate or responsible drinking between jurisdictions introduce further complications, especially as flows of information have become increasingly international. See Furtwængler, N. A. F. F. & Visser, R. O. 2013. 'Lack

of International Consensus in Low-Risk Drinking Guidelines', *Drug and Alcohol Review*, 32, 11–18.

4   For proponents of constructive drinking hypotheses, the readiness with which the population accepts the premise that reducing alcohol consumption is healthy attests to the dominance of public health paradigms and the narrowness of their definitions of health.

5   Yeomans, H. 2019. 'New Year, New You: A qualitative study of Dry January, self-formation and positive regulation', *Drugs: Education, Prevention and Policy,* 26, 460–8 clarifies that the discourse of TSI participant as altruistic hero is more prominent in campaigns with strong philanthropic orientations; TSIs such as Dry January are by contrast more focused on the self.

6   Dryathlon had limited campaigns taking place at other times, notably September beginning in 2015 and October beginning in 2018, a move that put the initiative in direct competition with Macmillan's Go Sober. See Weakley, K. 2018. *CRUK Changes Dryathlon to Clash with Macmillan's Go Sober* [Online]. London: Civil Society News. Available: https://www.civilsociety.co.uk/news/cancer-research-uk -to-run-dryathlon-in-october-clashing-with-macmillan.html (Accessed 7 April 2021).

7   Common forms of slacktivism that attract suspicion and scorn include reposting content (images or text) that signal alignment with a cause or support for victims of a tragic event without either (a) understanding the cause or events or (b) doing anything concrete, such as making a donation to a charity or relief effort, in addition to the show of temporary online solidarity.

Chapter 7

1   Jillian's appeals as 'cheerleader' are not only affective or emotional but also align well with neo-liberal logics of privatized preventative action or early intervention rather than allowing unaddressed problems to become matters for the state.

2   FebFast, which supports a Victorian charity, has a much stronger support base in Melbourne and other parts of Victoria than it does in the rest of Australia. Dry July now operates nationally but began as a local initiative in the eastern suburbs of Sydney, with the funds raised going to support the purchase of a television in the cancer centre of the local hospital. These kinds of locally impactful and tangible charity projects are one of the best ways to motivate donations.

3   Australia might be accused of having a larrikinish preference for slightly self-serving forms of embodied philanthropy. Movember, the now global month-long moustache growing fundraiser, began in Melbourne. Similarly, Sydney's annual City 2 Surf charity run regularly attracts over 80,000 participants.

Chapter 8

1 Room makes clear that, in a technical sense, 'social drinking' is not a synonym for moderate or responsible drinking. This is in contradiction to the common or vernacular use of the term today. Rather, 'social drinking', which may indeed entail the consumption of significant quantities of alcohol, 'is carried on with others and is heavily influenced by their expectations' (Room 1975: 360).

References

40 Brez Alkohola. 2021. *40 Brez Alkohola* [Online]. Ljubljana. Available: https://brezalkohola.si/o-akciji/ [Accessed 14 March 2021].

ABS. 2015. 'Apparent Alcohol Consumption Hits a 50 Year Low', Canberra: Australian Bureau of Statistics.

Act For Peace 2021. *Ration Challenge* [Online]. Canberra: Act for Peace. Available: https://actforpeace.rationchallenge.org.au/ [Accessed 12 April 2021].

Adler, M. 1991. 'From Symbolic Exchange to Commodity Consumption: Anthropological Notes on Drinking as a Symbolic Practice', in Barrows, S. & Room, R. (eds), *Drinking: Behaviour and Belief in Modern History*, Berkeley: University of California Press, 376–98.

AIHW. 2008. '2007 National Drug Strategy Household Survey: First Results', *Drug Statistics Series no. 20. Cat no. PHE 98*, Canberra: Australian Institute of Health and Wellness.

AIHW 2014. 'National Drug Strategy Household Survey: Detailed Report 2013', *Drug Statistics Series*, Canberra: Australian Institute of Health and Wellness.

Ajzen, I. 1985. 'From Intentions to Actions: A Theory of Planned Behavior', in Kuhl, J. & Beckermann, J. (eds), *Action Control: From Cognition to Behavior*, Berlin & Heidelberg: Springer, 11–39.

Alcohol Change UK. 2020a. *Information for Charities* [Online]. London: Alcohol Change UK. Available: https://alcoholchange.org.uk/get-involved/campaigns/dry-january/go-dry-for-charity/information-for-charities [Accessed 16 October 2020].

Alcohol Change UK. 2020b. *What is Dry January?* [Online]. London: Alcohol Change UK. Available: https://alcoholchange.org.uk/get-involved/campaigns/dry-january/about-dry-january/what-is-dry-january [Accessed 7 August 2020].

Alcohol Change UK. 2020c. *Why Do Dry January?* [Online]. London: Alcohol Change UK. Available: https://alcoholchange.org.uk/get-involved/campaigns/dry-january/why-do-dry-january-1/why-do-dry-january [Accessed 17 August 2020].

Alcorn, G. 2019. 'I Was Only Going to Give Up Alcohol for a Month but I Wasn't Prepared for the Impact It Had', *Guardian Australia*, 31 July.

Altimari Adler, D. M. 2019. *Plato's Timaeus and the Missing Fourth Guest: Finding the Harmony of the Spheres*, London: Brill.

American Liver Foundation. 2020. *Go Dry – Home* [Online]. New York: American Liver Foundation. Available: https://alfgodry.org/ [Accessed June 29 2020].

Amienyo, D., Camilleri, C. & Azapagic, A. 2014. 'Environmental Impacts of Consumption of Australian Red Wine in the UK', *Journal of Cleaner Production*, 72, 110–19.

References

Anderson, P., De Bruijn, A., Angus, K., Gordon, R. & Hastings, G. 2009. 'Impact of Alcohol Advertising and Media Exposure on Adolescent Alcohol Use: A Systematic Review of Longitudinal Studies', *Alcohol and Alcoholism*, 44, 229–43.

Andreoni, J. 1989. 'Giving with Impure Altruism: Applications to Charity and Ricardian Equivalence', *Journal of Political Economy*, 97, 1447–58.

Andreoni, J. 1990. 'Impure Altruism and Donations to Public Good: A Theory of "Warm-Glow Giving"', *The Economic Journal*, 100, 464–77.

Anne-Lise. 2014. 'Défi 28 jours: On commence l'année 2014 par une bonne action!', *Montreal Addicts: Curieuses, gourmandes, rêveuses* [Online]. Available from: http://montreal-addicts.com/defi-28-jours-jean-lapointe/ [Accessed 18 January 2017].

Arcese, G., Lucchetti, M. C. & Martucci, O. 2012. 'Analysis of Sustainability Based on Life Cycle Assessment: An Empirical Study of Wine Production', *Journal of Environmental Science and Engineering*, B1, 682–9.

Aristotle. 1991. *On Rhetoric: A Theory of Civic Discourse*, Oxford: Oxford University Press.

Atkinson, A. J., Huang, S.-M., Lertora, J. & Markey, S. (eds) 2012. *Principles of Clinical Pharmacology*, Cambridge, MA: Academic Press.

Aviles, G. 2020. *For Some, the New Dry January isn't Actually Dry* [Online]. New York: NBC News. Available: https://www.nbcnews.com/pop-culture/pop-culture-news/some-new-dry-january-isn-t-actually-dry-n1111741 [Accessed 11 November 2020].

Azar, D., White, V., Bland, S., Livingston, M., Room, R., Chikritzhs, T., Durkin, S., Gilmore, W. & Wakefield, M. 2013. '"Something's Brewing": The Changing Trends in Alcohol Coverage in Australian Newspapers 2000–2011', *Alcohol and Alcoholism*, 49, 336–42.

Bandura, A. 1977. 'Self-Efficacy: Toward a Unifying Theory of Behavioral Change', *Psychological Review*, 84, 191–215.

Bandura, A. 1986. *Social Foundations of Thought and Action: A Social Cognitive Theory*, Englewood Cliffs, NJ: Prentice-Hall.

Bandura, A. 2006. 'Self-Efficacy Scales', in Urdan, T. & Pajares, F. (eds), *Self-Efficacy Beliefs of Adolescents*, Charlotte, NC: Information Age Publishing, 307–37.

Barrows, S. & Room, R. (eds) 1991. *Drinking: Behavior and Belief in Modern History*, Berkeley: University of California Press.

Barry, A. E. & Goodson, P. 2010. 'Use (and Misuse) of the Responsible Drinking Message in Public Health and Alcohol Advertising: A Review', *Health Education & Behavior*, 37, 228–303.

Barthes, R. 1957. *Mythologies*, Paris: Seuil.

Barthes, R. 1991. *Mythologies*, New York: Noonday Press.

Bartram, A., Eliott, J. & Crabb, S. 2017. '"Why Can't I Just Not Drink?" A Qualitative Study of Adults' Social Experiences of Stopping or Reducing Alcohol Consumption', *Drug and Alcohol Review*, 36, 449–55.

Bartram, A., Hanson-Easey, S. & Eliott, J. 2018. 'Heroic Journeys Through Sobriety: How Temporary Alcohol Abstinence Campaigns Portray Participant Experiences', *International Journal of Drug Policy*, 55, 80–7.

References

BBC. 2012. 'Detoxing in January is Futile, Says Liver Charity', *Health*.

BC Cancer Foundation. 2020. *Lose the Booze – Home* [Online]. Vancouver: BC Cancer Foundation. Available: https://secure2.convio.net/bccf/site/SPageServer/?pagename =ltb18_home [Accessed 29 June 2020].

Beck, U. 2002. *Risk Society: Towards a New Modernity*, London: Sage.

Beck, U. 2009. *World at Risk*, Cambridge: Polity.

Bekkers, R. 2006. 'Traditional and Health-Related Philanthropy: The Role of Resources and Personality', *Social Psychology Quarterly*, 69, 349–66.

Belarmino, J. J. 2013. 'Essay Review: Imitation and Education: A Philosophical Inquiry into Learning by Example', *Journal of Aesthetic Education*, 47, 111–26.

Bennett, R. & Savani, S. 2011. 'Sources of New Ideas of Charity Fundraising: An Empirical Study. *Creativity and Innovation in Management*, 20, 121–38.

Bernard, J. 1991. 'From Fasting to Abstinence: The Origins of the American Temperance Movement', in Barrows, S. & Room, R. (eds), *Drinking: Behavior and Belief in Modern History*, Berkeley: University of California Press, 337–53.

Berridge, V. 2005. *Temperance: Its History and Impact on Current and Future Alcohol Policy*, London: Joseph Rowntree Foundation.

Berridge, V. 2013. *Demons: Our Changing Attitudes to Alcohol, Tobacco, and Drugs*, Oxford: Oxford University Press.

Big Easy Dryout. 2017. *Big Easy Dryout: No Alcohol, Lots of Motivation* [Online]. New Orleans: Causevox.com. Available: https://bigeasydryout.causevox.com/ [Accessed 14 March 2021].

Bird, L. B. 2019. *8 Mocktails You Need to Try This Dry July* [Online]. Sydney: Urban List. Available: https://www.theurbanlist.com/sydney/a-list/best-mocktails-sydney [Accessed 3 August 2020].

Birkwood, S. 2014. *Analysis: The Three Dry Campaigns – Compare and Contrast* [Online]. London: Third Sector. Available: http://www.thirdsector.co.uk/analysis -three-dry-campaigns-compare-contrast/fundraising/article/1317844 [Accessed 19 September 2017].

Bishop, M. & Green, M. 2015. 'Philanthrocapitalism Rising', *Society*, 52, 541–8.

Blainey, A. 2000. 'The "Fallen" Are Every Mother's Children: The Woman's Christian Temperance Union's Campaign for Temperance, Women's Suffrage and Sexual Reform in Australia, 1885–1905', PhD thesis, LaTrobe University.

Blommaert, J. 2005. *Discourse: A Critical Introduction*, Cambridge: Cambridge University Press.

Body, A. & Breeze, B. 2016. 'What Are "Unpopular Causes" and How Can They Achieve Fundraising Success?', *International Journal of Nonprofit and Voluntary Sector Marketing*, 21, 57–70.

Boisserie-Lacroix, C. & Inchingolo, M. 2019. 'Empathy for a Reason? From Understanding Agency to Phenomenal Insight', *Synthese*, 198(8), 7097–118.

Booker, L. 2019. *Try Dry: The Official Guide to a Month Off Booze*, London: Square Peg.

Bourdieu, P. 1977. *Outline of a Theory of Practice*, Cambridge: Cambridge University Press.

Bourdieu, P. 1984. *Distinction: A Social Critique of the Judgement of Taste*, Cambridge, MA: Harvard University Press.

Breeze, B. & Scaife, W. 2015. 'Encouraging Generosity: The Practice and Organization of Fund-Raising across Nations', in Wiepking, P. & Handy, F. (eds), *The Palgrave Handbook of Global Philanthropy*, London: Palgrave Macmillan, 570–96.

Bretherton, G. 1991. 'Against the Flowing Tide: Whiskey and Temperance in the Making of Modern Ireland', in Barrows, S. & Room, R. (eds), *Drinking: Behavior and Belief in Modern History*, Berkeley, CA: University of California Press, 147–64.

British Liver Trust. 2018. *4.2 Million People in the UK to Give Up Alcohol for Dry January 2019* [Online]. London: British Liver Trust. Available: https://britishlivertrust.org.uk/millions-to-do-dry-january-2019/ [Accessed 4 August 2020].

Broadbent, T. 2018. *Dry January Dan* (YouTube Video). Tamar Broadbent. Available: https://www.youtube.com/watch?v=FRko6tO5B9A.

Brown, B. J. & Baker, S. 2012. *Responsible Citizens: Individuals, Health and Policy Under Neoliberalism*, London: Anthem Press.

Brownie, B. & Graydon, D. M. 2015. *The Superhero Costume: Identity and Disguise in Fact and Fiction*, London: Bloomsbury.

Brubaker, R. 2020. 'Digital Hyperconnectivity and the Self', *Theory and Society*, 49, 771–801.

Bryant, L. 2020. *Dryathlon* [Online]. Brighton: Killer Creative. Available: https://www.killercreative.co.uk/project/dryathlon/ [Accessed 14 September 2020].

Bunds, K. S., Brandon-Lai, S. & Armstrong, C. 2016. 'An Inductive Investigation of Participants' Attachment to Charity Sports Events: The Case of Team Water Charity', *European Sport Management Quarterly*, 16, 364–83.

Burdick, J. & Sandlin, J. A. 2013. 'Learning, Becoming, and the Unknowable: Conceptualisations, Mechanisms, and Process in Public Pedagogy Literature', *Curriculum Inquiry*, 43, 142–77.

Cancer Research UK. 2020a. *Does Alcohol Cause Cancer?* [Online]. London: Cancer Research UK. Available: https://www.cancerresearchuk.org/about-cancer/causes-of-cancer/alcohol-and-cancer/does-alcohol-cause-cancer [Accessed 12 July 2020].

Cancer Research UK. 2020b. *Dryathlon* [Online]. London: Cancer Research UK. Available: https://www.cancerresearchuk.org/get-involved/do-your-own-fundraising/dryathlon [Accessed 7 June 2020].

Cancer Research UK. 2020c. *Dryathlon: Fundraising Tools and Ideas* [Online]. London: Cancer Research UK. Available: https://www.cancerresearchuk.org/get-involved/do-your-own-fundraising/dryathlon/fundraising-tools-and-ideas [Accessed June 7 2020].

Carah, N., Meurk, C. & Angus, D. 2017. 'Online Self-Expression and Experimentation as "Reflectivism": Using Text Analytics to Examine the Participatory Forum Hello

Sunday Morning', *Health: An Interdisciplinary Journal for the Social Study of Health, Illness and Medicine*, 21, 119–35.

Carlisle, S., Snooks, H., Evans, A. & Cohen, D. 2007. 'Evaluation, Evidence and Learning in Community-Based Action Research', In: Cropper, S. & Porter, A. (eds), *Community Health and Wellbeing: Action Research on Health Inequalities.* Bristol: Policy Press, 147–70.

Carter, B. 2014. 'New Name for Parched March as it Enters Fifth Year', *Hospitality Magazine.* Sydney.

Case, P., Angus, C., De Vocth, F., Holmes, F., Michie, S. & Brown, J. 2021. 'Has the Increased Participation in the National Campaign "Dry January" been Associated with Cutting Down Alcohol Consumption in England?' *Drug and Alcohol Dependence*, https://doi.org/10.1016/j.drugalcdep.2021.108938 [Accessed 6 August 2021].

Castells, M. 2007. 'Communication, Power and Counter-Power in the Network Society', *International Journal of Communication*, 1, 238–66.

Castells, M. 2015. *Networks of Outrage and Hope: Social Movements in the Internet Age*, Cambridge, Polity.

Chapman, S. 2015. 'Cancer Research UK's Dryathlon', *I Wish I'd Thought of That - Case Studies.* SOFII (Showcase of Fundraising Innovation and Inspiration).

Charmaz, K. 2008. 'Grounded Theory as an Emergent Method', In: Hesse-Biber, S. N. & Leavy, P. (eds), *Handbook of Emergent Methods.* New York: Guilford Press, 155–72.

Cheers, C., Callinan, S. & Pennay, A. 2020. 'The "Sober Eye": Examining Attitudes towards Non-drinkers in Australia', *Psychology & Health.*

Chell, K. & Mortimer, G. 2014. 'Investigating Online Recognition for Blood Donor Retention: An Experiential Donor Value Approach', *International Journal of Nonprofit and Voluntary Sector Marketing*, 19, 143–63.

Cherrier, H., Carah, N. & Meurk, C. 2017. 'Social Media Affordances for Curbing Alcohol Consumption: Insights from Hello Sunday Morning Blog Posts', In: Lyons, A. C., McCreanor, T., Goodwin, I. & Moewaka Barnes, H. (eds), *Youth Drinking Cultures in a Digital World: Alcohol, Social Media and Cultures of Intoxication.* New York: Routledge

Cherrier, H. & Gurrieri, L. 2013. 'Anti-consumption Choices Performed in a Drinking Culture: Normative Struggles and Repairs', *Journal of Macromarketing*, 33, 232–44.

Cherry, E. 2015. 'I was a Teenage Vegan: Motivation and Maintenance of Lifestyle Movements', *Sociological Inquiry*, 85, 55–74.

Choudry, A. 2015. *Learning Activism: The Intellectual Life of Contemporary Social Movements*, Toronto: University of Toronto Press.

Chouinard, J.-S. 2014. *Défi 28 jours: 4 Keys to Success* [Online]. Montreal: Adviso.ca. Available: http://www.adviso.ca/en/blog/2014/05/07/4-elements-succes-28-jours-les -longs-ta-vie-2/ [Accessed 20 September 2017].

Chouinard, J.-S. & Théorêt-Poupart, A. 2013. *Soberary – les 28 jours les plus longs de ta vie: Public Event Invitation* [Online]. Facebook. Available: https://www.facebook .com/events/135458343283685/ [Accessed 22 September 2017].

Cin, S. D., Worth, K. A., Dalton, M. A. & Sargent, J. D. 2008. 'Youth Exposure to Alcohol Use and Brand Appearances in Popular Contemporary Movies', *Addiction*, 103, 1925–32.

Clarke, J. 2005. 'New Labour's Citizens: Activated, Empowered, Responsibilized, Abandoned?', *Critical Social Policy*, 25, 447–63.

Cody, K. & Jackson, S. 2016. 'The Contested Terrain of Alcohol Sponsorship of Sport in New Zealand', *International Review for the Sociology of Sport*, 51, 375–93.

Cohen, S. 2002. *Folk Devils and Moral Panics: The Creation of the Mods and Rockers*, Abingdon, UK: Routledge.

Cook, L. 2012. 'European Press Review – 22/01/2012. Radio France Internationale', Available: http://en.rfi.fr/europe/20120122-european-press-review [Accessed 3 September 2017].

Costigan, C. L. & Cox, M. J. 2001. 'Fathers' Participation in Family Research: Is There a Self-Selection Bias?', *Journal of Family Psychology*, 15, 706–20.

Cowra Guardian. 2014. 'Dryving a Change in Drinking Culture', *Cowra Guardian*, 4 July.

Crawford, R. 1980. 'Healthism and the Medicalization of Everyday Life', *International Journal of Health Services*, 10, 356–88.

Crawford, R. 2006. 'Health as a Meaningful Social Practice', *Health: An Interdisciplinary Journal for the Social Study of Health*, 10, 401–20.

Dahl, R. 1964. *Charlie and the Chocolate Factory*, London: Puffin.

Dawnay, E. & Shah, H. 2005. *Behavioural Economics: Seven Principles for Policy Makers*. London: New Economics Foundation.

De Visser, R. O. & Nicholls, J. 2020. 'Temporary Abstinence During Dry January: Predictors of Success; Impact on Well-Being and Self-Efficacy', *Psychology & Health*, 1–13.

De Visser, R. O. & Piper, R. 2020. 'Short- and Longer-Term Benefits of Temporary Alcohol Abstinence During "Dry January" Are Not Also Observed Among Adult Drinkers in the General Population: Prospective Cohort Study', *Alcohol and Alcoholism*, 55, 433–8.

De Visser, R. O., Robinson, E. & Bond, R. 2016. 'Voluntary Temporary Abstinence from Alcohol During "Dry January" and Subsequent Alcohol Use', *Health Psychology*, 35, 281–9.

De Visser, R. O., Robinson, E., Smith, T., Cass, G. & Walmsley, M. 2017. 'The Growth of "Dry January": Promoting Participation and the Benefits of Participation', *European Journal of Public Health*, 27, 929–31.

De Visser, R. O. & Smith, J. A. 2007. 'Young Men's Ambivalence Toward Alcohol', *Social Science & Medicine*, 64, 350–62.

Dean, J. 2020. *The Good Glow: Charity and the Symbolic Power of Doing Good*, Bristol: Policy Press.

Dean, M. 1999. *Governmentality: Power and Rule in Modern Society*, London: Sage.

Défi 28 jours. 2017. *Notre Cause* [Online]. Montreal: Fondation Jean Lapointe. Available: http://defi28jours.com/notre-cause/ [Accessed 20 September 2017].

Department Of Health. 2014. *Alcohol: Initiatives to Minimise the Harmful Effects of Alcohol Consumption in Australian Society* [Online]. Canberra: Australian Government: Department of Health. Available: http://www.health.gov.au/internet /main/publishing.nsf/Content/health-pubhlth-strateg-drugs-alcohol-index.htm [Accessed 9 December 2014].

Dewey, J. 1934. *Art as Experience*, New York, Reprint edition by Penguin, 2005.

Dingle, A. E. 1977. *The Rise and Fall of Temperance Economics*, Melbourne: Monash University.

Dixon, B. 2005. '"Detox", a Mass Delusion', *The Lancet Infectious Diseases*, 5, 261.

Doran, M. 2017. 'Healthy Harold, Life Education Australia Saved from Planned Funding Cuts', *ABC News*, 30 May.

Douglas, M. (ed.) 1987. *Constructive Drinking: Perspectives on Drink from Anthropology*, Cambridge: Cambridge University Press.

Douglas, M. & Wildavsky, A. 1983. *Risk and Culture: An Essay on the Selection of Technological and Environmental Dangers*, Berkeley, CA: University of California Press.

Downing, A. 2019. *Dry January Could Actually be a Bad Idea so Pass Us the Aperol* [Online]. Body + Soul. Available: https://www.bodyandsoul.com.au/health/womens -health/dry-january-could-actually-be-a-bad-idea-so-pass-us-the-aperol/news-story /76db642e2e149f3fcf22e380706b4212 [Accessed 11 November 2020].

DrinkWise Australia. 2009. *Parental Influence Campaign* [Online]. South Melbourne: DrinkWise. Available: https://drinkwise.org.au/our-work/parents-campaign/# [Accessed 7 June 2020].

DrinkWise Australia. 2021. *Drinking and Teens: Australian Parents Encouraged to Display Good Role Modelling Behaviours at Home* [Online]. South Melbourne: DrinkWise Australia. Available: https://drinkwise.org.au/our-work/drinking-and -teens-australian-parents-encouraged-to-display-good-role-modelling-behaviours -at-home/# [Accessed 14 March 2021].

Dry Feb Canada. 2015. *Dry Feb Official Twitter Feed* [Online]. Toronto: Dry Feb Canada. Available: https://twitter.com/dryfebca?lang=en [Accessed 2 December 2020].

Dry January. 2016. *Dry January – Fundraising* [Online]. London: Alcohol Concern. Available: https://www.alcoholconcern.org.uk/Pages/Site/dry-january/Category/ fundraising [Accessed 25 November 2016].

Dry January. 2017. *Our Story* [Online]. Alcohol Concern. Available: https://www .alcoholconcern.org.uk/Pages/FAQs/Site/dry-january/Category/dry-january-story [Accessed 8 September 2017].

Dry January France. 2020. *Dry January France – Home* [Online]. Paris: Fédération Addiction. Available: https://dryjanuary.fr/ [Accessed 29 June 2020].

Dry January Suisse. 2021. *Dry January*, [Online]. Bern: Dry January Suisse. Available: https://dryjanuary.ch/fr/ [Accessed 14 March 2021].

Dry July. 2009. *Dry July Annual Report 2009*. Sydney: Dry July.

Dry July. 2013. *Dry July – About* [Online]. Sydney: Dry July. Available: https://www.dryjuly.com/about [Accessed 30 March 2014].

Dry July. 2014a. *Dry July 2013/2014 Annual Report*. Sydney: Dry July.

Dry July. 2014b. *Dry July: Wellbeing!* [Online]. Sydney: Dry July. Available: http://wellbeing.dryjuly.com/ [Accessed 28 December 2014].

Dry July. 2015a. *About* [Online]. Sydney: Dry July. Available: http://au.dryjuly.com/about [Accessed 15 January 2015].

Dry July. 2015b. *Dry July 2014/2015 Annual Report*. Sydney: Dry July.

Dry July. 2016. *Dry July 2015/2016 Annual Report*. Sydney: Dry July.

Dry July. 2017a. *Dry July – Homepage* [Online]. Sydney: Dry July. Available: https://www.dryjuly.com/ [Accessed 30 August 2017].

Dry July. 2017b. *Our Beneficiaries* [Online]. Sydney: Dry July. Available: https://www.dryjuly.com/our-beneficiaries [Accessed 29 September 2017].

Dry July. 2020. *Golden Tickets* [Online]. Sydney: Dry July Foundation. Available: https://www.dryjuly.com/golden-tickets [Accessed 5 October 2020].

Dry July Foundation. 2011. *Dry July Annual Report 2010/11*. Sydney: Dry July Foundation.

Dry July Foundation. 2017. *Dry July Foundation 2017 Annual Report*. Sydney: Dry July Foundation.

Dry July Foundation. 2020. *Dry(ish) July* [Online]. Sydney: Dry July Foundation. Available: https://www.dryjuly.com/dryish-july [Accessed 27 July 2020].

Dry July Foundation. 2021. *Dry July Foundation Impact Report 2020*. Sydney: Dry July Foundation.

Dry July New Zealand. 2014. *Dry July NZ Trust Annual Report 2013–14*. Auckland.

Dryathlon. 2016a. *Dryathlon – Home* [Online]. London: Cancer Research UK. Available: http://www.cancerresearchuk.org/support-us/find-an-event/charity-challenges/dryathlon [Accessed 17 December 2016].

Dryathlon. 2016b. *Willpower Test* [Online]. London: Cancer Research UK. Available: http://www.cancerresearchuk.org/support-us/find-an-event/charity-challenges/dryathlon/willpower-test [Accessed 25 November 2016].

Dubecki, L. 2013. 'T-Totalled: Profits Plunge as Drinkers Abstain for Charity', *The Age*, 25 February.

Dufour, M. C. 1999. 'What is Moderate Drinking? Defining "Drinks" and Drinking Levels', *Alcohol Research and Health*, 23, 5–14.

Dugard, P., File, P. & Todman, J. 2012. *Single-Case and Small-n Experimental Designs: A Practical Guide to Randomization Tests*, New York: Routledge.

Dykstra, C. & Law, M. 1994. 'Popular Social Movements as Educative Forces: Towards a Theoretical Framework', in Hyams, M. (ed.), *35th Annual Adult Education Research Conference, 1994, Knoxville, TN*, Knoxville, TN: University of Tennessee, 121–6.

Edman, J. 2015. 'Temperance and Modernity: Alcohol Consumption as a Collective Problem, 1885–1913', *Journal of Social History*, 49, 20–52.

References

Edwards, H. H. & Kreshel, P. J. 2008. 'An Audience Interpretation of Corporate Communication in a Cause-Related Corporate Outreach Event: The Avon Breast Cancer 3-Day Walk', *Journalism & Communication Monographs*, 10, 175–244.

Ehkäisevän Päidetyön Järjestöverkosto. 2020. *Behöver Jag den Här? [Do I need this?]* [Online]. Helsinki: Ehkäisevän Päidetyön Järjestöverkosto. Available: https://www.ept-verkosto.fi/en/doineedthis/ [Accessed 5 October 2020].

Eikenberry, A. M. 2009. *Giving Circles: Philanthropy, Voluntary Association, and Democracy*, Bloomington, IN: Indiana University Press.

Einstein, M. 2012. *Compassion, Inc.: How Corporate America Blurs the Line Between What We Buy, Who We Are, and Those We Help*, Berkeley, CA: University of California Press.

Elgin, C. Z. 1993. 'Understanding: Art and Science', *Synthese*, 95, 13–28.

Ellwood, C. A. 1901. 'The Theory of Imitation in Social Psychology', *American Journal of Sociology*, 6, 721–41.

Emanuel, J. 2014. 'The Fast Way to Fundraising', *Third Sector Magazine*. Sydney: Octomedia.

Engs, R. C. 2000. *Clean Living Movements: American Cycles of Health Reform*, Westport, CT: Praeger.

Eriksen, S. 1990. 'Drunken Danes and Sober Swedes? Religious Revivalism and the Temperance Movements as Keys to Danish and Swedish Folk Cultures', in Stråth, B. & Holmberg, C. (Eds). *Disco II Conference on Continuity and Discontinuity in the Scandinavian Democratisation Process, 1989 Kungälv, Sweden*. Gothenburg: Department of History, Gothenburg University, 55–94.

Fahey, D. M. 2006. 'Temperance Internationalism: Guy Hayler and the World Prohibition Federation', *The Social History of Alcohol and Drugs*, 20, 247–75.

Fawsitt, M. 2008. 'Charity Raises a Sobering Message in Fundraiser', *The Courier-Mail*, 29 September, 42.

Featherstone, M. (ed.) 2000. *Body Modification*, London: Sage.

Featherstone, M. 2007. *Consumer Culture and Postmodernism*, London: Sage.

FebFast. 2009. *FebFast Annual Report 2008/2009*. Melbourne: FebFast.

FebFast. 2013. *Why It's Good For You* [Online]. Available: http://febfast.org.au/whyitsgoodforyou/ [Accessed 10 October 2013].

FebFast. 2015. *Fast-Quotes* [Online]. Melbourne: FebFast. Available: http://febfast.org.au/fast-quotes/ [Accessed 14 January 2015].

Filo, K., Fechner, D. & Inoue, Y. 2020. 'Charity Sport Event Participants and Fundraising: An Examination of Constraints and Negotiation Strategies', *Sport Management Review*, 23, 387–400.

Fishbein, M. & Ajzen, I. 1975. *Belief, Attitude, Intention, and Behaviour: An Introduction to Theory and Research*, Reading, MA: Addison-Wesley.

Fitzgerald, R. & Jordan, T. L. 2009. *Under the Influence: A History of Alcohol in Australia*, Sydney: Harper Collins.

Flood, C. 2020. 'What Happened After My First Dry January', *Beautiful Hangover* [Online]. Available from: https://medium.com/beautiful-hangover/what-happened

-after-my-first-dry-january-e0992f67743c#:~:text=The%20joke%20in%20the
%20refrain,pretty%20warped%20relationship%20with%20booze [Accessed
9 November 2020].

Flowers, R. & Swan, E. (eds) 2015. *Food Pedagogies*, London: Ashgate.

Fondation Jean Lapointe. 2015. *Défi les 28 jours les plus longs de ta vie* [Online].
Montreal: Fondation Jean Lapointe. Available: http://fondationjeanlapointe.org
/evenements/defi-les-28-jours-les-plus-longs-de-ta-vie/ [Accessed 5 November
2015].

Fondation Jean Lapointe. 2020. *Défi 28 jours (homepage)* [Online]. Montreal: Fondation
Jean Lapointe. Available: https://www.defi28jours.com/ [Accessed 7 August 2020].

Fors, V. & Pink, S. 2017. 'Pedagogy as Possibility: Health Interventions as Digital
Openness', *Social Sciences*, 6, 59–62.

Foucault, M. 2000. 'The Subject and Power', in Faubion, J. D. (ed.), *Power*. New York:
The New Press, 326–48.

Foucault, M. 2008. *The Birth of Biopolitics: Lectures at the Collège de France, 1978–79*,
Basingstoke, UK: Palgrave Macmillan.

Frank, R. 1996. 'Motivation, Cognition, and Charitable Giving', in Schneewind, J. (ed.),
Giving: Western Ideals of Philanthropy. Bloomington, IN: Indiana University Press,
130–52.

Friedland, J. 2015. *Eatymology: The Dictionary of Modern Gastronomy*, Naperville, IL:
Sourcebooks.

Frizzell, N. 2014. 'Sober October: When Did Giving Up Alcohol Become a Heroic Act?',
The Guardian, 1 October.

Frow, J. 2007. 'Australian Cultural Studies: Theory, Story History 1', *Postcolonial Studies*,
10, 59–75.

Fry, M.-L. 2011. 'Discourses of Consumer's Alcohol Resistant Identities', *Journal of
Nonprofit & Public Sector Marketing*, 23, 348–66.

Fry, M.-L. 2014. 'Case Study: Hello Sunday Morning! – Towards "Practices" of
Responsible Drinking', in Brennan, L., Binney, W., Parker, L., Aleti, T. & Nguyen,
D. (eds), *Social Marketing and Behaviour Change: Models, Theory and Applications*.
Cheltenham, UK: Edward Elgar, 109–17.

Fuller, A. 2021. *Sobriety Savings: The Financial Case For Sobriety? Calculate Your Savings*
[Online]. New York: Finder.com (US). Available: https://www.finder.com/sobriety
-savings [Accessed 9 April 2021].

Fundraising & Philanthropy Magazine. 2020. 'Dry July Foundation Gets New CEO
Following Ezy Raise Acquisition', *Fundraising & Philanthropy Magazine*, New
Lambton, NSW.

Furtwængler, N. A. F. F. & Visser, R. O. 2013. 'Lack of International Consensus in
Low-Risk Drinking Guidelines', *Drug and Alcohol Review*, 32, 11–18.

Gardner, K. E. 2006. *Early Detection: Women, Cancer, and Awareness Campaigns in
the Twentieth Century United States*, Chapel Hill, NC: University of North Carolina
Press.

References

Garnett, C., Crane, D., West, R., Michie, S., Brown, J. & Winstock, A. 2015. 'Normative Misperceptions About Alcohol Use in the General Population of Drinkers: A Cross-Sectional Survey', *Addictive Behaviors*, 42, 203–6.

Garrison, J. 2015. 'Dewey's Aesthetics of Body-Mind Functioning', in Scarinz, A. (ed.), *Aesthetics and the Embodied Mind: Beyond Art Theory and the Cartesian Mind-Body Dichotomy*, Dordrecht, Netherlands: Springer, 39–53.

Gelley, A. (ed.) 1995. *Unruly Examples: On the Rhetoric of Exemplarity*, Stanford, CA: Stanford University Press.

Gentile, D. 2016. *Congratulations on Your Dry January, Loser* [Online]. New York: Thrillist. Available: https://www.thrillist.com/drink/nation/congratulations-on-your-dry-january-loser [Accessed 24 September 2020].

Giroux, H. A. 1993. 'Consuming Social Change: The "United Colors of Benetton"', *Cultural Critique*, 26, 5–32.

Giroux, H. A. & Pollock, G. 2010. *The Mouse that Roared: Disney and the End of Innocence*, Lanham, MD: Rowman & Littlefield.

Glanz, K., Rimer, B. K. & Viswanath, K. (eds) 2008. *Health Behavior and Health Education: Theory, Research and Practice*, San Francisco, CA: Jossey-Bass.

Glass, S. 2016. *Dry January: 101 Alcohol-Free Tips to Get You to February*, New York: Portico.

Go Sober. 2016. *Go Sober For October – Home* [Online]. London: Macmillan Cancer Support. Available: https://www.gosober.org.uk/?no_redirect=true [Accessed 21 December 2016].

Go Sober. 2019. *Fundraising Ideas* [Online]. London: MacMillan Cancer Support. Available: https://www.gosober.org.uk/fundraising-ideas [Accessed 7 June 2019].

Gold, S. S. 2018. 'How to Survive Weekends When You're Doing Dry January', *Health*. Des Moines, IA: Meredith.

Goodman, N. 1976. *Languages of Art: An Approach to a Theory of Symbols*, Indianapolis: Hackett.

Goodwin, A., Snelgrove, R., Wood, L. & Taks, M. 2017. 'Leveraging Charity Sports Events to Develop a Connection to a Cause', *Event Management*, 21, 175–84.

Goodwin, I., Griffin, C., Lyons, A., McCreanor, T. & Barnes, H. M. 2016. 'Precarious Popularity: Facebook Drinking Photos, the Attention Economy, and the Regime of the Branded Self', *Social Media + Society*, 2(1), 1–13.

Gordon, J., Harvey, C., Shaw, E. & Maclean, M. 2016. 'Entrepreneurial Philanthropy', in Jung, T., Phillips, S. D. & Harrow, J. (eds), *The Routledge Companion to Philanthropy*, London: Routledge, 334–47.

Government of Australia: Department of Health. 2013. *National Binge Drinking Strategy* [Online]. Canberra: Government of Australia: Department of Health. Available: http://www.alcohol.gov.au/internet/alcohol/publishing.nsf/Content/cli [Accessed 1 December 2014].

Graham, A. 2012. *The Problem with Dry July (Revisited)* [Online]. Australian Wine Review. Available: https://www.ozwinereview.com/2012/06/problem-with-dry-july-revisited.html [Accessed 9 November 2020].

Gual, A. 2007. 'Is Alcohol Foodstuff?', *Addiction*, 102, 1190–1.

Guillaume, D. 2019. 'RTL', in Sportouch, B. (ed.), *Le grand jury*. Paris, 17 November 2019.

Gusfield, J. R. 1981. *The Culture of Public Problems: Drinking-Driving and the Symbolic Order*, Chicago, IL: University of Chicago Press.

Gusfield, J. R. 1986. *Symbolic Crusade: Status Politics and the American Temperance Movement*, Urbana & Chicago, IL: University of Illinois Press.

Haenfler, R. 2019. 'Changing the World One Virgin at a Time: Abstinence Pledgers, Lifestyle Movements, and Social Change', *Social Movement Studies*, 18, 425–43.

Haenfler, R., Johnson, B. & Jones, E. 2012. 'Lifestyle Movements: Exploring the Intersection of Lifestyle and Social Movements', *Social Movement Studies*, 11, 1–20.

Hamilton, I. 2016. 'Dry January: Is it Worth Giving Up Alcohol for a Month?', *The Conversation*, 1 January 2016.

Hamilton, I. 2019. 'Dry January: A Convenient Distraction for the Alcohol Industry', *The Conversation*, 2 January 2019.

Hamilton, I. & Gilmore, I. 2016. 'Could Campaigns Like Dry January Do More Harm Than Good?', *British Medical Journal*, 352, i143.

Hampton, T. 1990. *Writing from History: The Rhetoric of Exemplarity in Renaissance Literature*, Ithaca, NY: Cornell University Press.

Hansen, J., Winzeler, S. & Topolinski, S. 2010. 'When The Death Makes You Smoke: A Terror Management Perspective on the Effectiveness of Cigarette On-Pack Warnings', *Journal of Experimental Social Psychology*, 46, 226–8.

Haraway, D. J. 1976. *Crystals, Fabrics, and Fields: Metaphors of Organism in Twentieth-Century Developmental Biology*, New Haven, CT: Yale University Press.

Hargreaves, J. & Vertinsky, P. 2007. *Physical Culture, Power, and the Body*, London: Routledge.

Hargreaves, T. 2011. 'Practice-ing Behaviour Change: Applying Social Practice Theory to Pro-Environmental Behaviour Change', *Journal of Consumer Culture*, 11, 79–99.

Harvey, I. 2002. *Labyrinths of Exemplarity*, Albany, NY: State University of New York Press.

Head, A. 2021. 'Here's Why Dry Jan May Not Be the Best Idea This Year, According to a Doctor', *Marie Claire (UK)*. Digital Edition. London: Future Publishing.

Heath, D. 2012. *Drinking Occasions: Comparative Perspectives on Alcohol and Culture*, 2nd edn., New York, NY: Routledge.

Hello Sunday Morning. 2019. 'Is There a Dark Side to Dry July?', *Hello Sunday Morning Blog* [Online]. Available from: https://hellosundaymorning.org/2019/06/26/dark-side-dry-july/ [Accessed 12 July 2020].

Hessari, N. M. & Petticrew, M. 2017. 'What Does the Alcohol Industry Mean by "Responsible Drinking"? A Comparative Analysis', *Journal of Public Health*, 40, 90–7.

Hesse-Biber, S. N. & Leavy, P. (eds) 2008. *Handbook of Emergent Methods*, New York: Guilford Press.

References

Hickey-Moody, A., Savage, G. C. & Windle, J. 2010. 'Pedagogy Writ Large: Public, Popular and Cultural Pedagogies in Motion', *Critical Studies in Education*, 51, 227–36.

Hill, L. & Casswell, S. 2004. 'Alcohol Advertising and Sponsorship: Commercial Freedom or Control in the Public Interest?', in Heather, N. & Stockwell, T. (eds), *The Essential Handbook of Treatment and Prevention of Alcohol Problems*, Chichester, UK: Wiley, 339–62.

Hillgrove, T. & Thomson, L. 2012. *Evaluation of the Impact of FebFast Participation. Final Report*, Melbourne, VIC: Victorian Health Promotion Foundation (VicHealth).

Højer, L. & Bandak, A. 2015. 'Introduction: The Power of Example', *Journal of the Royal Anthropological Institute*, 21, 1–17.

Hooper, D. 2020. *The Best Dry January Campaigns of 2020* [Online]. Broadfield Park: BeverageDaily.com. Available: https://www.beveragedaily.com/Article/2020/02/06/Best-Dry-January-campaigns-2020-Seedlip-Heineken-BrewDog [Accessed 23 September 2020].

Hunt, A. 1999. *Governing Morals: A Social History of Moral Regulation*, Cambridge: Cambridge University Press.

Hunt, G. 2020. *Dry July - A Doubly Good Idea*, Canberra: Commonwealth of Australia Department of Health.

Hvid Junuar. 2020. *Hvid Januar - Home* [Online]. Copenhagen: Sundhedsstyrelsen [Danish Health Authority]. Available: https://hvidjanuar.dk/ [Accessed 29 June 2020].

IkPas. 2019. *IkPas – Home* [Online]. Tilburg: Stichting Positieve Leefstijl. Available: ikpas.nl [Accessed 29 June 2020].

IkPas. 2020. *Waarom Meedoen? [Why Participate?]* [Online]. Tilberg: Stichting Positieve Leefstijl. Available: https://ikpas.nl/waarom-meedoen/ [Accessed 5 October 2020].

Irish Heart Foundation. 2016. *On The Dry – Homepage* [Online]. Dublin: Irish Heart Foundation. Available: http://www.onthedry.ie/ [Accessed 7 February 2017].

Irish Heart Foundation. 2017. *On The Dry – Official Twitter Feed*. On The Dry.

Jacobson, J. L. 2010. 'Moustachioed Men and Marathon Moms: The Marketing of Cancer Philanthropy', MA, Wilfrid Laurier University.

Johnson, S. 2018. 'Dimensions of Altruism: Do Evaluations of Prosocial Behavior Track Social Good or Personal Sacrifice?', *SSRN* [Online].

Jordi, R. 2011. 'Reframing the Concept of Reflection: Consciousness, Experiential Learning, and Reflective Learning Practices', *Adult Education Quarterly*, 61, 181–97.

Kant, I. 1781. *Critique of Pure Reason*, London: George Bell.

Kant, I. 2007. *Critique of the Power of Judgment*, Cambridge: Cambridge University Press.

Karlan, D. & Mcconnell, M. A. 2014. 'Hey Look at Me: The Effect of Giving Circles on Giving', *Journal of Economic Behavior & Organization*, 106, 402–12.

Karno, M. P. 2018. 'It's Not for Everyone: Advancing Research on Cognitive Bias Modification. A Commentary on Wiers et al. (2018)', *Journal of Studies on Alcohol and Drugs*, 79, 346–7.

Katzev, R. & Wang, T. 1994. 'Can Commitment Change Behavior? A Case Study of Environmental Actions', *Journal of Social Behavior and Personality*, 9, 13–26.

Kazdin, A. E. 1982. *Single-Case Research Designs: Methods for Clinical and Applied Settings*, Oxford: Oxford University Press.

Kazemi, D. M., Borsari, B., Levine, M. J., Li, S., Lamberson, K. A. & Matta, L. A. 2017. 'A Systematic Review of the mHealth Interventions to Prevent Alcohol and Substance Abuse', *Journal of Health Communication*, 22, 413–32.

Keane, H. 2000. 'Setting Yourself Free: Techniques of Recovery', *Health*, 4, 324–46.

Keane, H. 2009. 'Intoxication, Harm and Pleasure: An Analysis of the Australian National Alcohol Strategy', *Critical Public Health*, 19, 135–42.

Kékpont: Alkohol Drog Karantén. 2020. *Száraz November* [Online]. Budapest. Available: http://kekpont.hu/szaraz-november/ [Accessed 27 June 2020].

Kim, H. S. A. & Wohl, M. J. A. 2015. 'The Bright Side of Self-Discontinuity: Feeling Disconnected with the Past Self Increases Readiness to Change Addictive Behaviors (Via Nostalgia)', *Social Psychological and Personality Science*, 6, 229–37.

Kimball, M. 2016. 'No Booze for 40 Days: Take this Challenge to See Health Benefits of Popular Lenten Sacrifice', *The Times-Picayune*, 19 January.

Kimball, M. 2017. '#AlcoholFreeFor40 Challenge Begins March 1: Are You In?', *Times-Picayune*, 1 March.

Kimball, M. 2020. 'Get healthy! Ochsner's Alcohol Free for 40 Challenge Is Underway; See Tips to Get Started', *nola.com*, 27 February.

King, S. 2006. *Pink Ribbons, Inc.: Breast Cancer and the Politics of Philanthropy*, Minneapolis, MN: University of Minnesota Press.

Klawiter, M. 1999. 'Racing for the Cure, Walking Women, and Toxic Touring: Mapping Cultures of Action Within the Bay Area Terrain of Breast Cancer', *Social Problems*, 46, 104–26.

Kneale, J. & French, S. 2015. 'Moderate Drinking Before the Unit: Medicine and Life Assurance in Britain and the US c.1860–1930', *Drugs: Education, Prevention and Policy*, 22, 111–17.

Koenig, D. 2021. *Covid, Politics Make Dry January Harder Than Ever* [Online]. New York: WebMD. Available: https://www.webmd.com/lung/news/20210122/covid-politics-make-dry-january-harder-than-ever [Accessed 12 April 2021].

Krøijer, S. 2015. 'Revolution is the Way You Eat: Exemplification among Left Radical Activists in Denmark and in Anthropology', *Journal of the Royal Anthropological Institute*, 21, 78–95.

Krout, J. A. 1925. *The Origins of Prohibition*, New York: Alfred A. Knopf.

Kuhn, T. S. 1996. *Structure of Scientific Revolutions*, Chicago: University of Chicago Press.

Lamme, M. O. 2014. *Public Relations and Religion in American History: Evangelism, Temperance, and Business*, Philadelphia: Routledge.

Lansdown, E. 2018. *Social Badges – Dryathlon, Cancer Research UK* [Online]. London: Behance. Available: https://www.behance.net/gallery/65310825/Social-badges

-Dryathlon-Cancer-Research-UK?tracking_source=search_projects_recommended %7Cdryathlon [Accessed 22 September 2020].

Laraña, E., Johnston, H. & Gusfield, J. R. (eds) 1994. *New Social Movements: From Ideology to Identity*, Philadelphia: Temple University Press.

Laycock, T. 1857. *Social and Political Relations of Drunkenness: Two Lectures*, Edinburgh: Myles Macphail.

Leach, D. K. 2013. 'Prefigurative Politics', in Snow, D. A., Porta, D. D., Klandermans, B. & McAdam, D. (eds), *The Wiley-Blackwell Encyclopedia of Social and Political Movements*. Malden, UK: Wiley-Blackwell, 1004–6.

Leder, D. 1990. *The Absent Body*, Chicago: University of Chicago Press.

Lees, P. 2012. *Why Sober October Doesn't Work* [Online]. Sydney: NineMSN. Available: http://health.ninemsn.com.au/healthnews/8554460/why-ocsober-doesnt-work [Accessed 30 April 2014].

Leiss, W. 1983. 'The Icons of the Marketplace', *Theory, Culture & Society*, 1, 10–21.

Leiss, W., Kline, S., Shally, S. & Botterill, J. 2005. *Social Communication in Advertising: Consumption in the Mediated Marketplace*, New York: Routledge.

Lender, M. E. & Karnchanapee, K. R. 1977. '"Temperance Tales": Antiliquor Fiction and American Attitudes toward Alcoholics in the Late 19th and Early 20th Centuries', *Journal of Studies on Alcohol*, 38, 1347–70.

Lenucha, R. & Thow, A. M. 2019. 'How Neoliberalism is Shaping the Supply of Unhealthy Commodities and What this Means for NCD Prevention', *International Journal of Health Policy Management*, 8, 514–20.

Lepper, J. 2018. 'JustGiving Waives Fees for Disaster Fundraising Following Criticism', *Charity Digital* [Online]. Available from: https://charitydigital.org.uk/topics/topics/justgiving-waives-fees-for-disaster-fundraising-following-criticism-5366 [Accessed 15 October 2020].

Levine, H. G. 1978. 'The Discovery of Addiction: Changing Conceptions of Habitual Drunkenness in America', *Journal of Studies on Alcohol*, 39, 143–74.

Levine, H. G. 1993. 'Temperance Cultures: Concern about Alcohol Problems in Nordic and English-Speaking Cultures', in Lader, M., Edwards, G. & Drummond, D. C. (eds), *The Nature of Alcohol and Drug-Related Problems*, New York: Oxford University Press, 16–36.

Lew, M. 2014. 'How Do You Go Dry for a Month When Your Desk Looks Like This?', *Bon Appétit*. New York: Condé Nast.

Life Education Australia. 2017. *Ocsober – How to Raise $700* [Online]. Pacific Fair, QLD: Life Education Australia. Available: www.ocsober.com.au/how-to-raise-700/ [Accessed 7 October 2017].

Life Education Australia. 2018. *Ocsober: Lose the Booze to Help Aussie Kids*. Brisbane: Life Education Australia.

Life Education Australia. 2019. *Ocsober in 2019* [Online]. Life Education Australia. Available: https://www.ocsober.com.au/#jump [Accessed 29 June 2020].

Lindsay, J. 2010. 'Healthy Living Guidelines and the Disconnect with Everyday Life', *Critical Public Health*, 20, 475–87.

Livingston, M. & Callinan, S. 2015. 'Underreporting in Alcohol Surveys: Whose Drinking is Underestimated?', *Journal of Studies on Alcohol and Drugs*, 76, 158–64.

Luke, C. 1996. *Feminisms and Pedagogies of Everyday Life*, Albany, NY: SUNY Press.

Lupton, D. 1995. *The Imperative of Health: Public Health and the Regulated Body*, London: Sage.

Lupton, D. 2014. 'The Pedagogy of Disgust: The Ethical, Moral and Political Implications of Using Disgust in Public Health Campaigns', *Critical Public Health*, 25, 1–11.

Lupton, D. 2016. *The Quantified Self: A Sociology of Self-Tracking*, Cambridge: Polity.

Lyons, J. D. 1990. *Exemplum: The Rhetoric of Example in Early Modern France and Italy*, Princeton, NJ: Princeton University Press.

Macaskill, W. 2016 *Doing Good Better: How Effective Altruism Can Help You Help Others, Do Work That Matters, and Make Smarter Choices about Giving Back*, New York: Random House.

Macdonald, B. 2018. 'Interview with Dry July Founder Brett MacDonald', by Unity Gym. Sydney: Facebook Live, 31 July 2018, https://www.facebook.com/unitygym/videos/1901681406558310.

MacDonald, B. 2020. 'Looking for a New Fundraising Platform?', *Ezyraise Blog* [Online]. Available from: https://www.ezyraise.com/post/looking-for-a-new-fundraising-platform [Accessed 28 September 2020].

MacDonald, T. K. & Zanna, M. P. 1998. 'Cross-Dimension Ambivalence Toward Social Groups: Can Ambivalence Affect Intentions to Hire Feminists?', *Personality and Social Psychology Bulletin*, 24, 427–41.

Maher, C., Ryan, J., Kernot, J., Podsiadly, J. & Keenihan, S. 2016. 'Social Media and Applications to Health Behavior', *Current Opinion in Psychology*, 9, 50–5.

Manning, E. 2019. 'If You're an Alcoholic Dry January Could Kill You', *Yahoo! News*, 2 February 2019.

Mansbridge, J. 1998. 'On the Contested Nature of Public Good', in Powell, W. W. & Clemens, E. S. (eds), *Private Action and the Public Good*, New Haven, CT: Yale University Press, 3–19.

Martin, G. 2015. *Understanding Social Movements*, New York: Routledge.

Martin, M. W. 1994. *Virtuous Giving: Philanthropy, Voluntary Service, and Caring*, Bloomington, IN: Indiana University Press.

Marvasti, F. F. & Stafford, R. S. 2012. 'From "Sick Care" to Health Care: Reengineering Prevention into the U.S. System', *New England Journal of Medicine*, 367, 889–91.

Massumi, B. 2002. *Parables For The Virtual: Movement, Affect, Sensation*, Durham, NC: Duke University Press.

May, M. 2016. *Dry January Campaign Opens Up to Other Charities Through Virgin Money Giving* [Online]. UK Fundraising. Available: https://fundraising.co.uk/2016/11/02/dry-january-campaign-opens-charities-virgin-money-giving/#.WJLLoedrVKZ [Accessed 2 February 2017].

References

Maziak, W. & Ward, K. D. 2009. 'From Health as a Rational Choice to Health as an Affordable Choice', *American Journal of Public Health*, 99, 2134–9.

McCambridge, J. & Day, M. 2008. 'Randomized Controlled Trial of the Effects of Completing the Alcohol Use Disorders Identification Test Questionnaire on Self-Reported Hazardous Drinking', *Addiction*, 103, 241–8.

Mehta, G., MacDonald, S., Maurice, J., Al-Khatib, S., Piao, S., Rosselli, M., Nair, D., Jalan, R., Sumpter, C., Khera-Butler, T., Cronberg, A. & Moore, K. 2015. 'Short Term Abstinence from Alcohol Improves Insulin Resistance and Fatty Liver Phenotype in Moderate Drinkers', *66th Annual Meeting of the American Association for the Study of Liver Disease*, San Francisco, CA.

Mellor, P. A. & Shilling, C. 2010. 'Body Pedagogics and the Religious Habitus: A New Direction for the Sociological Study of Religion', *Religion*, 40, 27–38.

Meltzoff, A. N. & Prinz, W. (eds) 2002. *The Imitative Mind: Development, Evolution and Brain Bases*, Cambridge: Cambridge University Press.

Meslin, E. M., Rooney, P. M. & Wolf, J. G. 2008. 'Health-Related Philanthropy: Toward Understanding the Relationship Between the Donation of the Body (and Its Parts) and Traditional Forms of Philanthropic Giving', *Nonprofit and Voluntary Sector Quarterly*, 37, 44S–62S.

Moderation Management. 2016a. *What is Moderation Management?* [Online]. Moderation Management. Available: http://www.moderation.org/about_mm/whatismm.html [Accessed 24 November 2016].

Moderation Management. 2016b. *Why Dryuary?* [Online]. Grandville, MI. Available: http://dryuary.org/wp/why-dryuary/ [Accessed 24 November 2016].

Mohan, J. & Breeze, B. 2016. *The Logic of Charity: Great Expectations in Hard Times*, Basingstoke, UK: Palgrave Macmillan.

Mol, A. 2002. *The Body Multiple: Ontology in Medical Practice*, Durham, NC: Duke University Press.

Moore, S. E. H. 2008. *Ribbon Culture: Charity, Compassion and Public Awareness*, New York: Springer.

Munsterman, I. D., Groefsema, M. M., Weijers, G., Klein, W. M., Swinkels, D. W., Drenth, J. P. H., Schellekens, A. F. A. & Tjwa, E. T. T. L. 2018. 'Biochemical Effects on the Liver of 1 Month of Alcohol Abstinence in Moderate Alcohol Consumers', *Alcohol and Alcoholism*, 53, 435–8.

Murphy, D. A., Hart, A. & Moore, D. 2016. 'Shouting and Providing: Forms of Exchange in the Drinking Accounts of Young Australians', *Drug and Alcohol Review*, 36, 442–8.

Nafus, D. & Sherman, J. 2014. 'This One Does Not Go Up To 11: The Quantified Self Movement as an Alternative Big Data Practice', *International Journal of Communication*, 8, 1784–94.

Nettleton, S. & Hardey, M. 2006. 'Running Away with Health: The Urban Marathon and the Construction of "Charitable Bodies"', *Health: An Interdisciplinary Journal for the Social Study of Health, Illness and Medicine*, 10, 441–60.

Newby-Clark, I. R., McGregor, I. & Zanna, M. P. 2002. 'Thinking and Caring About Cognitive Inconsistency: When and for Whom Does Attitudinal Ambivalence Feel Uncomfortable?', *Journal of Personality and Social Psychology*, 82, 157–66.

NHMRC. 2007. *Australian Alcohol Guidelines for Low-Risk Drinking: Draft for Public Consultation*, National Health and Medical Research Council (Ed.). Canberra.

NHMRC. 2009. *Australian Guidelines to Reduce Health Risks from Drinking Alcohol*, National Health and Medical Research Council (Ed.), Canberra: Australian Government.

NHMRC. 2015. 'Eat For Health, Australian Dietary Guidelines', in National Health and Medical Research Council (ed.), *Ageing*, Canberra: Australian Government, 17 July 2015, https://www.eatforhealth.gov.au/sites/default/files/content/The%20Guidelines/n55_agthe_large.pdf

NHS. 2019. *The Risks of Drinking Too Much: Alcohol Support* [Online]. London: NHS (National Health Service). Available: https://www.nhs.uk/live-well/alcohol-support/the-risks-of-drinking-too-much/ [Accessed 9 September 2020].

Nicholls, E. & Conroy, D. 2021. 'Possibilities and Pitfalls? Moderate Drinking and Alcohol Abstinence at Home Since the COVID-19 Lockdown', *International Journal of Drug Policy*, 88, 103025.

Nickel, P. M. & Eikenberry, A. M. 2009. 'A Critique of the Discourse of Marketized Philanthropy', *American Behavioral Scientist*, 52, 974–89.

Nickerson, R. S. 1998. 'Confirmation Bias: A Ubiquitous Phenomenon in Many Guises', *Review of General Psychology*, 2, 175–220.

Nightlife.ca. 2013. 'Le mois de février sans alcool: les 28 jours les plus longs de ta vie' [Online]. Montreal: Nightlife.ca. Available: https://nightlife.ca/2013/01/31/le-mois-de-fevrier-sans-alcool-les-28-jours-les-plus-longs-de-ta-vie/ [Accessed 23 September 2020].

Noble, G. 2015. 'Pedagogies of Civic Belonging: Finding One's Way Through Social Space', in Watkins, M., Noble, G. & Driscoll, C. (eds), *Cultural Pedagogies and Human Conduct*, London: Routledge, 32–44.

Noble, G. & Watkins, M. 2003. 'So, How Did Bourdieu Learn to Play Tennis? Habitus, Consciousness and Habituation', *Cultural Studies Review*, 17, 520–39.

Nolsoe, E. 2020. *Nearly Half of 'Dry January' Attempts Failed* [Online]. London: YouGov. Available: https://yougov.co.uk/topics/food/articles-reports/2020/02/07/nearly-half-dry-january-attempts-failed [Accessed 11 November 2020].

Noyes, D. 2016. 'Gesturing Toward Utopia: Toward a Theory of Exemplarity', *Narodna Umjetnost*, 53, 75–95.

NZ Drug Foundation. 2015. *Five Wonderful Years of FebFast NZ* [Online]. Auckland: NZ Drug Foundation. Available: https://www.drugfoundation.org.nz/news-media-and-events/five-wonderful-years-of-febfast/ [Accessed 18 September 2017].

O'Malley, P. & Valverde, M. 2004. 'Pleasure, Freedom and Drugs: The Uses of "Pleasure" in Liberal Governance of Drug and Alcohol Consumption', *Sociology*, 38, 25–42.

Ocsober. 2016. *Ocsober – Home* [Online]. Sydney: Life Education. Available: http://www.ocsober.com.au/ [Accessed 21 December 2016].

Oei, T. P. S. & Jardim, C. L. 2007. 'Alcohol Expectancies, Drinking Refusal Self-Efficacy and Drinking Behaviour in Asian and Australian Students', *Drug and Alcohol Dependence*, 87, 281–7.

Olivola, C. Y. 2011. 'When Noble Means Hinder Noble Ends: The Benefits and Costs of a Preference for Martyrdom in Altruism', in Oppenheimer, D. M. & Olivola, C. Y. (eds), *The Science of Giving: Experimental Approaches to the Study of Charity*, New York: Psychology Press, 49–62.

Olivola, C. Y. & Shafir, E. 2013. 'The Martyrdom Effect: When Pain and Effort Increase Prosocial Contributions', *Journal of Behavioral Decision Making*, 26, 91–105.

Olivola, C. Y. & Shafir, E. 2018. 'Blood, Sweat, and Cheers: The Martyrdom Effect Increases Willingness to Sponsor Others' Painful and Effortful Prosocial Acts', *SSRN* [Online]. Available: https://papers.ssrn.com/sol3/papers.cfm?abstract_id=3101447.

Olson, M. 1965. *The Logic of Collective Action: Public Goods and the Theory of Groups*, Cambridge, MA: Harvard University Press.

Oppenheimer, G. M. & Bayer, R. 2020. 'Is Moderate Drinking Protective Against Heart Disease? The Science, Politics and History of a Public Health Conundrum', *Milbank Quarterly*, 98, 39–56.

Ore, J. 2015. *Why I've Given Up Alcohol During 'Drynuary' For Ten Years Running* [Online]. Business Insider. Available: http://www.businessinsider.com/drynuary-no-alcohol-in-january-2015-12/?r=AU&IR=T [Accessed 26 September 2017].

Pados, E., Kovács, A., Kiss, D., Kassai, S., Fövény, M. K., Dávid, F., Karsai, S., Terebessy, A., Zsolt Demetrovics, Griffiths M. D. & Rácz, J. 2020. 'Voices of Temporary Sobriety: A Diary Study of an Alcohol-Free Month in Hungary', *Substance Use & Misuse*, 55, 839–50.

Palmer, C. & Dwyer, Z. 2019. 'Good Running?: The Rise of Fitness Philanthropy and Sports-Based Charity Events', *Leisure Sciences: An Interdisciplinary Journal*, 42, 607–23.

Pantzar, M. & Ruckenstein, M. 2015. 'The Heart of Everyday Analytics: Emotional, Material and Practical Extensions in Self-Tracking Market', *Consumption, Markets & Culture*, 18, 92–109.

Pearson, M. R. 2013. 'Use of Alcohol Protective Behavioral Strategies Among College Students: A Critical Review', *Clinical Psychology Review*, 33, 1025–40.

Pennay, A., Lubman, D. I. & Frei, M. 2014. 'Alcohol: Prevention, Policy and Primary Care Responses', *Australian Family Physician*, 43, 356–61.

Petersen, A. 1996. 'Risk and the Regulated Self: The Discourse of Health Promotion as Politics of Uncertainty', *Journal of Sociology*, 32, 44–57.

Petersen, A. & Lupton, D. 1996. *The New Public Health: Health and Self in the Age of Risk*, London: Sage.

Pettigrew, S. & Pescud, M. 2016. 'The Salience of Alcohol-Related Issues Across the Adult Lifespan', *Health Education Journal*, 75, 117–28.

Pilzer, P. Z. 2002. *The Wellness Revolution: How to Make a Fortune in the Next Trillion Dollar Industry*, New York: Wiley.

Plastic Free July. 2021. *Plastic Free July (Homepage)* [Online]. South Freemantle, WA: Plastic Free Foundation. Available: https://www.plasticfreejuly.org/ [Accessed 12 April 2021].

Plato 360 BCE. *Timaeus*. Salt Lake City, UT: Project Gutenberg.

Polonsky, M. J. & Wood, G. 2001. 'Can The Overcommercialization of Cause-Related Marketing Harm Society?', *Journal of Macromarketing*, 21, 8–22.

Prestwich, P. E. 1980. 'French Workers and the Temperance Movement', *International Review of Social History*, 25, 35–52.

Proquest Australia & New Zealand Newsstand. 2014. (Results of a database search conducted on 10 December 2014).

Pryor, L. 2010. 'What Shall We do with the Drunken Abstainer? A Dry July Pickle', *Sydney Morning Herald*, 24 July.

Radley, A. & Marie, K. 1995. 'Charitable Giving by Individuals: A Study of Attitudes and Practice', *Human Relations*, 48, 685–709.

Reidy, C., Daly, J., Berry, F. & Brennan, T. 2012. 'NSW Sustainable Households Program 2012: Literature Review, Prepared for the NSW Office of Environment and Heritage by the Institute for Sustainable Futures', Sydney: NSW Office of Environment and Heritage.

Reinarman, C. 1988. 'The Social Construction of an Alcohol Problem: The Case of Mothers Against Drunk Drivers and Social Control in the 1980s', *Theory and Society*, 17, 91–119.

Reynolds, D. & Reason, M. (eds) 2012. *Kinesthetic Empathy in Creative and Cultural Practices*, London: Intellect Books.

Rich, E. 2011. '"I See Her Being Obesed!": Public Pedagogy, Reality Media and the Obesity Crisis', *Health*, 15, 3–21.

Rigolot, F. 1998. 'The Renaissance Crisis of Exemplarity', *Journal of the History of Ideas*, 59, 557–63.

Robert, J. 2013. 'Individualistic Philanthropy: The Paradox of Embodied Participation for Health-Related Fundraising Campaigns', *International Journal of Nonprofit and Voluntary Sector Marketing*, 18, 261–74.

Robert, J. 2014. 'Oppositional Symbolic Values of Language Display, or The Case of "English" Drinking in France', *Social Semiotics*, 24, 209–24.

Robert, J. 2015. 'The Loi Evin: Ambiguous Pedagogies of Responsible Drinking', in Flowers, R. & Swan, E. (eds), *Food Pedagogies*, London: Ashgate, 113–30.

Robert, J. 2016a. 'Temporary Sobriety Initiatives as Public Pedagogy: Windows of Opportunity for Embodied Learning', *Health*, 20, 413–29.

Robert, J. 2016b. 'Temporary Sobriety Initiatives: Emergence, Possibilities and Constraints', *Continuum*, 30, 646–58.

Robert, J. 2018. 'Practices and Rationales of Embodied Philanthropy', *International Journal of Nonprofit and Voluntary Sector Marketing* [Online], 23. Available: https://onlinelibrary.wiley.com/doi/abs/10.1002/nvsm.1595.

References

Roberts, J. S. 1982. 'Drink and the Labour Movement: The *Schnaps* Boycott of 1909', in Evans, R. J. (ed.), *The German Working Class 1888–1933: The Politics of Everyday Life*, London: Croom Helm, 80–107.

Rogers, Z. 2014. 'Wearing Your Heart on Your Sleeve: The Effects of Conspicuous Compassion on Identity Signalling and Charitable Behavior', PhD thesis, Graduate Center, City University of New York.

Room, R. 1975. 'Normative Perspectives on Alcohol Use and Problems', *Journal of Drug Issues*, 5, 358–68.

Room, R. 2010. 'The Long Reaction Against the Wowser: The Prehistory of Alcohol Deregulation in Australia', *Health Sociology Review*, 19, 151–63.

Room, R. 2011. 'Addiction and Personal Responsibility as Solution to the Contradictions of Neoliberal Consumerism', *Critical Public Health*, 21, 141–51.

Room, R. 2015. 'The Cultural Framing of Addiction', in Granfield, R. & Reinarman, C. (eds), *Expanding Addiction: Critical Essays*, New York: Routledge, 43–50.

Rose, N. 1999. *Powers of Freedom: Reframing Political Thought*, Cambridge: Cambridge University Press.

Rose, N. & Miller, P. 1992. 'Political Power Beyond the State: Problematics of Government', *British Journal of Sociology*, 43, 271–303.

Ryan, G. W. & Bernard, H. R. 2003. 'Techniques to Identify Themes', *Field Methods*, 15, 85–108.

Sandlin, J. A., Schultz, B. D. & Burkick, J. 2011. 'Understanding, Mapping, and Exploring the Terrain of Public Pedagogy', in Sandlin, J. A., Schultz, B. D. & Burdick, J. (eds), *Handbook of Public Pedagogy*, New York: Routledge, 338–75.

Sandlin, J. A. & Walther, C. S. 2009. 'Complicated Simplicity: Moral Identity Formation and Social Movement Learning in the Voluntary Simplicity Movement', *Adult Education Quarterly*, 59, 298–317.

Santi, P. & Horel, S. 2020. '"Dry January", malgré le véto de l'Elysée', *Le Monde*, 20 January.

Saukko, P. 2003. *Doing Research in Cultural Studies: An Introduction to Classical and New Methodological Approaches*, London: Sage.

Savic, M., Room, R., Mugavin, J., Pennay, A. & Livingston, M. 2016. 'Defining "Drinking Culture": A Critical Review of Its Meaning and Connotation in Social Research on Alcohol Problems', *Drugs: Education, Prevention and Policy*, 23, 270–82.

Saxon, G. D. & Wang, L. 2014. 'The Social Network Effect: The Determinants of Giving Through Social Media', *Nonprofit and Voluntary Sector Quarterly*, 43, 850–68.

Scaife, W., Mcgregor-Lowndes, M., Barraket, J. & Burns, W. 2016. *Giving Australia 2016: Literature review*, Brisbane: The Australian Centre for Philanthropy and Nonprofit Studies, Queensland University of Technology, Centre for Social Impact Swinburne University of Technology and the Centre for Corporate Public Affairs.

Scharf, K. & Smith, S. 2016. 'Relational Altruism and Giving in Social Groups', *Journal of Public Economics*, 141, 1–10.

Schmitz, J. 2020. 'Is Charitable Giving a Zero Sum Game? The Effect of Competition Between Charities on Giving Behavior', *Management Science* [Online]. [Accessed 23 October 2020].

Septembris Eij Oo. 2020. *Septembris Eij Oo – Homepage* [Online]. Tallin: Tervise Arengu Instituut [National Institute for Health Development]. Available: https://septembriseijoo.alkoinfo.ee/ [Accessed 29 June 2020].

Sheinbaum, H. 2020. *The Dry Challenge: How to Lose the Booze for Dry January, Sober October, and Any Other Alcohol-Free Month*, London: Harper Design.

Sherman, C. & Wedge, D. 2017. *Ice Bucket Challenge: Pete Frates and the Fight Against ALS*, Lebanon, NH: ForeEdge.

Shilling, C. 2005. *The Body in Culture, Technology & Society*, London: Sage.

Shilling, C. 2007. 'Sociology and the Body: Classical Traditions and New Agendas', in Shilling, C. (ed.), *Embodying Sociology: Retrospect, Progress and Prospects*, Oxford: Blackwell Publishing, 1–18.

Shilling, C. 2010. 'Exploring the Society-Body-School Nexus: Theoretical and Methodology Issues in the Study of Body Pedagogics', *Sport, Education and Society*, 15, 151–67.

Shilling, C. 2013. *The Body and Social Theory*, London: Sage.

Shilling, C. 2017. 'Body Pedagogics: Embodiment, Cognition and Cultural Transmission', *Sociology*, 51, 1205–21.

Shusterman, R. 2008. *Body Consciousness: A Philosophy of Mindfulness and Somaesthetics*, Cambridge: Cambridge University Press.

Simonton, D. K. 1979. 'Multiple Discovery and Invention: Zeitgeist, Genius, or Chance', *Journal of Personality and Social Psychology*, 37, 1603–16.

Skinner, B. F. 2012. *Science and Human Behaviour*, New York: Simon & Schuster.

Smith, J. A. 1996. 'Beyond the Divide Between Cognition and Discourse: Using Interpretive Phenomenological Analysis in Health Psychology', *Psychology & Health*, 11, 261–71.

Smith, K. C., Cukier, S. & Jernigan, D. H. 2014. 'Defining Strategies for Product Through "Drink Responsibly" Messages in Magazine Ads for Beer, Spirits and Alcopops', *Drug and Alcohol Dependence*, 142, 168–73.

Sober October UK. 2020. *Sober October UK – Official Facebook Page* [Online]. London: McMillan Cancer Support. Available: https://www.facebook.com/gosoberuk [Accessed 14 September 2020].

Solberg, R. J. 1970. *The Dry Drunk Syndrome*, Center City, MN: Hazelden.

Stokes, A. 2014. 'Dry July: Proving to Your Kids that You Are in Control', *Sydney Morning Herald*, 8 July.

Stolz, S. A. 2015. 'Embodied Learning', *Educational Philosophy and Theory*, 47, 474–87.

Stroud, S. R. 2011. 'Kant on Education and the Rhetorical Force of the Example', *Rhetoric Society Quarterly*, 41, 416–38.

Stukus, D. R. 2019. 'The Role of Medical Professionals in Social Media', in Stukus, D. R., Patrick, M. D. & Nuss, K. E. (eds), *Social Media for Medical Professionals: Strategies for Successfully Engaging in an Online World*, New York: Springer, 65–82.

Suchej Únor. 2020. *Suchej Únor – Home* [Online]. Prague: Liga Otevřených Mužů [League of Open Men]. Available: https://suchejunor.cz/ [Accessed 29 June 2020].

Sulik, G. 2011. *Pink Ribbon Blues: How Breast Cancer Culture Undermines Women's Health*, New York: Oxford University Press.

Sulkunen, I. 1990. *History of the Finnish Temperance Movement: Temperance as a Civic Religion*, Lewiston, NY: Edwin Mellen Press.

Sulkunen, P. & Warpenius, K. 2000. 'Reforming The Self and the Other: The Temperance Movement and the Duality of Modern Subjectivity', *Critical Public Health*, 10, 241–438.

Swan, M. 2013. 'The Quantified Self: Fundamental Disruption in Big Data Science and Biological Discovery', *Big Data*, 1, 85–99.

Szto, C. & Gray, S. 2014. 'Forgive Me Father for I Have Thinned: Surveilling the Bio-Citizen Through Twitter', *Qualitative Research in Sport, Exercise and Health*, 7, 321–37.

Tarde, G. D. 1903. *The Laws of Imitation*, New York: Holt.

Thompson, M. M., Zanna, M. P. & Griffin, D. W. 1995. 'Let's Not Be Indifferent About (Attitudinal) Ambivalence', in Krosnick, J. & Petty, R. E. (eds), *Attitude Strength: Antecedents and Consequences*, Hillsdale, NJ: Erlbaum, 361–86.

Throsby, K. 2018. 'Giving Up Sugar and the Inequalities of Abstinence', *Sociology of Health & Illness*, 40, 954–68.

Tolvin, J. 2020. *Jussi Tolvin Blogi: Tipaton Tammikuu Britanniassa* [Online]. Helsinki: Tipaton Tammikuu. Available: https://www.tipaton.fi/page/5/ [Accessed 14 June 2020].

Tonkin, L. 2008. 'What It's Like to ... Give Up Alcohol for a Month', *Newcastle Herald*, 22 July, 43.

Tournée Minérale. 2021. *Tournée Minérale* [Online]. Brussels: Univers santé. Available: https://tournee-minerale.be/ [Accessed 14 March 2021].

Towers, A., Philipp, M., Dulin, P. & Allen, J. 2018. 'The "Health Benefits" of Moderate Drinking in Older Adults may be Better Explained by Socioeconomic Status', *The Journals of Gerontology: Series B*, 73, 649–54.

Travis, T. 2009. *The Language of the Heart: A Cultural History of the Recovery Movement from Alcoholics Anonymous to Oprah Winfrey*, Raleigh, NC: University of North Carolina Press.

Tyrrell, I. 1991. *Woman's World, Woman's Empire: The Woman's Christian Temperance Union in International Perspective, 1880–1930*, Chapel Hill, NC: University of North Carolina Press.

University Hospital Southampton. 2018. *Liver Expert Warns Dry January can be "Perfect Decoy" for Problem Drinkers*, Southampton: NHS Foundation Trust.

Vahdati, S. 2014. *Dryathlon: Week 1* [Online]. Cambridge: The Tab. Available: https://thetab.com/uk/cambridge/2014/01/09/dryathlon-week-1-32066 [Accessed 23 March 2021].

Valverde, M. 1998. *Diseases of the Will: Alcohol and the Dilemmas of Freedom*, Cambridge: Cambridge University Press.

Van Deursen, D. 2019. 'Where is the Bias? Measuring and Retraining Cognitive Biases in Problem Drinkers', PhD thesis, University of Amsterdam.

Van Stekelengurg, J. & Roggeband, C. 2013. 'Introduction: The Future of Social Movement Research', in Van Stekelengurg, J., Roggeband, C. & Klandermans, B. (eds), *The Future of Social Movement Research: Dynamics, Mechanisms, and Processes*, Minneapolis, MN: University of Minnesota Press, xi–xxii.

Varamäki, R. n.d. 'Alcohol-Free January', *Innovative Projects*. Berlin: Deutsche Hauptstelle fuer Suchtfragen.

Veganuary. 2021. *Veganuary Homepage* [Online]. London. Available: https://veganuary .com/ [Accessed 12 April 2021].

Vismanen, P. 2009. 'Ensin oli huikaton helmikuu', *Turun Sanomat*, 2 February.

Wagenaar, A. C., Salois, M. J. & Komro, K. A. 2009. 'Effects of Beverage Alcohol Price and Tax Levels on Drinking: A Meta-Analysis of 1003 Estimates from 112 Studies', *Addiction*, 104, 179–90.

Wagner, D. 1997. *The New Temperance: The American Obsession with Sin and Vice*, Boulder, CO: Westview Press.

Ward, M. 2020. *The Dark Side of Dry January*. Available: https://medium.com/mental -health-and-addictions-community/the-dark-side-of-dry-january-ac4b8efdf1b5. Published 9 January 2020. [Accessed 3 November 2020].

Warin, M. 2011. 'Foucault's Progeny: Jamie Oliver and the Art of Governing Obesity', *Social Theory & Health*, 9, 24–40.

Warnick, B. R. 2008. *Imitation and Education: A Philosophical Inquiry into Learning by Example*, Albany, NY: State University of New York Press.

Warrington, R. 2018. *Sober Curious*, New York: Harper Collins.

Watkins, M., Noble, G. & Driscoll, C. 2015. *Cultural Pedagogies and Human Conduct*, London: Routledge.

Weakley, K. 2018. *CRUK Changes Dryathlon to Clash with Macmillan's Go Sober* [Online]. London: Civil Society News. Available: https://www.civilsociety.co.uk/ news/cancer-research-uk-to-run-dryathlon-in-october-clashing-with-macmillan .html [Accessed 7 April 2021].

Wellbeing Brewing Co. 2018. *Dry January Crew* [Online]. Maryland Heights, MO: WellBeing Brewing Co. Available: https://www.facebook.com/groups /583377382111598 [Accessed 2 December 2020].

Wexler, M. N., Oberlander, J. & Shankar, A. 2017. 'The Slow Food Movement: A "Big Tent" Ideology', *Journal of Ideology* [Online], 37.

WHO, 2018. *Global Status Report on Alcohol and Health 2018*, Geneva: World Health Organization.

Wiers, R. W., Houben, K., Fadardi, J. S., Beekb, P., Mijkerhemtulla & Cox, W. M. 2015. 'Alcohol Cognitive Bias Modification Training for Problem Drinkers Over the Web', *Addictive Behaviors*, 40, 21–6.

Wilson, T. M. 2005. *Drinking Cultures: Alcohol and Identity*, Oxford: Berg.

Winter, T. (director), *Boardwalk Empire, 2010–2014*, HBO.

Wirgau, J. S., Farley, K. W. & Jensen, C. 2010. 'Is Business Discourse Colonizing Philanthropy? A Critical Discourse Analysis of (PRODUCT) RED', *Voluntas*, 21, 611–30.

Woiak, J. 1994. '"A Medical Cromwell to Depose King Alcohol": Medical Scientists, Temperance Reformers, and the Alcohol Problem in Britain', *Histoire sociale/Social History*, 27, 337–65.

Wolburg, J. M. 2005. 'How Responsible are "Responsible" Drinking Campaigns for Preventing Alcohol Abuse?', *Journal of Consumer Marketing*, 22, 176–7.

Yeomans, H. 2011. 'What Did the British Temperance Movement Accomplish? Attitudes to Alcohol, the Law and Moral Regulation', *Sociology*, 45, 38–53.

Yeomans, H. 2013. 'Blurred Visions: Experts, Evidence and the Promotion of Moderate Drinking', *The Sociological Review*, 61, 58–78.

Yeomans, H. 2019. 'New Year, New You: A Qualitative Study of Dry January, Self-Formation and Positive Regulation', *Drugs: Education, Prevention and Policy*, 26, 460–8.

YouGov. 2017. *New Year's Resolutions Survey*, London: YouGov.

YouGov. 2019. *Do You Plan to Participate in Dry January (abstaining from drinking any alcohol for the month of January 2020)?* [Online]. YouGov (USA). Available: https://today.yougov.com/topics/food/survey-results/daily/2019/12/23/a6177/2 [Accessed 5 November 2020].

YouGov France. 2021. *'Dry January': les Français relèvent-ils le défi cette année?* [Online]. Paris: YouGov France. Available: https://fr.yougov.com/news/2021/01/11/dry-january-les-francais-relevent-ils-le-defi/ [Accessed 11 April 2021].

Young, L. B. 2011. 'Joe Sixpack: Normality, Deviance, and the Disease Model of Alcoholism', *Culture & Psychology*, 17, 378–97.

Young, M. P. 2006. *Bearing Witness Against Sin: The Evangelical Birth of the American Social Movement*, Chicago: University of Chicago Press.

Young, R. M., Oei, T. P. & Crook, G. M. 1991. 'Development of a Drinking Self-Efficacy Questionnaire', *Psychopathology and Behavioral Assessment*, 13, 1–15.

YSAS. 2011. *YSAS Annual Report 2010–2011*. Melbourne, VIC: Youth Support and Advocacy Service Pty Ltd.

Zanec Soft Tech Private Limited. 2017. *Dry January & Beyond*. 2.2 edn. London: Alcohol Concern.

Index

40 Brez Alkohola   46, 56–7, 120–1, 181

abstinence   2, 5, 65, 72, 76, 97–8, 176; *see also* moderation; prohibition; sobriety; temperance; Temporary Sobriety Initiatives
  detoxing and cleansing   48, 49, 112, 115, 140, 170
  as deviant behaviour   42, 51, 66, 79–80, 98–101, 109–10
  on drinking occasions   98–9
  exemplary   11–15, 77, 109, 179
  as intrinsically worthwhile   42
  total   72, 74, 75
addiction   39, 57, 72, 75, 91–2, 97–8
affect   12, 26, 27, 77–101, 120, 137, 146, 153, 156, 163
alcohol; *see also* alcoholism; non-alcoholic beverages; temperance; Temporary Sobriety Initiatives
  alcoholism   39, 62, 70, 75, 80, 98, 127
  anxiety about   5–6, 62–3
  and association with other enjoyable activities   98–9, 107, 168
  and cancer   70
  as commodity   90–1, 176
  drinking as social norm   99, 109–10, 155–7
  as drug   88, 91, 176
  and drunkenness   75, 95–6, 105–6, 109
  as food   88, 91
  and health effects   56, 111–12
  and interpersonal relations   95–101
  moral panic about   16, 20, 62–3
  and responsible drinking   5–7, 9–10, 13–14, 33–4, 64–6, 103–10, 113–15, 156
  and social capital   7, 33
  and social problems   33, 57, 62–3, 106
  ubiquity of   57, 81
  and violence   33, 48, 62, 64, 174

Alcohol Change   50, 53, 70, 73, 93, 147–8, 166, 182, 185; *see also* Défi de Janvier; Dry January; Dry January (Switzerland); IkPas
Alcohol Concern   49, 71, 147; *see also* Dry January
Alcohol Free for 40   12, 49, 54–6, 69, 90, 120–2, 145, 181, 192
Alcohol-Free January   46; *see also* Tipaton Tammikuu
Alcoholics Anonymous   97, 159
alcoholism   39, 62, 70, 75, 80, 98, 127
Alcohol Use Disorders Identification Test (AUDIT)   39, 75
America   39, 46, 54, 99, 121, 131, 138, 183, 184, 192
  drinking culture   61, 111
  healthcare system   56, 175
  prohibition   2, 5, 17, 62, 67
  temperance movements   3, 5–7, 17, 38, 52, 54, 62, 63, 67, 74, 111, 126, 158, 165
American Liver Foundation   54, 58, 138, 184; *see also* Go Dry
Anderson, Eliza   47, 80
Andreoni, James   137
Aristotle   22–3
Australia
  anti-temperance attitudes   62, 159, 170
  drinking culture   2, 5–6, 20, 33, 42, 62, 66, 87, 88, 99, 105, 111, 115, 119, 139, 191
  temperance movements   5, 61
  TSI campaigns in   1, 20, 46, 52, 53, 64, 70, 74, 80, 115, 131, 137, 139, 146, 149, 150, 170, 183–5, 189, 191–2

Bandura, Albert   91–2
Barrows and Room   63
Bartram, Hanson-Easey and Eliott   114
BC Cancer Foundation   53, 58; *see also* Lose the Booze

Index

Belgium 3, 53, 55, 187
Berridge, Virginia 61–2, 64, 68, 70
Big Easy Dryout 46, 181
binge drinking 1, 5, 20, 33, 46, 48, 62,
    71, 82, 115, 154, 158, 160, 161,
    174, 178
binge sobriety 3, 44, 158
Boisserie-Lacroix and Inchingolo 97
Booker, L. 93, 156
Britain 3, 9, 14, 38, 45, 46, 48–54, 62–4,
    70, 73, 93, 111, 118, 127, 131,
    137, 148, 150, 166, 178, 182–4,
    186, 194
    drinking culture 82, 160
    temperance movements 17, 61, 63,
        68, 72, 82
British Liver Trust 48, 71, 160
Broadbent, Tamar 160
Brubaker, Rogers 125

Canada 45, 50, 53, 84, 116
Cancer Research UK 53, 57, 58, 65, 70,
    148, 183; *see also* Dryathlon
Castells, Manuel 47
charities; *see* Temporary Sobriety
    Initiatives, fundraising and
    philanthropy
Chouinard, Jean-Sébastien 50, 80, 122
cognitive bias 157
Covid-19 74, 173–4, 185, 193
cultural entrepreneurs 79, 80, 82, 84
cultural studies 15–17
Czech Republic 53, 186

Dean, Jon 123, 125, 142
Défi 28 jours 12, 45, 47, 181–2; *see also*
    Jean Lapointe Foundation;
    Soberary
    fundraising and philanthropy 70, 80,
        98, 116
    history 50, 52, 80, 116–17, 122–3,
        161
    modified participation in 74
    objectives 12, 58
    social media 81, 116–17, 122–3
    timing 73, 98
    tracking technologies used by 68
Défi de Janvier 182
Denmark 53, 173, 185

detoxing and cleansing 48, 49, 112, 115,
    140, 170
de Visser, Richard 56, 71
direct action 79, 132
DrinkWise 33
Dryathlon 12, 45, 183
    badges 43, 124, 126–7
    branding 69, 117–18
    fundraising and philanthropy 53, 57,
        65, 117–19, 129, 137,
        139, 148
    health and wellness 42, 69, 70, 117,
        120
    heroism of participants 117–18, 120,
        126
    modified participation 58
    participant feedback 45
    social media 43, 124
    social validation of participants 126–7
    tracking technologies used by 68
Dry Feb 12, 84, 182, 183; *see also* Dry
    July
    branding 113
    history 53, 185
    timing 45
Dry January 3, 12, 14, 45–7, 118, 119,
    137, 182, 183, 185; *see also*
    Défi de Janvier; Dry January
    (Switzerland); IkPas; Raitis
    Tammikuu
    branding 54
    English and French versions of 14,
        52, 53, 82, 84, 148, 160, 182
    fundraising and philanthropy 58,
        139, 147, 148
    health and wellness 12, 39, 70, 71, 73,
        92–3, 138, 160, 161, 178
    history 49–50, 52, 54, 80
    objectives 53, 55, 70, 92–3, 126, 156
    participant feedback 165
    timing 137, 139
    tracking technologies used by 68
Dry January (Switzerland) 52, 84, 182–3
Dry January Feel Good February 183
Dry July 1–3, 37, 41, 46, 113, 183; *see
    also* Dry July New Zealand
    fundraising and philanthropy 57, 70,
        116, 123–4, 129, 136, 139, 142,
        146–50, 167, 174

228   *Index*

health and wellness 58, 69–70, 149–50
heroism of participants 117, 149–50, 167–8, 174
history 48, 51, 53, 80, 123, 149
modified participation 74, 150
motivations for joining 1–2, 84, 127, 139, 149, 167
publicity around 57, 123, 127, 161
purchasable reprieves 44, 57, 114, 117, 125, 136, 150, 167
social media 124–5, 127
vision statements 57
Dry July New Zealand 53, 57
Drynuary 54, 97, 183
Dryuary 54, 144, 184
Dykstra and Law 30

education 23, 26; *see also* exemplarity; learning; public pedagogies
Elgin, Catherine 24, 85, 103, 110
embodied learning 20, 32, 56, 84–91, 94–101, 171, 175–9
embodied philanthropy 2, 50, 56, 129–32, 138–41, 143–4, 146, 148–51, 164, 169
England; *see* Britain
Estonia 53, 186
Europe 5, 30, 38, 52, 53, 56, 70, 88, 158, 175
exemplarity 11–15, 19–35, 103, 179
counterexamples 153–64
definition of examples 21–3, 28
in embodied public pedagogy 28–35, 78, 84–91, 94–101, 121, 131, 174–9
learning by example 23–8, 34–5
mass 14, 31, 113, 122, 153, 172, 175
as model for a future self 78, 91–4, 96, 101
negative 15, 29, 33

Featherstone, M. 30
FebFast 3, 12, 45, 52, 184; *see also* FebFast New Zealand
branding 112–13
fundraising and philanthropy 41, 58, 70, 119–20, 132–4, 140–1, 146, 150

health and wellness 43, 65, 69, 83, 87–9, 95–6, 98, 111, 134, 138, 140, 169
heroism of participants 66
history 47, 48, 50, 80
objectives 58
recruitment 83–4
social media 84, 89
FebFast New Zealand 45, 52
Finland 3, 14, 20, 46–8, 61, 64–5, 72–3, 76, 111, 187
Flood, Chelsea 159
Fondation Jean Lapointe 50, 52, 98, 117, 182
Fors and Pink 84, 85
France 3, 14, 52, 53, 68, 70, 82, 148, 160–1, 165, 178, 182, 192
Frank, Robert 143

Germany 46, 72, 183
Global Financial Crisis 64
Go Dry 54, 58, 138, 184
Gold, S. S. 65
Go Sober 53, 184–6
branding 42, 54, 113, 115
fundraising and philanthropy 41, 65, 119, 137, 183
heroism of participants 42, 54, 115
modified participation in 74
Granfelt, A. A. 65, 71
Grove, Phil 48, 80
Guillaume, D. 164
Gusfield, Joseph 6–7, 62

Haenfler, Johnson and Jones 14, 30, 31, 79
Haenfler, R. 30
Hamilton, Ian 71
Hampton, Timothy 91
Haraway, Donna 26
Harvey, Irene 26
health education 8, 33
Healy, Fiona 47, 80, 184
Heath, Dwight 4
Hello Sunday Morning 71, 126, 159
Højer and Bandak 12, 26
Hungary 3, 53, 165, 186
Hunt, Greg 70
Hvid Januar 173, 185

Ice Bucket Challenge   9, 116
IkPas   49, 53, 70, 120, 138, 185
imitation   5, 11–12, 20, 22, 23, 25–8,
        31, 38, 59, 61, 75, 82–4, 101,
        121–2, 153–5, 168, 179; *see also*
        exemplarity
Ireland   3, 38, 45–6, 183
Irish Heart Foundation   45, 54, 186; *see
        also* On the Dry
irresponsible drinking   5, 6; *see also*
        binge drinking; responsible
        drinking

Janopause   48
Jean Lapointe Foundation   50, 52, 98,
        117, 182

Kant, Immanuel   23
Kimball, Molly   54, 56, 57, 69, 90, 121,
        122, 181
King, Samantha   131
Krøijer, Stine   14, 30–1
Kuhn, Thomas   25–6

Laraña, Johnston and Gusfield   30
Laycock, Thomas   68
learning   19; *see also* exemplarity
    embodied   20, 32, 56, 84–91, 94–101,
        171, 175–9
    imitative   22, 26–8 (*see also* role
        models)
    and reflection   55–6
    and rewards   27
Lent   2, 12, 38, 39, 46–50, 120–1, 160
Lenucha and Thow   105
Levine, Harry   5, 61, 63
Life Education   52, 56, 148, 149, 185; *see
        also* Ocsober
lifestyle movements   14, 30–2, 34–5, 78,
        79, 83, 84, 101, 113–15, 121–2
Livesey, Joseph   68, 72
Lose the Booze   53, 58, 185

Macdonald, Brett   48, 53, 80, 183
McGilvary, Kenny   48, 80
Macmillan Cancer Support   53, 183, 184,
        186; *see also* Go Sober
Mansbridge, Jane   139
Martin, Mike   143

martyrdom   41, 57, 65, 104, 116–21, 135,
        136, 149–50
Massumi, Brian   26
moderation   5–7, 64–6, 77, 113, 156, 164,
        176, 177; *see also* responsible
        drinking; temperance
Moderation Management   39, 54, 97,
        159, 184; *see also* Dryuary
Mohan and Breeze   9, 143
Moore, Sarah   132
morality
    and alcohol consumption   62–7,
        108–10 (*see also* temperance)
    religious   8, 27
    secular   8–9, 110
multiple discovery hypothesis   50

narrative sense of self   28, 154
National Binge Drinking Strategy,
        Australia   115
neo-liberalism   5, 7, 8
    and health care   8–9, 50, 56, 104–12,
        114, 117, 128, 175
    neo-liberal neo-temperance   4, 9,
        69–70, 175–9
    and personal responsibility   104–10, 174
    and philanthropy   104, 130–1
    and privatisation of public
        services   130
neo-temperance   7, 62–7, 71, 75–6, 79;
        see also temperance; Temporary
        Sobriety Initiatives
    neo-liberal neo-temperance   4, 9,
        69–70, 175–9
Netherlands   3, 49, 53, 111, 148, 182, 185
network hypothesis   50–3, 59
New Year's resolutions   2, 38, 48–50, 111
New Zealand   38, 45, 48, 52, 53, 57, 61,
        111, 183, 184
New Zealand Drug Foundation   52, 184;
        see also Febfast New Zealand
No Alcohol April   185
non-alcoholic beverages   43, 54, 58,
        65–6, 75, 95, 99–100, 113–14,
        125, 156
Nordic countries   61, 73
Noyes, Dorothy   6, 22, 83, 103, 107, 124

Ocsober   3, 45, 139, 185–6, 189

benefits of participation 56
branding 113
educative rhetoric 115, 148–9
fundraising and philanthropy 115, 148
heroism of participants 116
history 52
Olivola, C. Y. 129
Olivola and Shafir 135
On the Dry 45, 54, 186
Ore, John 54, 183
Oschner Health 56, 145; *see also* Alcohol Free for 40

Packer, James 149
Perry, Neil 149
Petersen, A. 105
Petersen and Lupton 106
philanthropy; *see* Temporary Sobriety Initiatives, fundraising and philanthropy
Plastic Free July 179
Plato 22–4
prefigurative politics 79, 81, 115, 127
prohibition 2, 5, 27, 61, 62, 64, 67, 68, 76; *see also* abstinence; temperance
  post-prohibition societies 104–5
public pedagogies 19–35
  and embodied examples 20, 28–32, 84–91
  scholarship on 19–20

Quantified Self movement 7–8
Quebec 45, 50, 116

Raitis Helmikuu 73
Raitis Tammikuu 73
rational choice models 27, 69
Ration Challenge, The 179
recognizability 12, 24
research methodology 187–94
responsible citizenship 8–9, 64, 112
responsible drinking 5–7, 9–10, 13–14, 33–4, 64–6, 103–10, 113–15, 156; *see also* moderation; temperance
Rigolot, François 21, 23
Robert, Julie 129

Robinson, Emily 49–50, 80
role models 11–15, 20, 22, 31, 33
Room, Robin 6, 74, 110

sacrifice 5, 10, 13, 39, 41, 55, 57, 92, 116–17, 120–1, 127, 135, 149, 155, 164, 169, 174, 175, 179
Scotland 185
Septembris ei joo 186
shared responsibility for health and well-being 173
Shilling, C. 29, 30, 32, 34, 78, 93, 95
Slovenia 3, 20, 38, 46–7, 181
Soberary 50, 116, 181; *see also* Défi 28 jours
Sober Buddy Challenge 186
sober-curious movements 2, 71, 126, 159
Sober March 185, 186
sobriety 57, 88, 92, 100, 117, 177; *see also* abstinence; temperance; Temporary Sobriety Initiatives
social media 9–10, 16, 42–4, 47, 51, 65, 81, 84, 89, 103, 116–17, 122–8
Spencer, Adam 123
spirits 61, 66, 68, 72, 90, 113
Stroud, Scott 23
Suchej únor 53, 186
sugar 55, 69, 82, 88, 106, 108, 112, 134, 179, 184
Sulkunen and Warpenius 63
Switzerland 52, 53, 84, 148, 182
Száraz November 70, 186–7

teetotalism 2, 5, 66, 74, 77, 80, 82, 109, 155, 169; *see also* abstinence; temperance
temperance 2, 5, 6, 14, 17, 59, 61–6, 72; *see also* neo-temperance; responsible drinking; sobriety; Temporary Sobriety Initiatives
  alcohol boycotts and strikes 72–3, 76
  in America 5–7, 17, 62, 63, 67, 74, 126, 158
  anti-temperance 62
  in Australia 5, 61, 62, 159, 170
  in Britain 17, 61, 63, 68, 72, 82
  and class 63–4, 67, 73, 145
  in English-speaking and Nordic societies 61, 63

Index

episodic 72–4
and exemplification 74–5, 110
in Finland 46–7, 72–3, 76
in France 68
in Germany 72
and healthy lifestyle 7, 138
Hollywood portrayals of 2
and mental health 138
and morality 5, 7, 62–7, 69, 79
and moral panic about alcohol 16, 20, 62
pledges 126
political and social campaigns 72
and rehabilitated drunkards 80
and respectability 7, 63–5, 67, 75–6, 126–7
scientific 67–71, 73
temperance cultures 61, 75
temperance organizations 68
in the twenty-first century 5–10, 104–10
temporary abstinence campaigns; *see* Temporary Sobriety Initiatives
Temporary Sobriety Initiatives 2–4
and abstinence 176
and alcoholics 39, 127, 159–60
and altruism 12, 48, 58, 82, 129, 130, 135, 137–9, 142–4, 148–9, 169
analysis of TSI publications and media 193
in Anglophone countries 46, 55, 82, 175
in Australia 1, 20, 46, 52, 53, 64, 70, 74, 80, 115, 131, 137, 139, 146, 149, 150, 170, 183–5, 189, 191–2
and awareness-raising 132–4
badges 43–4, 124, 126–7, 165
and binge sobriety 44, 158
and blood tests 56, 69, 89
catalogue of official TSIs 46, 181–7
changing drinking cultures 10, 15, 32, 34, 38, 42, 70, 80–1, 101, 115, 119, 129, 136, 164, 166, 168, 174, 175, 178
characteristics of 2, 12
and class 69, 145, 175, 178
competition between different TSIs 136–9, 176
and conventional media 122–3, 160–1

as corrective to overindulgence 49, 111, 160–1
and counterexamples 153–64, 166, 172
critiques of 71, 157–64, 167–8, 178
and cultural norms of drinking 155–7
and data collection 42
detoxing and cleansing 48, 49, 112, 115, 140, 170
discourse around 8–10, 15–16
donors and beneficiaries 8, 9, 129, 135, 137, 143–4
and drug and alcohol treatment organizations 52, 54, 58, 70–1, 97, 164
duration 12–13, 44–5
and education 4, 10–15, 34, 45, 68, 70
electronic direct messaging of participants 42–3
embodied nature of 2, 13–15, 17, 34, 50, 56, 77–8, 84–91, 94–101, 121, 129–32, 138–41, 143–4, 146, 148–51, 164, 169, 174–9
and empathy 57, 71, 78, 94–5, 97–8, 100, 132, 147, 179
end of the campaign 44–5, 71, 90, 92, 93, 158, 161–4
environmental impacts 90–1
and episodic temperance 72–4
exemplary nature of 11–17, 28–35, 44, 45, 59, 65, 74–5, 77–8, 82–91, 94–101, 112–13, 121–31, 151, 153, 164, 169, 171–2, 174–9
as experiments 86–7
financial impacts of 90–1, 144–5
founders 50–1, 79–84, 177–8
and framing of alcohol 54–5
fundraising and philanthropy 4, 8–10, 17, 39, 41–2, 44, 52–9, 65, 71, 116–17, 119–21, 128, 129–51, 176
and habits 93–4, 155–6
and health and wellness 3, 7, 10, 17, 39, 42–4, 67–76, 89–90, 111–12, 140, 149, 170
and health education 77–101, 176
and heroism 39, 41–3, 54, 57, 65, 103–4, 114–18, 127, 143, 177
history 16, 20, 46, 50–2

and humour   69, 81, 89, 124, 127, 139
and integrity   146–7, 168–9
and legitimacy   123–4, 127, 157–8
and martyrdom   41, 57, 65, 104,
     116–21, 135, 136, 149–50
as model for a future self   78, 91–4,
     96, 101
modified participation in   44, 58, 73–4
motivations for joining   38–9, 82–4,
     110–16, 130, 137–46, 167, 170,
     178
and negative exemplarity   15, 17, 171
and neo-liberalism   4, 5, 7, 9, 15, 69,
     104–10, 175–9
as neo-temperance initiatives   6–7,
     16–17, 66, 76, 174
non-Anglophone   70
non-completion of   164–72
origins   9, 46, 50, 79–82
outcomes   44–5
participant communities   43
participant feedback   45
participant narratives   15–16
participants' relationships with
     alcohol   71
and performative moderation   65–6,
     124, 128, 175
as phenomenon   38–46
and philanthropic abstainers   130–9
and post-campaign binges   44, 71,
     158, 161–4, 178
public nature of   123–5
and purchasable reprieves   44, 55,
     57–8, 99, 114, 125, 136, 166–9
recruitment of participants   40, 83–4,
     120, 123, 134–5, 148, 168, 177–8
research on   3, 187–94
and responsible use of alcohol   64–5,
     77, 103–4
responsiveness and adaptation
     of   146–50
and rewards   27, 39, 104, 107–8, 114,
     117, 137–8, 145, 161, 177
and sacrifice   5, 10, 13, 39, 41, 55, 57,
     92, 116–17, 120–1, 127, 135,
     149, 155, 164, 169, 174, 175, 179
and scientific reasoning   68–71

and selfish philanthropists   139–46,
     178
and social media   9–10, 16, 42–4, 47,
     51, 65, 103, 122–8
social orientation of   54–8, 77
and social validation of
     participants   7–8, 57–8, 64–5,
     126–7
sponsors, official   20, 33, 56, 158
sponsors of participants   10, 58, 116,
     118, 129, 131, 134–6, 147, 169
spread of   46–54
and support-building   136–9
team participation in   134–5, 136,
     141, 169
and temperance movements   61, 158
timing   44, 46, 95, 139
tracking technologies used by   8–10,
     41, 42, 68, 129
unruly examples   153–72
who can participate   39–41, 118–19
Théorêt-Poupart, Antoine   50, 73, 80,
     122, 161
Throsby, K.   82
Tipaton Tammikuu   46, 55, 138, 187
Tournée Minérale   53, 55, 187
TSIs; *see* Temporary Sobriety Initiatives

UK; *see* Britain
USA; *see* America

Valverde, M.   64, 75
van Stekelengurg and Roggeband   122
Veganuary   178–9
violence, alcohol-related   33, 48, 62, 64,
     174
Virgin Money Giving   147; *see also*
     Alcohol Concern

Wagner, David   7, 63, 66
Warnick, Bryan   28, 29, 82, 123–4, 154–5
wowserism   62, 159, 170
Wright, Mark   71, 160

Yeomans, Henry   75, 92
YSAS Pty Ltd   47, 50, 134, 184; *see also*
     FebFast

Printed in the USA
CPSIA information can be obtained
at www.ICGtesting.com
LVHW051625010324
773307LV00002B/180